# Learning from the Past, Present, and Future to Drive Profits To New Levels

The content of this book is centered around three seemingly diverse themes. The first theme is why it's so important for companies to learn from the past, the present, and the future. The author covers some of the key learnings from the distant and current past, and how these learnings changed the course for many companies. He discusses new learnings that have been developed in our current state and will continue to be brought forward. He provides a look into the future, just to make sure companies understand that they should always be looking for better ways to function.

The second theme is centered around problem-solving, problem prevention, and decision-making. That is, how to successfully define problems that already exist in your current reality, how to prevent problems from occurring in the future, and how to make much more effective decisions. Problems have plagued many companies for many years and knowing how to follow a structured approach to solve them should prove to be very useful. And perhaps even more important than solving problems, is how companies can go about preventing the problems from occurring in the first place. Think about how your company might look if the plethora of problems to solve didn't exist. And with current or potential problems, many decisions must be made.

The final theme in this book is how to successfully implement the Theory of Constraints, and then combine Lean Manufacturing, Six Sigma, and the Theory of Constraints. The Theory of Constraints should be considered the "missing link" in most improvement initiatives. The author presents, in detail, why combining the Theory of Constraints with Lean and Six Sigma and all of the associated improvement tools and techniques, will take your company to new levels of profitability. He introduces two new roadmaps. One roadmap is on how to implement the Theory of Constraints, while the other new roadmap is how to implement my Ultimate Improvement Cycle.

# Learning from the Past, Present, and Future to Drive Profits To New Levels

## Roadmaps for Solving and Preventing Problems, Making Better Decisions, and Implementing the Ultimate Improvement Cycle

Bob Sproull

Routledge
Taylor & Francis Group

A PRODUCTIVITY PRESS BOOK

First published 2024
by Routledge
605 Third Avenue, New York, NY 10158

and by Routledge
4 Park Square, Milton Park, Abingdon, Oxon, OX14 4RN

*Routledge is an imprint of the Taylor & Francis Group, an informa business*

© 2024 Bob Sproull

ISBN: 978-1-032-61180-8 (hbk)
ISBN: 978-1-032-61179-2 (pbk)
ISBN: 978-1-003-46238-5 (ebk)

DOI: 10.4324/9781003462385

Typeset in Garamond
by Deanta Global Publishing Services, Chennai, India

## Dedication

As we progress through our lives, we meet people who have an impact on our lives. Sometimes, the impact is negative, but those people who made a really positive impact are the ones that truly matter. In my life, the most positive impact has been from my wonderful, loving, and supportive wife, Beverly. Why has she been the person who had the most positive influence on my life? The answer to that question could fill many pages but let me zero in on just a few very apparent things. Beverly has been the most supportive person I have ever met.

Her unconditional love is beyond what I ever expected before I met her. When we first got married, back in 1968, I truly didn't know what to expect from a wife. But what I did get was the most loving person I have ever met! Beverly gave me three wonderful children and as they were growing up, she taught them how to love others which has carried on in each of their marriages. She also taught each of them how to be great parents, by teaching them the value of listening, loving, and being devoted to their wonderful spouses.

On September 18, 2021, I lost the love of my life to the complications of the terrible disease known as dementia. During the final three years of Beverly's life, I became her caregiver and when she passed away, we were fortunate enough to have our three children, Rob, John, and Emily at her bedside. Thank you, Beverly, for everything you did for our family and know that we all miss you every single day. In your honor, I dedicate this book to you, Beverly, and can't wait to see you again in the future.

# Contents

# About the Author

**Bob Sproull**, for much of his life, was an Independent Consultant and the co-owner of Focus and Leverage Consulting. Because Bob's beloved wife had contracted dementia, Bob had to retire so he could become a caregiver for his wife of 53 years until she passed away in 2021. Bob is a certified Lean Six Sigma Master Black Belt and a Theory of Constraints Jonah.

Bob has served as a Vice President of Quality, Engineering, and Continuous Improvement for two different manufacturing companies; has an extensive consulting background in Healthcare, Manufacturing, and Maintenance and Repair Organizations (MRO); and focuses on teaching companies how to maximize their profitability through an integrated Lean, Six Sigma, and Constraints Management improvement methodology.

Bob is an internationally known speaker and author of numerous white papers and articles on continuous improvement. Bob's background also includes nine years with the Presbyterian University Hospital complex in Pittsburgh, Pennsylvania, where he ran the Biochemistry Department at the Children's Hospital, performed extensive research in breakthrough testing methods, and assisted with the development of organ transplant procedures.

Bob completed his undergraduate work at the University of Pittsburgh, Pennsylvania, and the University of Rochester, New York with a dual Math/ Physics major. A results-driven Performance Improvement professional with a diverse healthcare, manufacturing, MRO, and technical background, he has significant experience appraising under-performing companies and developing and executing highly successful improvement strategies based upon the integration of Lean, Six Sigma, and Constraints Management methodologies.

Bob is the author of six books: *The New Beginning*; *The Secret to Maximizing Profitability*; *The Problem-Solving, Problem Prevention, and Decision-Making Guide*; *Theory of Constraints, Lean, and Six Sigma Improvement Methodology*; *The Focus and Leverage Improvement Book*;

*The Ultimate Improvement Cycle: Maximizing Profits Through the Integration of Lean, Six Sigma, and the Theory of Constraints*; and *Process Problem-Solving: A Guide for Maintenance and Operations Teams.*

Bob is the co-author of *The New Beginning*; *Epiphanized: A Novel on Unifying Theory of Constraints, Lean, and Six Sigma* (First and Second Editions), and *Focus and Leverage: The Critical Methodology for Theory of Constraints, Lean, and Six Sigma (TLS).*

Bob holds a Bachelor of Science Equivalent in Math and Physics, University of Rochester, Rochester, New York; Bob is a Certified Lean Six Sigma Master Black Belt from Kent State University, a Certified Six Sigma Black Belt; and holder of a Sigma Breakthrough Technologies, Inc. TOCICO Strategic Thinking Process Program Certificate; TOC Thinking Processes (Jonah Course) L-3 Communications; Critical Chain Expert Certificate; and Realization Technologies Lean MRO Operations Certificate, University of Tennessee, Knoxville, Tennessee.

# Chapter 1

# Learning from the Past, Present, and Future

It has been said that, "Those who don't know history, or cannot remember it, or worse yet, choose to ignore it altogether, are all destined to repeat it." I'm not sure who first coined this phrase or parts of it, but it certainly is wisdom for the ages. The value of learning from history has the pronounced effect that all companies will move further, jump higher, and run faster than their competition. Remember when the Space Shuttle Challenger exploded seventy-three seconds into take-off; NASA learned from that disaster, made changes, and tried again. Also, when the Space Shuttle Columbia burned up on re-entry; once again, NASA learned, made changes, and tried again. Although learning is predictable, and even anticipated from misfortunes and disasters like these, do we really want to be in a cycle in which we learn only from disasters? Wouldn't it be better if we were able to anticipate future events before they happened, rather than respond to them after the fact? Knowing and understanding history, coupled with a desire to evolve into something greater and improved, is a fundamental prerequisite to being successful.

To be successful in manufacturing, some sense of history is a fundamental prerequisite for all manufacturing managers, but real success is actually achieved by anticipating the future. Because the manufacturing playing field is dynamic and constantly changing, we must be able to look into and anticipate what it might bring. And one way of doing this is by having an appreciation of the past. Knowing why something in the past worked, or

DOI: 10.4324/9781003462385-1

failed, truly helps to shape our future courses of action. But again, we'd rather improve by anticipating the future.

Americans and other societies have invented revolutionary manufacturing concepts that have contributed to much of the current state of our manufacturing companies. In fact, I believe that there are three key "discoveries," in particular, that have impacted how many companies operate successfully in today's world. Consider Frederick Taylor, who popularized the concept of *scientific management*. Taylor believed that companies should systematically break down a process into its component parts, and then improve the efficiency of each individual part. In addition, Taylor developed the concept of the work standard, based upon the "best method." Taylor was relentless in his pursuit of the "best way" to do things. His work standards represented the work rate that should be accomplished by a "first-class man."

Next, consider Andrew Carnegie. Before the mid-1850s, America's iron and steel industry was pretty much disparate and disjointed, with separate companies performing the individual processes of smelting, rolling, forging, and fabricating. Andrew Carnegie changed all of that, by *vertically integrating* these individual operations into a single company. In addition, Carnegie integrated even further into the iron and coal mines. The final piece of Carnegie's pie was his implementation of a *strict cost-accounting system*. In fact, one of his favorite platitudes was "Watch the costs and the profits will take care of themselves." The result of Carnegie's actions was for his steel company to become the lowest-cost provider of steel, and, in so doing, he was able to undercut his competition through high throughput and economies of scale. Whereas Carnegie focused on cost reduction, in today's world, I do not believe that this is the right approach. We will discuss the correct approach later in this book.

Finally, consider Henry Ford. Henry Ford recognized the importance of *throughput velocity*, by reducing all forms of *waste*, and the need to *keep everything in motion* while keeping *inventories low*. [1] John Yorke wrote on Agile Connection's website that Ford's ideas about process improvement made him a pioneer for *systems thinking* and agile software development. To quote Yorke, "Ford and his team created a flow-based production line and focused on removing constraints using a continuous improvement process. He was always pushing for the next improvement, constantly asking, 'What's next?'." Over a five-year period, Ford worked to identify every bottleneck in his production system. His obsession for improving flow was relentless and his focus on flow and continuous improvement led to some stunning results:

- The time to build a Model T car went from 12.5 hours to just 93 minutes, cutting nearly 11 hours of time out of an already-profitable system.
- In 1914, Ford produced more cars than everyone else – not just more cars than each of his competitors, but more cars than all three hundred of his competitors in the world combined.
- Ford employed 13,000 people compared with 66,000 people combined for all his competitors, and the productivity of his employees was five times the industry average.

Although these accomplishments were profound, Ford did so at the expense of product diversity. Ford correctly understood that high throughput, along with reduced inventory, would keep his costs lower than anyone else's, enabling him to increase his market share and profitability. But Ford's now-infamous statement, "The customer can have any color car he wants, as long as it's black," was a clear indicator that he didn't equate mass production with product diversity, which led to his company's abrupt fall in market share. Ford got the part about high throughput and low inventories right, but he failed to recognize that customers wanted choice.

Even though these three "discoveries" were very successful in their day, they are clear impediments to progress in today's manufacturing world. Today, we understand that improving individual efficiencies, based on work standards, can and does have detrimental effects on inventory costs and delivery rates. In fact, such improvements are actually at the epicenter of many manufacturing problems that exist today in many companies. Instead of maximizing *local efficiencies*, companies must focus on maximizing their *global efficiency*. In Chapter 18, we will discuss the concept of local versus global optima in much more detail.

Unfortunately, many companies are still attempting to maximize the efficiency of each individual process step, instead of maximizing the process as a whole. Worse yet, for many companies, efficiency is considered a key performance metric. The mass production mindset and its strict adherence to cost-accounting systems drive companies to use the wrong information for day-to-day decision-making. Finally, customers are entitled to what they want, when they want it, and at a cost they are willing to pay. As we learned from Ford, the mass production mindset creates less product diversity, late deliveries, and higher costs.

But the news from America isn't all dire. In fact, two men, in particular, contributed enormously to the world's understanding of the deleterious effects of excess variation. In the early 1930s, [2] Walter Shewhart published his now-famous *Economic Control of Quality of Manufactured Product*, in which he introduced the concept of the *control chart*. The importance of Shewhart's work cannot be overstated. Shewhart taught the world about variation and the need to know the difference between assignable and natural cause variation. Shewhart understood the need to bring the production process into a state of statistical control, where there is only natural cause variation present. Shewhart's control charts were developed as a tool for improvement, but, unfortunately, they were perceived only as a means of maintaining the *status quo*.

Almost fifty years later, [3] Dr W. Edwards Deming published his book, *Quality, Productivity, and Competitive Position* (later renamed *Out of the Crisis*), in which he presented a theory of management based on his now-celebrated *14 Points for Management*. Deming told us that management's failure to plan for the future results in loss of market share, followed by loss of jobs. Deming explained that management should not be judged merely by the quarterly dividend, but by innovative plans to stay in business, protect investments, ensure future dividends, and provide more jobs through improved products and services. He further stated, "Long-term commitment to new learning and new philosophy is required of any management that seeks transformation. The timid and the fainthearted, and the people that expect quick fixes, are doomed to disappointment."

In order to make the transition into the future, to the new era of manufacturing, it's important to remember the lessons of history, but what about this "new learning" of which Deming spoke? What is it we should be learning and where do we go to find it? If I had to recommend one text to all American managers, it would be [4] Hopp and Spearman's book, *Factory Physics – Foundations of Manufacturing Management*. I have long believed that factories are comprised of two distinct laboratories, a physics lab and a behavioral science lab, and Hopp and Spearman so eloquently confirmed this belief. Like all physics texts, *Factory Physics* contains various principles and laws of factory physics as they relate to manufacturing. It is my belief that Hopp and Spearman's book should be the quintessential manufacturing guide for the future, and, if you're a manufacturing manager at any level, this book should be considered required reading!

The factory physics principles and laws presented by Hopp and Spearman include relationships between inventory, throughput, and cycle time, as well as laws and principles governing things like flow, variability, capacity, utilization, rework, manpower, etc. – basically, all of the required elements associated with managing a manufacturing unit, plant, or division. [4] Hopp and Spearman summarize the key skills that will be required of the manager of the future, falling into three distinct categories:

1. *Basics.* The language and elementary concepts for describing manufacturing systems will be essential fundamentals going forward for all manufacturing managers.
2. *Intuition.* The single most important skill of all for manufacturing managers is intuition with regard to the behavior of manufacturing systems because it enables a manager to identify key leverage points, evaluate the impact of planned changes, and coordinate improvement efforts.
3. *Synthesis.* This is the ability of a manufacturing manager to bring together the disparate components of a manufacturing system into an effective whole. In part, synthesis is closely related to the ability to recognize and understand trade-offs and focus on critical parameters while still evaluating the system from a holistic point of view.

One of the most useful laws of all, presented by Hopp and Spearman, is Little's Law (actually, it is not a law at all; it is a mathematical tautology). Simply stated, Little's Law tells us that work-in-process (WIP) inventory is the product of throughput and cycle time:

$$WIP = Throughput\ (T) \times Cycle\ Time\ (CT)$$

Although this might be intuitive to many of you, its impact is far-reaching in terms of usefulness as a manufacturing aid. This law can be applied to a single station, an entire line, or even an entire plant, as long as all three inputs are measured in consistent units. Little's Law can be used to calculate queue length or WIP, by simply using the formula $WIP = T \times CT$, but, by rearranging the terms, it can also be used to estimate Cycle Time (i.e., $CT = WIP/T$) or Throughput (i.e., $T = (WIP/CT)$. In addition, it can be used to calculate planned inventory as well as inventory turns.

In the 1970s and 1980s, when American manufacturers were heavily involved in the Manufacturing Resource Planning (MRP) movement, something completely different was going on in Japan. Just-In-Time (JIT) is perhaps the most publicized manufacturing strategy in practice today, but it is also misunderstood by some manufacturers. Just-In-Time means having *the right product, at the right place, in the right amounts, at the right time, for the right price.* Taichii Ohno pioneered JIT, but its roots lie in America. Not from the automobile industry, as one might expect, but rather from American supermarkets. Ohno studied the replenishment systems in American super-markets and adapted them for Toyota's needs. Although reducing inventory is one of the main effects of JIT, it is as a direct consequence of reducing variation. JIT works because of *reduced variability* and *cycle times*.

[4] Hopp and Spearman have a wonderful section in their book on the corrupting influence of variability, but the important thing to understand about variability is that *variability always degrades the performance of a production system*. Why? Because it works to increase the average cycle time and WIP levels. Variability in a production system can be buffered by some combination of inventory, capacity, or time, but, if you do not reduce vari-ability, Hopp and Spearman tell us that you *will* pay in one or more of the following five ways (I have added a sixth way of my own):

1. Lost throughput.
2. Wasted capacity.
3. Inflated cycle times.
4. Larger inventory levels.
5. Longer lead times and/or poor customer service.
6. Inability to plan and produce needed production.

So, in the future, in order to stay competitive, we need to understand how and why we need to increase throughput, reduce cycle times, maximize flow, reduce and control variation, reduce waste, and optimize inventory. But we must do all of this with the needs of the customer at the forefront and within the confines of our available resources. Sound like a daunting task? It certainly can be if you don't understand basic factory physics. But, equally important, it is essential to have a coherent and structured plan for doing so. Just going out to the production floor and making changes, without first understanding why, can be disastrous. [4] Hopp and Spearman can certainly help you understand what changes should be made and why they should be made, but you still need a manufacturing strategy and an implementation plan.

Finally, back in the 1980s, I had an epiphany of sorts! Dr Eli Goldratt introduced the world to the Theory of Constraints, which changed my approach to improvement in very dramatic ways. In his and Jeff Cox's now-infamous business novel, [5] *The Goal*, Goldratt and Cox taught the world about the importance of identifying that part of your system that controls its output, the *system constraint*. He then taught the world that, once the system constraint is identified, it must be *exploited*. By "exploiting," Goldratt and Cox meant that you must work to reduce the limiting impact of your system constraint, and, when you do, the output of your system will grow exponentially.

Goldratt and Cox also taught the world about the concept of subordination by explaining that the rest of the steps in your processes must never out-pace your system constraint. Goldratt and Cox also explained that the constraint can never be in an idle state, so work must always be available when it's needed at the constraint. Goldratt and Cox then explained that, if you continue to improve the output of the constraint, eventually it will no longer be the limiting factor in your system. But, having said this, Goldratt and Cox taught us that, once the current constraint is "broken," a new one will appear immediately. And when this takes place, you must move your improvement efforts to this new system constraint.

Yes, as I explained earlier, the value of learning from history allows companies to move further, jump higher, and run faster than their competition. The combination of all of these discoveries and contributions will take companies to new levels of profitability if used with an open mind. In Chapter 17, I will demonstrate how I have taken my past learnings, sorted out the proverbial "good" from the "bad," and developed an integrated improvement methodology that has served me well throughout my career. In that same chapter, I will present a roadmap that describes how to implement my Ultimate Improvement Cycle.

In the next chapter, I'm going to discuss problems and how best to go about solving them. Problems exist everywhere and seem to always come upon us at the most inappropriate time. And how you go about solving them will be critical to the ultimate success of your organization. Following a structured approach will be paramount to your success.

# References

1. John Yorke, *Henry Ford: Master of Lean Agile Processes*, Agile Connection's website, October 11, 2017
2. Walter Shewhart *Economic Control of Quality Of Manufactured Product*, 1931
3. Dr W. Edwards Deming, *Quality, Productivity, and Competitive Position*, 1981
4. Hopp and Spearman's, *Factory Physics – Foundations of Manufacturing Management*, second edition
5. Goldratt and Cox, *The Goal*, North River Press, 1984

# *Chapter 2*

# The Key to Solving Problems

One thing for certain in today's world is that solving problems is something we all face every day. It matters not what type of job you might have, or even if you have no job at all. The fact of the matter is that problems surround everyone, and how you go about trying to solve them will dictate how successful your efforts will be. It should be obvious but, before you can solve a problem, the problem must be clearly defined in terms of the *type of problem* it is, as well as the *details* of the problem must be defined. You must include things like the *what, where, when, who*, etc., in order to adequately define the problem if you are to successfully navigate your problem-solving ship. The fact of the matter is that problem-solving does not have to be a difficult, time-consuming ordeal, but that's precisely how many people perceive this problem-solving exercise. Typically, what happens is that people try something – anything – just to see what happens, and then repeat the process until they either get irritated and quit or sometimes they luck onto the root cause. The absolute key to problem resolution is to follow a methodical, organized, and structured approach until your ultimate destination is reached and the problem is solved.

## Understanding Problems

One of the primary reasons people have difficulty solving problems is that they truly don't understand the nature of the problem. When someone commands, "Fix that problem now!", there's probably no connection between the problem that needs fixing and the person charged with fixing it. That

DOI: 10.4324/9781003462385-2

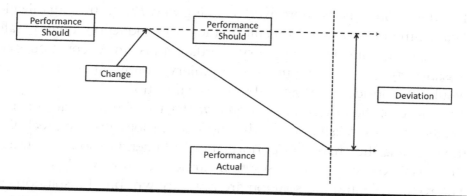

**Figure 2.1**

is, there is no ownership of the problem. Understanding *why* a problem is considered a problem is one of the first steps in solving it. This understanding helps create an appropriate sense of urgency for both the organization and the problem-solvers assigned to it. So, let's take a look at just what a problem really is.

If you look in a dictionary like Webster's, you will see a definition of a problem in very simple terms as "a matter proposed for solution: a puzzle." Although this simple definition describes what a problem is from a literal perspective, it provides barely enough insight to understand what a problem is in the real world. [1] Kepner and Tregoe, in their incredible book, *The Rational Manager – A Systematic Approach to Problem Solving and Decision Making,* define problems as "deviations from expected performance." Kepner and Tregoe present a simple model to illustrate the basic structure of a problem, as shown in Figure 2.1.

Kepner and Tregoe explain that "a performance standard is achieved when all conditions required for acceptable performance are operating as they should." This is true for everything in your work environment, including people, systems, equipment, departments, and so on. Their model, described in Figure 2.1, states that a level of performance is occurring, but then a change takes place and a new level of performance is observed. The difference between the old level of performance and the new level of performance is a *deviation*. So, is this deviation referred to as a problem? Let's answer that question.

In my experience, a problem is not merely a deviation from the expected level of performance. As a matter of fact, for a deviation to be classified as a problem, I believe it must satisfy one or more of the following three basic requirements:

1. The deviation must be perceived as being *negative* to the organization. That is, the deviation must result in a loss of production, quality, safety, etc., that translates into a delivery shortfall, a loss in revenue, customer dissatisfaction, a throughput issue, an injury, or any other "thing" that would be considered negative by the organization.
2. The cause of the deviation is *unknown*. That is, the root cause is not immediately established using the "normal" problem-solving techniques, thus causing the change in performance to linger. Obviously, if the cause isn't known, then the solution cannot be known either.
3. The root cause and the solution are both known, but the solution can't be implemented, because doing so would either cost too much or take too long to implement. As pressure mounts to have the problem fixed, the symptoms get treated, or another "quick fix" is found that, in turn, creates a prolonged episode of the problem.

If the root cause and the solution are known and implementing the solution doesn't take too long and/or cost too much, then the deviation is not considered a problem because it just gets fixed! In short, deviations in and of themselves may or may not become problems, but when you include the critical factors of cost, time, and revenues, deviations most likely will be considered problems.

What if an organization considers a deviation to be positive? In other words, the change that occurs results in better safety, better quality, increased production, or more revenue? Obviously, these conditions are not considered problematic at all. But beware: the bottom line is that when a positive deviation returns to its previously acceptable level of performance (and it will if you don't address and identify the root cause), the organization will now perceive it as being negative and, therefore, it will be considered a problem. Why? Because the positive shift in performance will now become the new expected level of performance. For this reason, it is imperative that **all** deviations be investigated for their root cause with the same level of intensity. In other words, all changes in performance (i.e., deviations) have the potential to become problems. Figure 2.2 is a graphical description of both negative and positive deviations.

In closing, this leads us to a couple of [2] problem-solving truths with more to follow later on in the chapter:

■ **Problem-Solving Truth 1:** All problems are the direct result of changes that occurred prior to the new level of performance.

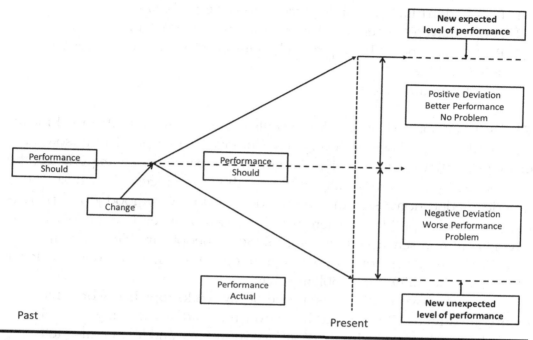

**Figure 2.2**

■ **Problem-Solving Truth 2:** Deviations in performance don't become problems unless they negatively impact the organization, their root cause is unknown, or it costs too much or takes too much time to fix them.

## Problem-Solving Skills

As a general rule, I believe that most people become excited when they solve a problem. There is actually a physiological reason that explains these emotions. When people get excited – when they do something that they feel good about, such as solving a problem – the brain emits endorphins. Endorphins are the purest opiate in the world, so people, in a sense, truly do get "high" when they solve a problem. Their level of satisfaction actually seems to be proportional to the size and complexity of the problem and how severe the problem was perceived by the organization.

But if people feel so good when they solve problems, then why is it that so many people look for ways to avoid them? [1] Kepner and Tregoe tell us that the answer depends on the presence of one or more of the following:

1. People don't have the skills needed to solve problems.
2. People haven't experienced success in solving problems.
3. People have never been positively reinforced when they successfully solved problems.
4. People are afraid to fail.

Why is it that some people lack the skills needed to solve problems? I mean, they do their jobs flawlessly every day, but give them a problem to solve and many times they're just lost. They're not stupid; based on my experience, the answer lies in the level of training (if any) they have received (or not). The American educational system certainly doesn't do a very good job of preparing one to solve problems! There is a difference between being educated, or having common sense, or being logical. Some people are blessed with an inordinate amount of common sense and logic, but others are not. The latter group must be trained in problem-solving.

I remember two participants in one of my workshops had worked for their company for 27 years and had never received any training on problem-solving. This is a sad state of affairs! [1] Kepner and Tregoe also tell us that some people are afraid to fail, so they shy away from attempting to solve problems. Why are they afraid to fail? Consider young children in Little League baseball, whose frantic parents criticize them for striking out or making an error. Similar behavior occurs in the workplace. Sometimes, even when problems are solved, negative feedback occurs with statements like, "What took you so long?" This kind of comment is not likely to inspire people to go out and look for new problems to solve! People must be made to feel good about themselves when they solve a problem, and they must be allowed to fail, or they will stop trying. In the process of learning, mistakes will be made, and if we learn from those mistakes and aren't criticized for them, we will move in a positive direction and continue learning.

## The Need for a Structured Approach

Problem-solving need not be a difficult, time-consuming ordeal, but that is exactly how many people perceive it. Usually, these same people try something – anything – just to see what happens, and then repeat the process until they either get frustrated and quit, or they luck onto the root cause. I have always believed that luck plays a major role in solving a problem, but the luck I'm referring to is **L**aboring **U**nder **C**orrect **K**nowledge, or LUCK! This represents a structured approach.

There are many advantages to using a structured approach in a problem-solving exercise. In fact, a structured approach will:

1. Reduce the probability that key factors to the problem will be overlooked.
2. Force us to re-evaluate and understand the basic process of the problem.
3. Discourage the reliance on hunches, intuition, and the "I know what the problem is" syndrome.
4. Increase the probability that the root cause or causes of the problem will be found.
5. Result in solved problems.

Contrary to popular belief, problem-solving success does not result from superior knowledge. Certainly, it helps to understand the process as well as the problem, but total knowledge of the object experiencing the problem is not a prerequisite for solving the problem. What is important is being able to use problem-solving tools effectively.

A structured approach to problem-solving will succeed only if such an approach is established as the norm and expected behavior. A shift in problem-solving expectations is just as important as teaching and learning new skills. Failure to set these expectations – that is, failure to demand that the root cause of the problem be uncovered – will seriously impede any effort to upgrade problem-solving in any organization.

In one company, I conducted five workshops on problem-solving. The GM was concerned that he hadn't seen a shift in success at problem-solving, so I attended one of his daily production meetings and listened as everyone presented a seemingly endless list of problems to solve. Surprisingly, never once was the question of root cause raised. However, when the GM began expecting root cause analysis, the shift to solved problems was immediate and swift. The leadership in any organization must ask this basic question, if the employees are going to routinely use this root cause analysis.

## More Problem-Solving Truths

The following [2] are five more truths regarding problem-solving:

- **Problem-Solving Truth 3:** Systematic methods only appear to take longer than the "change something and see what happens" approach.

- **Problem-Solving Truth 4:** Problem-solving success is not the result of superior knowledge.
- **Problem-Solving Truth 5:** Structured approaches to solving problems will only be successful if they are established as the norm.
- **Problem-Solving Truth 6:** Today's problem solutions could very well be tomorrow's problems if the right questions aren't asked.
- **Problem-Solving Truth 7:** Today's problems are yesterday's solutions implemented without data.

## The Logical Pathway of Problem-Solving

Now that you have seen the advantages of using a structured, systematic problem-solving approach, one that is founded upon basic reasoning and logic, let's look at a typical problem-solving format. Many problem-solving formats exist, but all use, in some form or another, the basic elements of a logical pathway. So, let's look at each one of these in more detail by describing what each element is intended to accomplish, along with some appropriate examples. We'll start by looking at my [2] Problem-Solving Roadmap that I first introduced in 2018. Figure 2.3 is the basic structure of my Problem-Solving Roadmap and it is my belief that, if you follow the logical steps outlined in this roadmap, you will become much more proficient and successful at solving problems.

The layout of my Problem-Solving Roadmap contains six major sections and seventeen individual steps. The six major sections include:

   I. Define, Describe, and Appraise the Problem.
  II. Investigate, Organize, and Analyze the Data.
 III. Formulate and Test a Causal Theory.
 IV. Choose the Most Probable Cause.
  V. Develop, Test, and Implement a Solution.
 VI. Implement, Document, and Celebrate.

Each of the major sections of my roadmap are intended to describe the major activities, whereas the individual steps describe the individual actions that must be taken in order to successfully solve an existing problem. Let's now look at each of the individual steps.

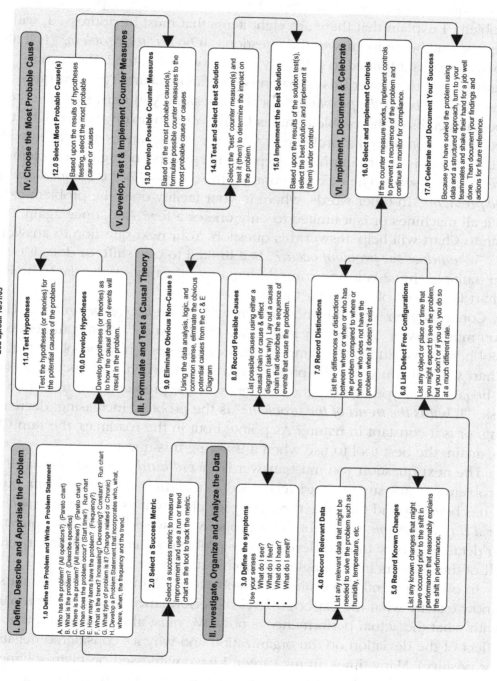

## Problem Solving Roadmap

Bob Sproull 10/31/05

### I. Define, Describe and Appraise the Problem

**1.0 Define the Problem and Write a Problem Statement**

A. Who has the problem? (All operators?) (Pareto chart)
B. What is the problem? (Describe specifics)
C. Where is the problem? (All machines?) (Pareto chart)
D. When does the problem occur? (Start time?) Run chart
E. How many items have the problem? (Frequency?)
F. What is the trend? Increasing? Decreasing? Constant? Run chart
G. What type of problem is it? (Change related or Chronic)
H. Develop a Problem Statement that incorporates who, what, where, when, the frequency and the trend.

**2.0 Select a Success Metric**

Select a success metric to measure improvement and use a run or trend chart as the tool to track the metric.

### II. Investigate, Organize and Analyze the Data

**3.0 Define the symptoms**

Use your senses
• What do I see?
• What do I feel?
• What do I hear?
• What do I smell?

**4.0 Record Relevant Data**

List any relevant data that might be needed to solve the problem such as humidity, temperature, etc.

**5.0 Record Known Changes**

List any known changes that might have occurred prior to the shift in performance that reasonably explains the shift in performance.

**6.0 List Defect Free Configurations**

List any object or place or time that you might expect to see the problem, but you don't or if you do, you do so at a much different rate.

**7.0 Record Distinctions**

List the differences or distinctions between where or when or who has the problem compared to where or when or who does not have the problem when it doesn't exist.

**8.0 Record Possible Causes**

List possible causes using either a causal chain or cause & effect diagram (ask why) Lay out a causal chain that describes the sequence of events that cause the problem.

### III. Formulate and Test a Causal Theory

**9.0 Eliminate Obvious Non-Cause s**

Using the data analysis, logic, and common sense, eliminate the obvious potential causes from the C & E Diagram

**10.0 Develop Hypotheses**

Develop hypotheses (or theories) as to how the causal chain of events will result in the problem.

**11.0 Test Hypotheses**

Test the hypotheses (or theories) for the potential causes of the problem.

### IV. Choose the Most Probable Cause

**12.0 Select Most Probable Cause(s)**

Based upon the results of hypotheses testing, select the most probable cause or causes

### V. Develop, Test & Implement Counter Measures

**13.0 Develop Possible Counter Measures**

Based on the most probable cause(s), formulate possible counter measures to the most probable cause or causes

**14.0 Test and Select Best Solution**

Select the "best" counter measure(s) and test it (them) to determine the impact on the problem.

**15.0 Implement the Best Solution**

Based upon the results of the solution test(s), select the best solution and implement it (them) under control.

### VI. Implement, Document & Celebrate

**16.0 Select and Implement Controls**

If the counter measure works, implement controls to prevent a recurrence of the problem and continue to monitor for compliance.

**17.0 Celebrate and Document Your Success**

Because you have solved the problem using data and a structured approach, turn to your teammates and shake their hand for a job well done. Then document your findings and actions for future reference.

**Figure 2.3**

# Define the Problem and Write a Problem Statement

In the first section of my roadmap, Define, Describe, and Appraise the Problem, I explain that there are eight items that must be addressed, with the first one being to answer the question, *"Who has the problem?"* Is it all operators or is it limited to primarily one or two operators? The recommended tool to answer this question is the Pareto Chart. The next question asks, *"What is the problem?"* For this question, you must describe the specific details of the problem that is facing your company. Stating why this problem is considered a problem or what are the negatives associated with this problem is a very important step toward understanding the problem you are trying to solve. The next question to answer is, *"What is the location of the problem?"* In other words, where in your facility does the problem exist? Is it all machines or is it limited to only one or a few? And, once again, the Pareto Chart will help answer this question. Your next question to answer is, *"When does the problem occur?"* Is it limited to one shift, or does it occur on multiple shifts? Is it occurring during a specific time of the day? The Run Chart is the tool of choice for this question.

Continuing on, you must now *identify the frequency of the problem*. Here, you must answer *"How many items have this problem?"* My recommended tool here is the Run Chart, simply because, if this is a new problem, the Run Chart will tell you when the problem started and when it has occurred since it began. Once you identify the frequency of the problem, you must now ask, *"What is the trend of the problem?"* Is the problem increasing, decreasing, or is it constant in nature? As pointed out in the roadmap, the Run Chart is, again, the best tool to use when answering this question.

The next question you must answer is *"What kind of problem is it?"* If the problem has just surfaced, it is classified as a *change-related problem*, but, if it has been around for some time, then we classify it as a *chronic problem*, or a *day-1 problem*. Once you have properly answered all of these questions in detail, it is now time to develop your problem statement that incorporates all of the answers into a single descriptive statement.

In order to identify and ultimately solve a problem effectively, we must know exactly what the expected level of performance should be, compared with what the actual performance is now. We must also understand the effect of the deviation on the organization and why it's considered negative (or positive). Many times, in my career, I have witnessed problem-solving teams fail to follow this step to completely understand why a problem is considered a problem for their organization.

# Describe and Define the Problem

Effectively describing and defining the problem is, in some respects, the most significant step in the problem-solving process. The problem description builds the foundation for the problem-solving activities that will follow, so it must be as complete and accurate as possible. For example, suppose you were given the task of solving a problem involving a motor that stopped functioning. Because you had solved a similar problem in the past, you assumed the root cause was a burned-out armature. By limiting yourself to actions that might be related to only things like a defective overload, or a short in the electrical system, you may miss other potential causes of the problem. What if the real root cause was seized bearings that resulted in excessive heat build-up, which, in turn, shut the motor down?

When describing the problem, it helps to view it from two separate perspectives: the object and the object's defect or fault. By asking a series of simple questions, it is possible to develop a more complete definition of the problem as follows:

a. *What* is the specific object with the problem and what feature of the object is considered to have a fault or defect? In other words, what is it, and what's wrong with it?

b. *Where* geographically and physically on the object is the problem or fault found?

c. *When* in time, and when in the process cycle of the object, was the problem first observed? Determining when the problem started is key to understanding the problem.

d. *How many* objects have the problem, and how many faults or defects are observed on the objects? In this step, be very specific in terms of the number of objects that currently exhibit the problem.

e. *What* is the trend and scope of the defect or fault? Is the problem rate increasing, decreasing, or remaining constant? Is there a distinct pattern for the defect or fault?

It is helpful to answer these questions by contrasting or comparing the object with the problem to another like it (or to a similar object) without the problem. That is, ask not only where the problem is, but also where it is not. Or, where would you expect to see the problem, but you do not? These comparisons help you zero in on *distinctions* that are important to consider in your effort to solve the problem. When this step is complete, you should then combine all that you have learned about the problem and then develop your *problem statement*. The problem statement becomes a sort of problem-solving compass for all of your future efforts required to eventually solve the problem.

## Select a Success Metric

Now that you have clearly and completely defined your problem, you must come up with a way to measure it that you can track, in order to determine the effect or impact of your changes. This success metric, which you should track on a Run Chart, is intended to demonstrate the impact of all changes you make along the way as you work to solve the problem at hand. The success metric can be something as simple as a percentage reduction of the problem or even a current metric you track that is tied to the problem being studied.

## Define the Symptoms

Solving problems is the culmination of many different activities, one of the most important of which is developing a list of symptoms related to the problem being solved. If you've ever been a patient in an emergency department (ED) at a hospital, then you have probably observed the actions of the ED doctors and nurses. Doctors understand that developing a list of symptoms is paramount to a precise diagnosis of their patients. What kind of information is of interest to the doctors? They, or the nurses, usually check your temperature, blood pressure, pulse rate, your eyes, ears, your abdomen, your lungs, etc. Doctors are clearly searching your body for symptoms that might lead them to the root cause of your ailment.

When I was working at Michelin many years ago, there was a man from the parent company who taught me the importance of using my senses to uncover potential future problems. When he arrived at our plant in Dothan, Alabama, I had been selected to show him around our manufacturing facility. He asked me to take him on a tour, so we went out onto the shop floor. He asked me if I had heard something and when I asked him what I was supposed to hear, he simply told me to stand where I was and when I heard it, to come get him. I was confused, but I did what he asked me to do. I stood in this location and listened to all of the sounds until, finally, I thought I heard the sound of gears grinding. I went and got him and then told him what I had heard. He smiled and said, "Good, Mr. Sproull, many people listen, but they don't really hear."

We then began walking again until we stopped near one of the many extruders in our facility. He asked me, "Mr. Sproull, do you smell it?" I asked him what I should be smelling. Once again, he smiled and said, "When you smell it, come get me." I stood there and patiently began sniffing until I smelled the odor of burning rubber. I went and got him, explained what I had smelled, and again, he smiled and said, "Very good, Mr. Sproull, many people sniff, but they don't really smell." With that, we moved toward a large extruder. He placed his hand on the extruder and said, "Do you feel it, Mr. Sproull?" I asked him what I was supposed to feel and, just like with the first two senses, he told me to come get him when I felt it. I touched the extruder and felt a vibration, but when I touched another, similar extruder, I didn't feel the same vibration. I also noticed a difference in temperatures, so I went and got him, and explained what I had felt. He smiled and said, "Very good, Mr. Sproull, many people touch, but they don't feel."

We then moved on to another machine used to hand-lay rubber materials on the carcass of a tire being built. It was near shift change, so we stood there, watching the operator. He turned to me and asked me if I saw it. And again, I asked him what it was I was supposed to be seeing. And again, he told me to come get him when I saw it. I stood and watched the operator's method, but, when the shift changed, and a new operator began building carcasses, the method being used was clearly different between the two operators. I then went and told this man what I had observed and again he smiled and said, "Very good, Mr. Sproull, many people look, but they don't really see."

This exercise taught me a very important lesson about using my senses to look for and find the various symptoms of problems. If you're in a typical manufacturing setting, you might detect common symptoms through smell, touch, sound, or sight, and sometimes even taste. Let's look at some common examples that you might uncover using your senses.

- *Smell*: If you smell the odor of burning rubber, you might look for worn or loose V-belts, or an electrical problem, or a problem with overheating bearings.
- *Touch*: If you feel abnormal vibration or elevated temperatures, you might look for worn bearings in a motor, loose bolts, misalignment of shafts, etc.

- *Sound*: If you hear a grinding or scraping noise, you might look for misalignments or misaligned gears, etc.
- *Sight*: You can detect many things by looking for abnormal fluid levels, excessive gaps, jerking motions, work method differences, and many other things.

The point here is that using your senses to detect symptoms is a very important part of problem-solving events.

## Record Relevant Data

In your experiences in problem solving, how many times have you gotten deep into a problem, only to discover that you were missing some key information and you had to go search for it? In this section of the Problem-Solving Roadmap, it is important to record any data that might be relevant and needed to solve the problem. Relevant data might include things like:

- Humidity data in the proximity of the problem being solved.
- Temperature data in the immediate proximity of the machine in question or the temperature of the machine itself.
- The speed of the machine in question.
- Any pressure settings of the machine in question.
- Guide settings of the machine in question.

## Record Known Changes

Many times, problems are the direct result of changes that have occurred prior to the new level of performance (i.e., the problem). The change or changes responsible for the new level of performance could have occurred immediately prior to the onset of the problem or it could have been a change made in the distant past. For this reason, *all* changes must be listed and investigated. It's always a good idea to have some sort of manual close by for the operators, maintenance mechanics, and others to record changes.

There are numerous reasons or ways that changes might have occurred, so let's look at some of these:

- *Adjustments to process settings.* These are sometimes very difficult to find, simply because not all changes are documented and recorded. This special category of changes is referred to as tampering and, believe me, it goes on in your facility. Again, make sure you have some kind of recording device close by so that all changes can be recorded when they occur.

- *Modifications or improvements to the process.* These types of changes include both well-studied and unstudied, well-documented and undocumented, well-planned and unplanned improvements that may have an impact on how equipment or processes run after they are implemented.

- *Major or minor maintenance work on processes.* This category of change includes things like simple tightening of nuts and bolts, adjustments to belts, or even major overhauls. It includes both simple and complex work done by maintenance and is sometimes not documented.

- *Preventive maintenance (PM) activities.* Preventive maintenance is by far one of the most important activities in every manufacturing facility. If done correctly, it is specific in nature and usually requires little effort in the search for documentation. But, as we all know, other things get done as part of PM that never get documented.

- *Changes to raw materials.* This is sometimes an elusive change because process changes at the supplier location are rarely communicated to the customer. My advice here is to implement a system with all of your suppliers to notify you of all changes made to their processes or materials.

- *Changes to environmental conditions.* Although we would like to believe that our products are robust over a wide range of temperatures and humidities, in many cases they simply aren't.

- *Shutdowns and start-ups.* Shutdowns and start-ups can create a real dilemma for the problem solver(s) simply because many times they are not documented. If things like pressure and temperature stabilization are important factors in your process, it is imperative that these stoppages and restarts are well documented. You cannot collect too much information, so start documenting changes.

- *Changes in operators.* The simple fact of the matter is that no two operators' work methods are ever quite the same, especially if the work to be done is labor intensive.

- *Changes in speeds or production rates.* Speed up! This seems to be the norm in many manufacturing companies and, if done under control and well documented, it shouldn't be a problem for you.

■ *Changes in utilities.* Sometimes, even in the best facilities, there are changes in things like air pressure, line voltage, etc., that remain undetected until they create a performance problem. Make it clear to your operators that any noticeable change in utilities must be documented.

Unfortunately, in many organizations, changes turn out to be a problem, simply because changes are made frequently, but many of these changes are not documented or, if they are, the documentation isn't complete. If this is the case (i.e., no or incomplete documentation of the change), then you may be forced to reconstruct the changes based on interviews with the process owners. It is enormously important to document any change made to your processes, including things like changes in raw material lots, actions taken to repair or improve processes, changes in equipment settings, and other changes. This is so critical that I cannot emphasize it enough! If your company does not thoroughly document changes, then you must force this improvement action. I always recommend using a Run Chart and recordong all known changes directly onto the Run Chart to demonstrate cause-and-effect relationships.

## List Defect-Free Configurations

When individual parts are linked together for the purpose of performing a distinct function, this linkage is referred to as a *configuration*. An example of a configuration might be the transmission in a car. It's an example of where individual components (e.g., shafts, cams, pinions, clutches, etc.) are linked together to allow a car to move forward and backward at different speeds. What if a problem developed where the car would go backward, but would not go forward? In this case, reverse would be considered a *defect-free configuration*. Identifying Defect-Free Configurations (DFCs) is a very important action because DFCs help us eliminate potential causes of problems.

In this section of the Problem-Solving Roadmap, list any object or place or time that you might expect to see the problem, but you don't or, if you do, you do so at a much different rate. These defect-free configurations can be very useful as you move along the problem-solving pathway. Maybe you have two supposedly identical machines producing the same product, but only one of the machines has the problem. Or maybe you have multiple operators running one machine, but one of the operators does not have the problem or does but at a much lower rate than other operators.

## Record Distinctions

Returning to our car example in the last section, if we were trying to understand the reason why it only moves backward, we might start by asking the question, "What is different or unique about why it will go backward, compared to why it won't move forward?" If we can answer this basic question, then chances are we will be able to pinpoint the most probable cause of the problem. The difference between where we have the problem and where we don't have the problem is referred to as a *distinction.*

In this section you should list the differences or distinctions between where or when or who has the problem, compared with where or when or who does not have the problem when it doesn't exist. These distinctions can prove to be very helpful in your problem-solving efforts. For example, suppose you have three machines producing the same product, but only one is having the problem. What needs to happen is a complete analysis of the machine with the problem, compared with the two where the problem does not exist. These two machines are the defect-free configurations, so you must find the distinctions that exist between the machine with the problem when compared to the two without the problem.

## Record Possible Causes

Once you've completed your analysis of the problem, you can now create a list of potential causes. This list must be one that is based on a logical, systematic look at all of the information you have been able to collect to this point. Ask yourself and carefully answer the question, "Based upon the information I have gathered, how could this change have caused this change in performance?" Because this list of possible causes has been logically developed, it reduces the chances of relying on hunches, intuition, or even guesses. If you need more data or information to develop this list more thoroughly and make it more useable, then go collect what you need. Effective possible cause lists are the combination of experience, good data, and the combined expertise of you and your co-workers. And don't be afraid to ask for help if you need it

– it's actually a sign of intelligence! Remember, problems represent the outcome of a series of multiple cause-and-effect relationships.

I have found that the most effective way to list possible causes is to use either a Causal Chain or a Cause-and-Effect Diagram. If you lay out a Causal Chain correctly, you will have described the sequence of events that caused the problem.

## Eliminate Obvious Non-Causes

The list of possible causes, constructed according to a logical and factual approach, should contain realistic potential causes. The next step is to reduce this list into a shorter list of most probable causes by testing each possible cause against a pre-determined set of test criteria. Using something as simple as "if-then" logical statements, you will be able to develop these test criteria quite simply. For example, use a question like this, "If I increase the voltage, then (some predictable event) should happen." Each possible cause must be looked at individually and only the causes surviving analysis will be considered as one of the most probable causes. The final list must then be tested using even more rigorous criteria to further zero in on the final root cause (or causes). An important point to remember is that you must never assume that a problem has only a single cause.

## Develop Hypotheses

In this step, you will develop your hypotheses (or theories) as to the how the step-by-step cause-and-effect chain of events could result in the problem you are trying to solve. It is my belief that the most effective way to accomplish this is by using the Causal Chain. Without this step-by-step cause-and-effect chain of events, it is usually not possible to develop your theory or theories as to why the problem exists.

For those of you without much experience in using causal chains, let's look at a simple example.

Figure 2.4 is an example of a causal chain. Working from right to left, we see that the problem we are trying to solve is that a press has stopped. When constructing causal chains, the object is listed (i.e., "Press") on top of the line and the state that it is in is listed directly beneath it. You then ask "Why?" the press has stopped. In this example, the press stopped because

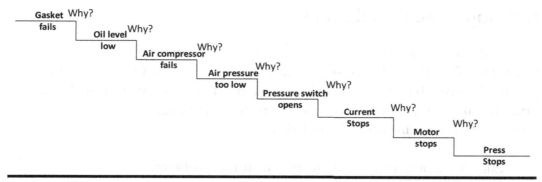

**Figure 2.4**

the motor stopped. You then continue asking "Why?" for each step until you reach the root cause, which in this example was that a gasket has failed. Causal chains can be a single stair-step, like our example, or they could have multiple stairways. We will discuss causal chains in much more depth later in this chapter.

## Test Hypothesis

A list of possible causes, constructed according to a logical and factual approach, should contain realistic potential causes. It is now time to test your hypotheses to shorten your list even further. Using something as simple as an "if-then" logic statement, you can develop your test criteria very easily. For example, ask yourself, "If I increase the voltage, then what should I expect the outcome to be?" Each potential cause must be looked at individually and only those causes surviving analysis will be considered as the most probable cause(s). The final list must be tested in depth to further zero in on the final root cause.

## Select the Most Probable Cause

Based on your results achieved from your hypothesis testing, it is now time to select the most probable cause or causes. It's important to remember that, even though you have worked hard to narrow your list of most probable causes down to a single entity, it is very possible that you will end up with more than one most-probable cause of your problem. But having said this, it is possible that your final list will contain multiple entities.

# Develop Possible Solutions

Based on the most probable cause or causes, it's now time to formulate potential solutions to the most probable cause or causes. Once the list of potential causes has been refined to a manageable level, you must decide upon the most appropriate actions, if any, to take. Several actions or combinations of actions are possible as follows:

1. Take no action and decide to live with the problem.
2. Take a short-term action that effectively will buy you some time.
3. Take a long-term corrective action that eliminates the problem.

Usually, we opt for a combination of actions 2 and 3. The priority is to stop the negative effect of the problem first and then to implement true preventive actions. Whatever the action taken, we should always consider its potential impact on the process and the controls that can be put in place to prevent a recurrence of the problem. An example of this is adding a check as part of the preventive maintenance on the equipment.

# Test and Select the Best Solution

Frequently, I have seen problem-solving teams go through a complete analysis of a problem, develop solutions, implement them, and then assume they have fixed the problem. I have a warning for you. *Never* implement a solution without validating that your solution does not have a negative impact on the process in question! Always perform a first-piece inspection (possibly a more extensive inspection) to assure that the product being produced meets all intended performance requirements.

I am reminded of a problem-solving team at a large sheet molding compound (SMC) supplier that was absolutely certain that its root cause analysis had led it to the problem-solving "Promised Land." The team had done an excellent job of determining why a bonding machine always seemed to bond components out of position. This team was so confident that they implemented the solution and left the premises to celebrate. After all, this had been one of the plant's single biggest problems, and the team had done what no other team had been able to do! While celebrating though, the equipment produced thirty-five scrap parts. The "improvement" had altered the position of another component, and the team had failed to test production after making the change! Remember this: today's solutions could very well be tomorrow's problems. And again, always test the impact of your solution before you declare success!

## Implement Appropriate Controls

Once the root cause has been identified and a solution is tested and implemented, it's extremely important that you also implement controls to prevent the problem from recurring. These controls might be, for example, an update to the preventive maintenance checklist or a control chart of the measurable variable associated with the problem. The critical point is that you never walk away from a solved problem without implementing preventive measures and/or controls. If the SMC problem-solving team had done this, they would not have experienced the thirty-five scraps!

## Celebrate, Recognize Success, and Document

One of the things I always recommend to companies is that, when a difficult problem is "solved," they should always recognize the success of the problem-solving team and celebrate their accomplishment. Why do I recommend this? When people are recognized positively for what they have done, they are incentivized to solve more problems. I have seen some companies actually present teams with monetary incentives as a way of recognizing what they have accomplished.

The final step in the problem-solving actions is to document what the team has accomplished. By using the sixteen steps in succession, a formal report can easily be written and saved as an example for future teams. Problem-solving teams start by identifying and fully defining the problem and then listing the symptoms and changes that they observed. Once these preliminary actions have been successfully completed, then the search for causes and solutions is accomplished. By following these steps, a formal report can be completed for future teams to follow.

## Reason, Good Judgment, and Common Sense

The best problem-solving tools in the world are of little value if we ignore reason, good judgment, and common sense. No tool should ever be complete without these important attributes. With that in mind, here are eight important problem-solving fundamentals that one must consider when attempting to solve a problem.

1. *Develop a complete definition of the problem.* If this is not the most important fundamental, it certainly is close to it. It is absolutely imperative that you completely understand the problem before you try to solve it. I am reminded of a problem-solving effort involving a motor attached to a robotic arm that was used to cut fiberglass parts. This particular motor had burned out five times and had been replaced five times. I was asked to get involved and assist the team working on this problem. My first question to the team was, "What do you mean when you say the motor burned out?" The team told me that the armature was shorting out. My second question was, "What did you see when you opened the motor casing?" The team's response was to stare at me like a deer in the headlights. It seems that no one had actually looked inside the casing to further define the problem. When we opened the motor, we found burned-out bearings. The team redefined the problem accordingly and was able to determine that a flow switch used to regulate coolant had been mislocated and that the motor bearings were not being cooled correctly.
2. *Develop accurate definitions of symptoms.* Symptoms are a sign that something has changed or gone wrong. They are the faults that we see, hear, smell, and feel (or taste, if you are a chef or cook). A machine that makes a funny noise; the smell of burning rubber or plastic; the feel of a vibration; a change in the appearance of a product's characteristic are all symptoms of a potential problem. The bottom line is that you should use all of your senses to find *all* of the symptoms.
3. *Look for simultaneous symptoms.* When you see multiple symptoms, they generally have a common cause. When two or more symptoms occur at the same time, they typically are the result of a common cause or origin, even if one is the result of the other, such as two presses powered by the same compressed air source both failing at the same time.
4. *Independent causes may or may not occur simultaneously.* When symptoms are not simultaneous in occurrence, then they most likely are the result of independent problems and causes.
5. *Find defect-free configurations (DFCs).* Configurations are individual parts linked together to perform a given function. A defect-free configuration is the combination of components in a nonfunctioning system, machine, or process that is still functioning correctly. DFCs

could also include another identical or similar process or piece of equipment.

6. *Look for distinctions.* When comparing a nonfunctioning piece of equipment with another one that is functioning (or to a similar piece of functioning equipment), ask yourself, "What is unique, different, or special about it?"

7. *List and investigate changes.* A change is any event that precedes the initial onset of a symptom of a problem. Because the change precedes the problem, it is a potential cause of the problem. It is important to remember that changes do not always occur immediately prior to the onset of the problem. The change may have happened long before the first symptom(s) appeared, and the first symptom may have appeared long before you even noticed it.

8. *Always test to determine cause(s).* Never rely solely on what you think might be happening. Think through the problem and then imagine what you should be seeing and test for it.

## Intermittent and Recurring Problems

Have you ever worked on a problem where symptoms appear, then disappear, the reappear, and so on? This is referred to as an *intermittent problem* and it can be very frustrating and sometimes difficult to both recognize and to solve. Once again, however, if you follow a systematic approach as I have laid out, you will significantly reduce the degree of difficulty. One of the keys to solving this type of problem is to spend lots of time on the process with the problem. To find the root cause of intermittent problems, you must determine the timing of the symptoms.

The following is a simple, yet effective, six-step procedure to do so.

1. Document each time the symptom(s) appear and disappear. It's important to record specific dates and times, including when the symptoms began and ended (i.e., the duration of the symptoms).

2. Document all the changes that occur prior to and immediately after the onset of the symptoms. Operator shifts, environmental conditions (e.g., temperature, humidity before and after symptoms arise), operating speeds, material changes, and the like are all potentially useful clues that may help solve the problem.

3. Create a simple time-based Run Chart, depicting start and stop times for each occurrence of the symptom(s).

4. Transpose the documented changes directly onto the Run Chart at the appropriate date and time coordinates.
5. Look for a correlation between the documented changes and the date/time that the symptoms occurred.

Analyze the plotted results. Is there a repeating pattern? That is, do the symptoms occur at the same time every day? Is the pattern periodic? Is the pattern cyclical?

## Recurring Problems

Sometimes, when a process or specific piece of equipment has allegedly been repaired, the same problem recurs with exactly the same symptoms as before. Recurring problems are always the direct result of inadequate or incomplete problem-solving techniques used in the first place. Typically, recurring problems exist because of one or more of the following actions:

■ The root cause of the problem was not found; therefore, only a symptom was treated.
■ The repair was inadequate or incomplete.
■ The diagnosis was made with insufficient or inaccurate information and thus was incorrect.
■ The root cause was purposely avoided. Sometimes, people avoid problems they don't know how to solve or repairs they don't know how to make. Sometimes, people even avoid problems because they are too tired, too lazy, or don't care.
■ The cost or time to make the repair was prohibitive, so as a result a temporary, cheaper, or quicker repair was made. We all know that cheaper repairs always cost more in the long run, and quicker repairs always take longer in the final analysis, don't we?

## Potential Problem-Solving Traps

Solving a problem, like any other activity, is not always as straightforward as some tools and techniques would lead you to believe. In the real world, there always seems to be obstacles or interferences that get in the way and/or lead the problem-solver on a wild goose chase. Although you can't eliminate these problem-solving "traps," it's important that you are aware that they exist. Being on guard against them will help you stay on the path to the true root cause of the problem. Typical traps that you should be aware of include the following:

■ *Erroneous information, facts, or data supplied by someone involved in the process with the problem.* This misinformation could be supplied deliberately in an attempt to sabotage the process for personal gain (e.g., to obtain time off due to equipment downtime, or unintentionally by someone just trying to be helpful who doesn't understand the importance of accurate information). Be wary of generalized statements such as, "It's always been like this," or "I think it happened last week," or any statements that are based on emotion. When in doubt, collect new data or seek new information from other sources.

■ *Defective replacement parts from the supplier.* Being trusting people, we automatically assume that, if we install a replacement part directly from the package it came in, it must be functional. Believe it or not, this is not always the case! If you are reasonably certain that one of the equipment parts is defective, and you install a replacement part that doesn't fix the problem, my advice to you is to remove the replacement part and have it tested for functionality, just to be sure.

■ *Defective measurement tools or gauges.* I am reminded of a team working on a rather large hydraulic press with a hot oil problem. The team had tried everything they could think of to solve the problem, but they could not locate its root cause. The team had made one fatal mistake in analyzing the problem: they had assumed that all of the gauges on the press were functioning properly and, in particular, that the pressure readings were accurate (one of the known causes for hot oil is excessive pressure). When I explained the concept of problem-solving traps to them, the team checked all the gauges and found the pressure gauge was not giving accurate information. The actual delivered pressure was much higher than the gauge reading. The team replaced the defective gauge, adjusted the pressure into the normal operating range, and the problem was solved. Incorrect data are actually more dangerous than no data because they lead you down the wrong path.

■ *Defective input material.* Raw material, which is accepted as being good when it is actually out-of-spec, can create a trap. Raw material characteristics that affect the final product can lead you to the wrong conclusions. For example, take one of the most important characteristics, viscosity. If the viscosity moves outside the acceptable range, the material will exhibit different flow properties inside the mold. One team I worked with was trying to solve a surface quality issue. Because the tag on the batch of SMC had an acceptable value for viscosity, the team assumed that the viscosity was not the root cause. When they retested the material, however, they found the viscosity to be too high, thus creating a material flow problem. This was the root cause of the problem. If one assumes that the material characteristic (e.g., viscosity) is acceptable when it isn't, wrong assumptions and conclusions will be the end product. When in doubt, retest!

■ *Incorrect drawings or schematics.* How often in your company have modifications been made to equipment without the related drawings or schematics being updated? Even subtle changes to the process wiring, hydraulics, or such must be added to the drawings in a timely manner. When this fails to occur, drawings and schematics become a trap for future problem-solvers.

■ *Incorrect logic on your part.* Even though you have thoroughly thought through a problem, it's possible that your assumptions may be erroneous or inaccurate. Therefore, it is always good practice to have someone review your thoughts and conclusions. Far from being a sign of weakness, doing so actually shows foresight.

Let's now review two of the most common problem-solving tools that can be immensely helpful when trying to resolve a problem. Specifically, we will review *cause-and-effect diagrams*, and *causal chains*.

## Cause-and-Effect Diagrams

One of the most popular and widely used problem-solving tools available is the *cause-and-effect (C & E) diagram*. C & E diagrams were developed by Dr. Kaoru Ishikawa, a noted Japanese consultant and author of *A Guide to Quality Control* (2). They have been used successfully by teams around the world. In honor of Dr. Ishikawa, this tool is sometimes referred to as an Ishikawa diagram, but it is also referred to as a "fishbone diagram," because its basic structure resembles the skeleton of a fish. Whatever you wish to call it, a C & E diagram is a useful tool that must be part of the problem-solver's tool kit.

Figure 2.5 (below) shows the basic structure of the C & E diagram, which is used to develop and organize potential causes of a problem. The potential causes are listed on the fishbones driving toward the problem (i.e., the effect). The effect or problem statement is stated to the right, while the potential causes are listed as "fishbones" to the left under the appropriate category headings. By arranging lists in this manner, there is often a greater understanding of the problem and possible contributing factors.

Typical C & E diagrams, as depicted in Figure 2.5, are constructed with four major categories of potential causes (the four Ms: Man, Method, Materials, and Machines), but the C & E diagram should be customized to the needs of the user. In other words, other categories can be added to further organize the potential causes. In our example, two other categories, Environment and Measurement, have been added.

The following are the steps used to create a C & E diagram:

1. Develop a statement of the problem which describes the problem in terms of what it is, where it is occurring, when it is occurring, and how extensive it is. This statement is the effect and is listed to the right on the C & E diagram.
2. Brainstorm and create a list of causal categories that will be used to develop the possible causes of the problem on the C & E diagram. For example, if the problem being studied was equipment-related, our categories might be listed as Electrical, Mechanical, Pneumatic, Man,

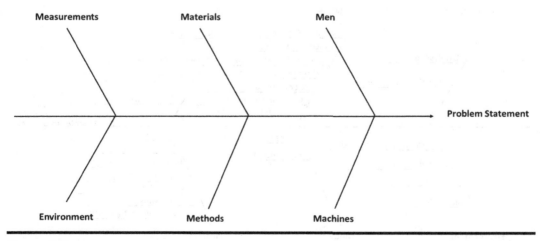

**Figure 2.5**

Methods, and Materials. The team must be creative when selecting the causal categories.

3. Construct the C & E diagram by:
   a. Placing the problem statement to the right of the fishbones.
   b. Listing the causal categories above and below the centerline or "spine" of the fishbone diagram.
   c. Brainstorm and list possible causes on the fishbones under the appropriate causal category headings.
4. Interpret the C & E diagram by:
   a. Looking for causes listed in the individual fishbones and testing the potential causes to determine if they have an impact on the effect.
   b. Gather additional data and information to validate the potential causes.

Let's now look at an example of a real C & E diagram (Figure 2.6). In our example, a team was attempting to solve a pinhole problem on a fiberglass part. Although the team had developed a more comprehensive problem statement, they simply stated the problem as "Pinholes in Gelcoat," and then brainstormed to develop a list of potential causes. Figure 2.6 below is the final C & E diagram that the team had completed. One-by-one, they tested the list of potential causes and narrowed it down to two possibilities: either contaminated gelcoat or contaminated catalyst. They replaced both ingredients and the problem was solved. Remember, like all problem-solving tools,

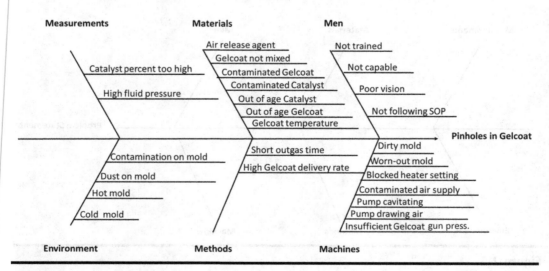

**Figure 2.6**

the C & E diagram will only identify potential causes. Only data and further information about the other causes will lead you to the actual root cause(s).

## Causal Chains

When problems are discovered and investigated, a chain of events usually always leads to the problem source or the root cause. One of the most effective techniques for uncovering the root cause of the problem is the causal chain or, as they are sometimes known, chains of causality. Causal chains are stepwise evolutions of problem causes. Causal chains are typically seen in two different chain-like patterns, as depicted in Figure 2.7.

Each step (or saw tooth) represents an object in a normal or abnormal state as depicted in Table 2.1. The object is placed above the step-line and its state is placed below the line, directly underneath the object. Some examples of objects and states might be:

Each step (or saw tooth) is the cause of the next step and the effect of the preceding step as described in Figure 2.8. That is, the information on the step to the left is always the cause of the information on the step to the

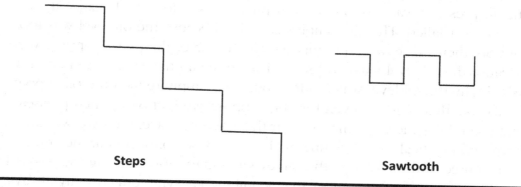

**Steps**　　　　　　　　　　**Sawtooth**

**Figure 2.7**

**Table 2.1**

| Object | State |
|--------|-------|
| Fuel line | Plugged |
| Circuit breaker | Tripped |
| Tire | Flat |
| Motor | Stopped |

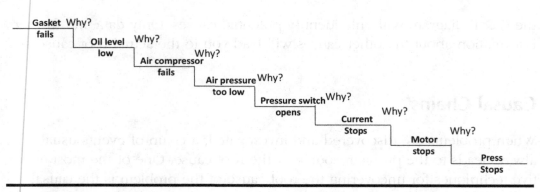

**Figure 2.8**

right. So, it starts with the problem (Press has stopped) and then continues in a stepwise fashion by asking "Why?" in terms of the current state.

An investigation of the problem reveals that a pressure switch had tripped the circuit breaker to the press's electric motor. In this example, we start with the problem symptom (the punch press has stopped) and continue in a stepwise direction to the left by asking "Why?" until we arrive at the root cause of the problem. The punch press stopped because the motor stopped. The motor stopped because the current stopped. The current stopped because the pressure switch was open. The pressure switch opened because the air pressure was too low. The air pressure was too low because the air compressor failed. The air compressor failed because the oil level was too low. So, there we have found that the root cause of the press stopping was because the oil level was too low. This team could have continued on and asked why the oil level was too low, but they simply refilled the oil supply.

To take this example even further, suppose we had two punch presses that used the same air compressor. If this were the case, then we would have two identical causal chains, which would be connected at the common source of the problem, the oil level being too low, causing the gasket to fail. It's important to remember that simultaneous symptoms usually always have a common cause. The bottom line is that, if you want to solve a problem, then use a structured approach to do so. Wandering aimlessly in a sea of uncertainty will only prove to get you lost. In my next chapter, I want to introduce what I refer to as the DNA of a good problem-solver.

## More Problem-Solving Truths

Before ending this chapter, I want to share other [2] problem-solving truths with you that could help you in your problem-solving efforts. Because I have already provided seven of these truths, I will begin this list with truth number 8.

■ **Problem-Solving Truth 8:** When describing a problem, always view the problem from two separate perspectives: the object and the object's defect or fault.

■ **Problem-Solving Truth 9:** Use all of your senses when searching for symptoms.

■ **Problem-Solving Truth 10:** Effective problem analysis attempts to relate the problem to symptoms, differences, changes, and times.

■ **Problem-Solving Truth 11:** It is important to understand that problems might have multiple root causes.

■ **Problem-Solving Truth 12:** Identifying potential root causes is the result of a logical and systematic look at all the available information. It is never the result of guessing.

■ **Problem-Solving Truth 13:** Don't ever be afraid to ask for help when solving problems. Asking for help is not a weakness, it is a sign of intelligence.

■ **Problem-Solving Truth 14:** Don't ever assume a problem has only one cause.

■ **Problem-Solving Truth 15:** The priority in problem solving is always stopping the negative effect(s) of the problem first, then implementing true solutions and preventive actions.

■ **Problem-Solving Truth 16:** Never implement a solution and then assume it is failsafe. Always confirm that your solution does not have a negative impact on the process in question. Always test the impact of your solution before you declare success.

■ **Problem-Solving Truth 17:** Never let any problem-solving tool completely replace your ability to reason and exercise good judgment.

■ **Problem-Solving Truth 18:** Symptoms are always a sign that something has changed or is wrong.

■ **Problem-Solving Truth 19:** Simultaneous symptoms usually have a common cause.

■ **Problem-Solving Truth 20:** Independent causes do not or may not occur simultaneously.

■ **Problem-Solving Truth 21:** Find defect-free configurations and then compare them to find differences and distinctions.

■ **Problem-Solving Truth 22:** Problem-solving traps create detours for problem-solvers. You can't eliminate them, but it helps to know they exist.

- **Problem-Solving Truth 23:** Incorrect data are actually more dangerous than no data because they lead you down the wrong path.
- **Problem-Solving Truth 24:** The key to finding the root cause of intermittent problems is determining the timing of symptoms and then relating them to changes.
- **Problem-Solving Truth 25:** Recurring problems are always the direct result of inadequate or incomplete problem-solving techniques.
- **Problem-Solving Truth 26:** Every problem is a treasure because it represents an opportunity for an organization to improve.
- **Problem-Solving Truth 27:** Effective problem-solving is the synergistic result of a functionally diverse team using a structured approach.
- **Problem-Solving Truth 28:** Membership of a problem-solving team should be limited to people who have a vested interest in the process with the problem.
- **Problem-Solving Truth 29:** When problems are discovered and investigated, a chain of events always leads to the problem source or root cause.
- **Problem-Solving Truth 30:** Most processes are dynamic and changing so it is important to study them over time. This is especially true with labor-intensive processes.
- **Problem-Solving Truth 31:** When plotting data using time as the variable on the x-axis, always put the data in production order before plotting them.
- **Problem-Solving Truth 32:** Everyone has opinions about the cause of problems, but opinions aren't facts, and facts and data are what ultimately lead to the root cause of problems.
- **Problem-Solving Truth 33:** When developing a problem statement, view the problem from two different perspectives: the object and the object's defect or fault.
- **Problem-Solving Truth 34:** Symptoms are the faults we observe, so use your senses to detect the symptoms.
- **Problem-Solving Truth 35:** Problems never occur without reason, and they always follow changes.
- **Problem-Solving Truth 36:** Identifying defect-free configurations (DFCs) is important because DFCs help us to eliminate potential causes of problems.
- **Problem-Solving Truth 37:** Always compare the process or object with the problem to the process or object without the problem, not vice versa. It's easier to see distinctions.

- **Problem-Truth 38:** Whenever possible, test to eliminate potential root causes.
- **Problem-Solving Truth 39:** Problems may have multiple root causes with each producing separate symptoms, and each requiring separate actions.
- **Problem-Solving Truth 40:** People will avoid problem-solving opportunities if they lack problem-solving skills, haven't successfully solved problems in the past, aren't recognized and appreciated when they do solve problems, or feel threatened by the situation.

There may be other problem-solving truths that I haven't listed, but these were the ones that I have learned throughout my career. In the next chapter, we will look into what the DNA of a good problem-solver should be.

# References

1. Charles H. Kepner and Benjamin B. Tregoe, *The Rational Manager – A Systematic Approach to Problem Solving and Decision Making*, McGraw Hill Book Company, 1965.
2. Bob Sproull, *The Process-Problem Solving, Problem-Prevention, and Decision-Making Guide – Organized and Systematic Roadmaps for Managers*, Taylor & Francis Group, LLC, 2018.

# Chapter 3

# The DNA of a Good Problem-Solver and Preventer

It is my belief that the truly good problem-solvers and problem-preventers in the world all share a special bond, a connection if you will, and this connection is not unexpected. It is because of specific behaviors and character traits that problem-solvers and -preventers all seem to have in common. I am convinced it is these qualities and behaviors that separate the true problem-solvers and preventers from problem-solving and prevention "wanna-bees" or "could-bees." If you've ever worked for Toyota, or have been a supplier to Toyota, then you will recognize these traits and behaviors easily. Why Toyota? Because Toyota is probably the best possible example of a company that truly "gets it," as it applies to their approach to business in general and, more specifically, problem-solving and problem-prevention.

In this chapter, I will present twelve distinct behaviors and/or personality traits that I believe are the basic genetic material shared and employed by effective problem-solvers and preventers. I also believe that, if a person or team can demonstrate and exploit these behaviors, the opportunity to become effective and successful at problem-solving and prevention will just happen. Each of these behaviors and traits (below), although not listed in order of importance, serves a different purpose or function as the individual or team searches for the answer to their problem-solving and prevention conundrums. These traits and/or behaviors are as follows:

1. Being objective and impartial.
2. Being analytical and methodical.

DOI: 10.4324/9781003462385-3

3. Being creative and imaginative.
4. Having dedication, commitment, focus, and perseverance.
5. Being curious and probing.
6. Having courage and daring.
7. Having a sense of adventure and exploration in both the present and future.
8. Being enthusiastic and passionate.
9. Having patience and perseverance.
10. Being vigilant and cautious, and expecting the unexpected.
11. Being an effective listener.
12. Being a critical thinker.

Let's look at each of these in more depth.

A problem-solver or preventer must always be *impartial and objective* and not have preconceived notions, ideas, or biases on what is causing the problem or what could cause the problem. Each problem has its own set of conditions or circumstances, and most of the time the answer lies in the data and information surrounding these conditions. Without objectivity, crucial observations might be ignored or even missed altogether. So many times, in my career, I have observed individuals and teams jumping to causes and solutions before even understanding the current or future problem. Keeping an open mind throughout the problem-solving and -prevention process is critical.

A good problem-solver or preventer must be *analytical* and *methodical* in their approach to solving or preventing problems. One of the keys to solving and preventing problems is the art of asking the right questions in a very systematic and methodical way. As we investigate existing problems or potential future problems, it is crucial to use a logical approach, as we move through the network of unknown facts and forever-present opinions of everyone involved. Asking questions, or should I say the right questions, is imperative if we are to expose the key facts relative to the problem we are trying to solve or prevent. Closely related to this is the need for detailed analysis. Once the information and data surrounding the problem are collected, they must be analyzed in a very systematic and orderly manner. A good problem-solver and preventer knows and understands which tools and techniques are available, how to use them, and when to utilize each one.

Solving and preventing problems requires *imagination, creativity,* and *ingenuity.* Solving and preventing problems sometimes requires abstract thinking and requires imaginative and inventive actions, especially as relates to developing an effective solution or prevention. Once you have determined the true root cause (or causes) of the current or future problem, it's time to be innovative and let your creative juices flow, as you develop successful solutions. The solution to your problem will demand ingenuity and resourcefulness, so you must be inventive.

Solving and preventing problems requires *dedication, perseverance, focus,* and *commitment* because the answers are sometimes obscure or hidden and, therefore, not always obvious. One must be determined to find the root cause(s) and be focused and committed to using a systematic approach. A good problem-solver or problem-preventer doesn't vacillate as the problem-solving and prevention journey unfolds; they stay the course and stay focused. Uncovering facts, in the face of uncertainty, requires tenacity and resolve, as the problem-solving or prevention effort unfolds.

A good problem-solver or problem-preventer is *curious* and *probing.* When one is curious, one is interested in understanding why things happen or could happen and will probe below the surface of the problem, looking for things that may not be obvious or evident. Solutions to problems all begin out of curiosity and desire to determine and understand what happened or could happen, and then understand why it happened or might happen. Until you understand why the problem has emerged or could occur, your chances of solving it are pretty much nil.

It takes *courage, daring,* and *"guts"* to be a good problem-solver or preventer. Since there is usually always a negative aura or atmosphere surrounding problems, people who are closest to and feel responsible for the area with the problem sometimes feel threatened. Because they are feeling vulnerable and exposed, they generally don't like to be questioned, but you must have the courage and fortitude to push forward and seek answers. When you ask someone questions about the problem or potential problem in their area of responsibility, many times the instinctive reaction is to take a defensive posture. You are typically perceived as prying and impugning their character. Of course, this isn't really the case, and if you ask the questions in a positive and non-threatening way, you can alleviate some of this perception.

Solving or preventing problems is a journey and an exploration into what happened or could happen, so having a *sense of adventure and exploration* in the present and future are fundamental to reaching your destination. I have often wondered how the early explorers, like Columbus or Lewis and Clark, must have felt as they sailed into unknown and uncharted waters or passed through unfamiliar and strange countryside, never knowing what they were going to encounter or be confronted with or even if they would be successful. A good problem-solver or problem-preventer needs to be like Columbus or Lewis and Clark, as they seek out the problem details. One of the things Toyota does better than any other company is its passion for "go and see." That is, Toyota spends an inordinate amount of time going to the source of the problem and studying it firsthand. It has been my experience that many problem-solving and prevention efforts fail simply because the team or individual doesn't spend enough time "going and seeing."

A good problem-solver and preventer must demonstrate *enthusiasm* and *passion* during the problem-solving or prevention journey. The problem-solver or problem-preventer must demonstrate a certain zest and zeal that becomes contagious and infectious to the rest of the team. By demonstrating and communicating enthusiasm to the team, you are inadvertently motivating and inspiring your team members. There will be times when the situation may appear hopeless to the team, but your positive outlook and enthusiasm will guide you and your team through the process.

Finding root causes and developing solutions to current or future problems are not always clear-cut, straightforward, or uncomplicated, so a good problem-solver or preventer must demonstrate *patience, persistence*, and *staying power.* You will, at times, be pressured to move faster than you would like to or need to, so you must be compelled to stay the course and stay focused on the destination. Part of learning to be a good problem-solver or problem-preventer is learning how to become disciplined and regimented. If you will take your time and systematically work through problems, your success rate will improve dramatically. Remember, *patience* truly is a virtue.

A good problem solver or preventer should be *vigilant* and *cautious* and should always *expect the unexpected.* Just when you think you may have exposed the root cause(s) of a problem, or have discovered the causal pathway of the current or future problem, new information or something unanticipated may come out of the blue and catch you off guard, if you aren't alert to this possibility. So be cautious and attentive that new information could come at any time, that will change your point of view.

An effective problem-solver or problem-preventer must have *good listening skills*. The solver or preventer must focus on who's answering your questions, to hear details of the situation, so that you fully understand the basics of the problem you are attempting to solve or prevent. It's important to remember that each problem has its own features and impacts each person involved differently. Your ability to listen effectively puts you in the best position to comprehend fully the challenges at hand.

The final piece to this solving or prevention pie is that, once you understand a problem, you must apply *critical thinking skills,* so that you can analyze and scrutinize the information you have gathered together. A cause-and-effect analysis will allow you to make effective decisions with both short- and long-term perspectives in mind.

These are the qualities and behaviors of a good problem-solver or problem-preventer, but not all of them are necessarily essential in one person to achieve successful solving or preventing of a problem. As a matter of fact, it's probably true that if the "team" possesses these qualities or behaviors, then success will follow. If one person is, for example, analytical, curious, patient, and dedicated, whereas someone else is objective and enthusiastic, and still another has courage, a sense of adventure, but is vigilant, then the team holistically satisfies these requisites. It sometimes "takes a village" to solve or prevent problems, so select your team members with all of these qualities in mind.

After developing this list of traits and characteristics, I came across an article that appeared in the June 1999 issue of *Quality Progress,* written by Abdul M. Chaudhry, entitled *To be a Problem Solver, Be a Classicist.* In this article, Chaudhry identified ten values or qualities that an ideal problem-solver or problem-solving team must collectively possess to solve or prevent a problem effectively. Chaudhry arranged these "Ten Classicist Problem-Solving Qualities" to form the acronym, *Classicist.* It is my belief that these qualities equally relate to problem prevention. Chaudhry's list of qualities were as follows:

1. Creative
2. Leader
3. Analytical
4. Structured
5. Systematic
6. Intuitive
7. Critical
8. Informative
9. Synthesizer
10. Team oriented

As you can see, the two lists share common beliefs as to what constitutes the right qualities or traits of effective problem-solvers and problem-preventers or problem-solving and problem-prevention teams. The key in both scenarios is to exploit these behaviors for the successful resolution of problems.

Problems exist everywhere and we all know when we're in the midst of one because we can feel and experience its chilling and unsettling presence. In the case of potential problems, we can anticipate these same things. We feel and experience the pressure, demands, and stress to fix the problem or prevent it, and, if we're not prepared, or if we don't know how to begin to solve it, or prevent it, it is not a good feeling at all. Maybe we're getting pressure from the boss who tells us to do "something and do it quickly!" Maybe the board of directors wants to know what's happening to profit margins. Or maybe we're getting emails, texts, or telephone calls from irate, infuriated customers about quality problems or orders behind schedule. Whatever the motivation, the normal response to this pressure for many of us is that we start making changes and hope for the best!

It's not unusual, for many of us, to make blind adjustments to otherwise stable processes or systems without understanding the simple cause-and-effect relationships that are driving the negative performance. The bottom line is that, characteristically, many of us tend to panic and do stupid things, foolish things, irresponsible things, that we might not do, if we thought through the problem more or didn't have all this pressure! Whatever the reason or motivation, it is clear that making pointless or unwarranted changes without understanding why is the worst reaction possible because it simply complicates and confuses the situation! *That's the problem with problems*: they have a tendency to change our behaviors and make us do things that we instinctively know are wrong. It's almost as if there is some supernatural or paranormal power at work here. To further complicate matters, there are different types of problems and each requires a different tactic if we are to resolve or prevent them happening quickly and effectively.

## The DNA of Problems

Just like problem-solvers and preventers, not all problems are created equal. That may seem intuitive or obvious to you, but, in many cases, it simply isn't. When I say that not all problems are created equal, I'm not referring to the basic problem itself, but rather the framework or structure of the problem. There are different categories or types of problems, and it is enormously important that you recognize and distinguish what type of problem you are working on, because the approach to one type of problem may not work for another type. Problems are divided into three fundamental categories as follows:

1. *Change-related problems* that have resulted from a *change* or adjustment from existing conditions.
2. *Chronic problems* that are persistent and have seemingly been around forever.
3. Problems that are both chronic and change-related, or what I call *hybrid problems*.

Let's take a little closer look at all three problem types.

## Change-Related Problems

I mentioned earlier that problems sometimes tend to create panic and we respond by making unnecessary changes. So, if these are not the behaviors we should be demonstrating, then what are the right behaviors? Before we answer this, let's review the basic concept of what a problem is. [1] Kepner and Tregoe, in their problem-solving classic, *The New Rational Manager,* characterize problems simply as *deviations from expected performance*, but let's look at this more closely. Kepner and Tregoe tell us that a performance standard is achieved when all of the conditions required for acceptable performance are operating as they *should*. This includes everything in our work environment including *people, materials, systems, processes, departments, pieces of equipment,* basically everything. Kepner and Tregoe further tell us that "if there is an alteration in one or more of these conditions, that is, if some kind of change occurs, then it is possible that performance will alter too." If performance goes from good to bad or positive to negative, then we feel the pressure. The more serious the effect of the decline in performance, the more pressure there is to find a cause and correct or prevent it.

Changes happen every day in our lives, so the question becomes, "When is the deviation that we observe, or anticipate in the future, considered to be a problem?" It has been my experience (and that of Kepner and Tregoe) that, in order for a deviation to be considered a problem, or potential problem, one or more of the following requirements must be satisfied:

1. The deviation or performance shift must be recognized and perceived as being *negative to the organization*. That is, the deviation must result in, or could result in, a negative effect to things like a loss in throughput, a deterioration in quality, a safety performance issue, etc., that translates directly into something like a missed delivery to a customer, a loss in revenue or margin erosion, a customer complaint, an injury, etc.

2. The cause of the performance deviation, or potential future deviation, *isn't known or obvious*. That is, the root cause is not immediately established using "normal" problem-solving or prevention techniques, which results in an extended period of time at the new negative or potentially new, performance level. Obviously, if the cause isn't known, then the solution won't be known either, so the current performance problem, or potential performance problem, lingers.

3. Both the root cause and the solution are known, but the *solution can't be implemented* because it either costs too much or will take too long. As pressure mounts to have the problem fixed, or prevented, more often than not, the symptoms get treated and a "quick fix" is implemented. This, in turn, usually prolongs the problem episode or sets the stage for it to return or actually deteriorate even further.

If the root cause and the solution are known and implementing it will not take too long, and/or cost too much, then the deviation is not deemed to be a problem because it simply gets fixed or prevented. In effect, it has no visibility within the organization, at least not in the upper echelon. But when you add the critical factors of cost, time, lost revenues, etc., deviations will most likely be portrayed and characterized as problems.

Let's look at an example of a change-related problem that currently exists. Suppose you are the plant manager of a company that manufactures electronic equipment for the automobile industry. Your plant's budgeted % EBITDA (Earnings Before Income Taxes and Depreciation) is tied to sales revenue and is variable but has been averaging roughly 25% per month throughout the year. This means that, if your annual sales are in the $100 M range, then the annual earnings are expected to be in the neighborhood of $25 M for the year. You've worked hard and you've pretty much hit budget in each of the first five months of the year. The board is pleased with the job you're doing, and you feel good about how well your plant is performing. In July, you get a frenzied call from your accountant telling you that the numbers are in for June, and they don't look good at all. You tell him to come to your office with the numbers so that you can both assess the results.

Figure 3.1 is the monthly % EBITDA graph and one look at it tells you that your accountant is right. What had been a picture of steady and stable on-budget earnings from January through May has abruptly and unexpectedly gone awry by taking a nosedive. You ask him what happened, but he has no idea. A sense of fear, apprehension, and, yes, panic comes over you, because you know that this very afternoon the board of directors is coming for their monthly review of your plant's performance. You tell your accountant that you need answers and that you need them right now!

The accountant leaves and you sit there and rack your brain, trying to understand what has happened. You know instinctively that something has changed, but what is it? You think to yourself, "% EBITDA was right on target through May, but in June, it dropped from 25% to 18%." Because the drop in performance was sudden and unexpected, you know you have to find out what *changed*. That's the problem with *change-related problems*, they are often sudden and unpredictable. And when the direction of change is toward the negative side of the ledger, they often cause people to panic.

But, sometimes, conditions improve, and positive changes occur, and things go better than expected. But, when performance rises or improves unexpectedly, it clearly does not trigger the same urgent response as the negative shift does. What if the reverse had been true for our plant manager? What if his % EBITDA had suddenly improved as in Figure 3.2? Would the

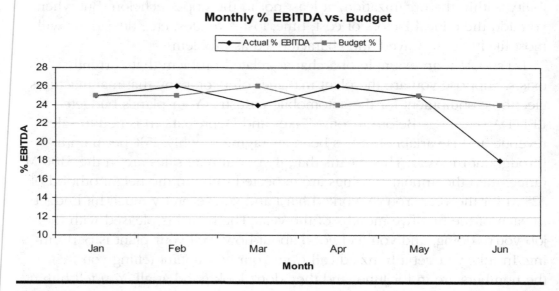

**Figure 3.1**

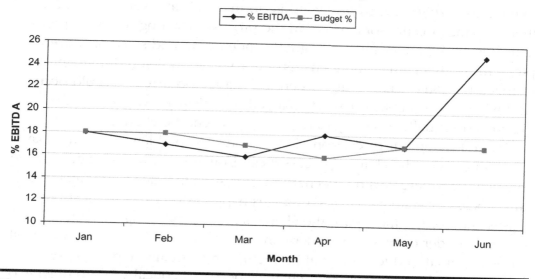

**Figure 3.2**

sense of urgency or panic have gripped him as when the % EBITDA had declined? Obviously, it wouldn't have, would it? Why do you suppose that this is true? It is because, reason number one, the negative recognition and perception requirement of a problem "trumps" both of the other reasons.

Since the plant manager would have known that the board would have been happy with the new % EBITDA, there would have been no negative feelings expressed by the board and therefore, little, if any, pressure to even find out why the positive deviation had occurred. But, beware, do not ignore or disregard positive deviations! "Why?" Because in my opinion, unexplained positive changes in performance have potentially the same consequences as negative changes. That is to say, if we don't understand what prompted the positive change in performance, then we certainly won't be able to understand or explain why the performance suddenly changed back to its original, "normal" level of performance and **it will happen at some point in the future.**

The "positive" performance level that had resulted from the original shift in performance will now become the new expected level of performance. So, when the performance metric shifts back to the performance from January through May, it then satisfies the first two requirements of a problem and, therefore, becomes classified as a problem. For this reason, it is essential to investigate positive deviations and uncover the root cause or causes.

Because these types of problems are always the result of a change, I refer to them as *change-related problems*. Performance is at a certain level and then a change occurs somewhere in the process, resulting in a new performance level. When trying to recognize, understand, and solve or prevent problems of this nature, the focus must always be on determining what changed (or could change) and when the change occurred or could occur. And when you do discover what changed or anticipate what could change, the solution usually is simply to reverse or prevent the change.

Before leaving our discussion of change-related problems, I need to say something about the change process itself. In many of the companies I have consulted for, there was no mechanism or system in place to routinely capture process or system changes. Changes happen every day in most businesses and, for the most part, the changes are a good thing, provided they are made under control. (By under control, I mean that the change was well conceived, analyzed for potential problems, and, equally important, fully documented.) Documentation of changes becomes critical when problems of this nature are encountered. The documentation should include the specifics of the change and the timing of the change. At the very least, the date should be documented, but if you can record more specific time information, like serial numbers or bar code numbers, then problems can be correlated directly to the change.

## Chronic Problems

There is another type of problem that is not necessarily the result of a change, but rather a problem that has been around ostensibly forever. Many times, when you ask someone how long this problem has existed, you get a response like, "We've always had this defect!" or "This machine has never produced what the others have." I have named this kind of problem a *chronic problem* and, for those of you that have ever been involved with the Fords or GMs or Chryslers of the world, you will recognize it immediately. [1] Kepner and Tregoe refer to this kind of problem as a *day-one problem*.

As the name implies, it's the kind of problem that is persistent and unending and it has defied all previous attempts at resolution. Maybe it's the launch of a new machine that is supposed to be identical to one or more already in place, but which, since the start-up, has never performed quite like the others. Or maybe the supplier of a raw material has two factories and product received from one factory has performed better than that from the other factory from the first delivery of the product. Figure 3.3 is a common example of this type of problem.

In this type of problem, there is still the expected level of performance (machine target) of the new machine, compared with the actual performance of the other machines making the same or a similar product. The deviation is the output between the lower-performing machine and the other two supposedly identical machines. The same rules for deciding whether or not a problem is a problem apply here, as well as the problem-solving tools and techniques.

The major difference between *change-related problems* and *chronic problems* is where we focus our efforts. In change-related problems, we focus most of our efforts on determining what changed or could change to create the new level of performance, and when the change occurred. But, when we have a situation where the performance of one item has never been what it "should" be, compared with one that performs to expectations, we can assume that one of the conditions necessary to attain the expected level of performance does not exist and never has. In this case, we must focus most of our efforts on the area of distinctions or differences between where, or when, or who has the performance problem, compared with where, or when, or who doesn't. That is, there is something distinct or different, when comparing the supposedly identical units, processes, methods, or materials.

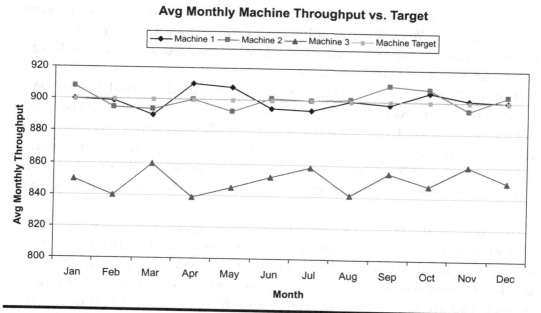

**Figure 3.3**

If we are to successfully solve or prevent chronic-type problems, then we must find the critical differences or distinctions between the two objects and take actions that are specifically aimed at eliminating or reducing the differences or preventing the same!

Finding these differences or distinctions requires observation and investigation of both the under-performing unit and the unit or units that are performing to expectations. If the under-performing item is an operator, for example, one effective method is to videotape both the operator with the problem and an operator without the problem, and then critique both methods. If the unit with the problem is a machine, then perhaps critical measurements on both the problem machine and the machine performing well are in order. Whatever the case, a comparison of where, or when, or who, has the problem, to where, or when, or who doesn't have the problem is necessary. And I might add that we make this comparison in that order. That is, we always start with where, or when, or who has the problem and compare our findings with where, or when, or who does not have the problem.

## Hybrid Problems

Now that we understand the differences between a *change-related problem* and the *chronic problem*, you might wonder if it's possible to have both types of problems acting together simultaneously. The answer is an emphatic and categorical "Yes!" When you have an expected level of performance that has never been achieved and it suddenly worsens, you are in the midst of what I refer to as a *hybrid problem*.

Consider the situation in Figure 3.4. Here, we see the actual % EBITDA by month, compared with budgeted % EBITDA. The actual % EBITDA has been below-budget by approximately 2.5% for the first seven months of the year. In August, the situation worsens and the gap between expected performance (i.e., % EBITDA) and actual performance grows to about 8%. A situation that, I'm sure, was filled with pressure and negative energy just became worse.

If you were the owner of these financials, imagine how you would feel and what your actions might be. You have two competing priorities here. On the one hand, you must determine what changed to make the already-dismal situation worse. On the other hand, you must close the gap in the budget. You are in the midst of a *hybrid problem*, with each part of it competing against the other. The logical approach would be to return to "ground

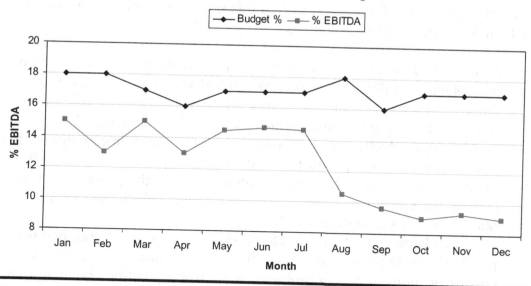

**Figure 3.4**

zero" by finding the change that caused the performance shift, reverse it if possible, and then develop a plan to improve the % EBITDA.

Although both are serious problems, one is short-term and requires immediate attention, while the other is chronic and requires thoughtful and considerate action! One thing to remember, when you are faced with a hybrid problem, is to separate the problem into its constituent parts. Disconnect the change-related problem from the chronic problem, because the solution to each will be different.

## The Four Cs of Problem-Solving

No matter what type of problem, or potential problem, you are faced with, there is usually always pressure and anxiety associated with it. You have demands placed on you that can be overwhelming at times. You must take action and implement countermeasures, but that doesn't preclude you from following some sort of logical process. You must remain calm and composed, and sometimes that is difficult to do in the face of a crisis. Most of the time, the immediate actions you take, after the problem surfaces, or could surface, are crucial. It is important to realize that the basic actions we take, in the face of all existing and future potential problems, follow the same logical cycle or sequence of *contain*, *cause*, *correct*, and *control*, the four Cs of problem-solving. Each step in this sequence requires your immediate and urgent attention as follows:

1. *Contain the Problem*: No matter whether the problem is located within your plant or facility, or has already reached your customer, the first action is to always contain or confine the problem. That is, you must stop or prevent the bleeding immediately and limit its scope. If the problem is a defective product, you must not permit it from entering the value stream of good product. It is always good practice to physically isolate the problem, if there is product involved. If the problem involves people, such as labor unrest, you must defuse it quickly, so that it doesn't grow to unmanageable levels.

2. *Find the Cause of the Problem*: Once you have caged and confined the problem, it is imperative that you find the root cause or origin of the current or future potential problem. Systematically define and analyze it and search for the cause or causes, or potential cause or causes. If it is a quality problem, for example, you must find the source of the problem or change that has occurred. If it's a people problem, you must understand what caused the unrest to surface.

3. *Correct or Prevent the Problem*: As soon as the cause of the problem, or potential problem, has been determined, you must take swift and pragmatic action to find an effective counter measure and implement it with expediency. Make certain that you don't just start making changes without justification or reason. Often, you will have options with one solution being short-term and the other more long-term. What you must decide is how urgently the solution must be implemented, and it could be that you find yourself implementing a temporary, short-term solution, just to get out of the crisis. It is OK to do this, as long as your intention is to implement the longer-term solution later.

4. *Control the Problem*: Once the problem has been resolved, or a potential problem has been prevented, always implement some kind of control that will prevent the problem from recurring. When problems persist and recur at customer locations, your credibility takes a hit, so avoid this by implementing a control.

Remaining calm in the face of problems is imperative, so if you will just stop and remember these four actions, you can transform or prevent a stressful and taxing situation into one of relative calm and tranquility. In the face of pressure, clear-headed thinking and practical actions are crucial, so simply remember the four Cs, namely *contain, cause, correct,* and *control,* and you will be in control of the situation. Although solving problems is critical, preventing them is equally important. In the next chapter, I will be presenting my Problem-Prevention Roadmap.

Before leaving this chapter, I want to present a data collection form that I included in my very first book, *Process Problem Solving – A Guide for Maintenance and Operations Teams.* The name of this tool is the Problem Analysis Flow Chart, or PAF Chart for short (Figure 3.5).

As the name implies, the purpose of the PAF Chart is to be able to record key items as called out on my Problem-Solving Roadmap. I have found throughout the years that, by recording information in a single location, it is much easier to coordinate the problem-solving or problem-preventing efforts.

Figure 3.6 is the reverse side of my PAF Chart. You will notice that two additional blocks have been added to the reverse side of the PAF Chart, with Block 9 being a listing of the most probable cause or causes and Block 10 being short-term corrections and long-term controls.

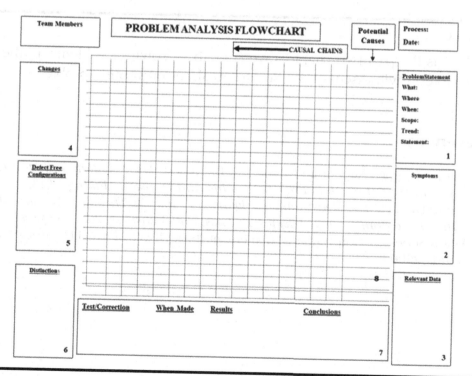

**Figure 3.5**

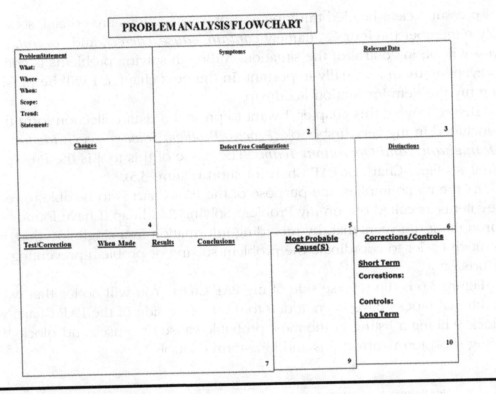

**Figure 3.6**

Whereas the past two chapters were all about solving problems, in the next chapter, I will discuss how best to go about preventing problems.

# References

1. Charles Higgins Kepner and Benjamin B. Tregoe, *The New Rational Manager: A Systematic Approach to Problem Solving and Decision Making*, 2013.
2. Smith, Debra – *The Measurement Nightmare, How the Theory of Constraints Can Resolve Conflicting Strategies, Policies, and Measures*, St. Lucie Press/ APICS Series on Constraints Management through CRC Press LLC, Boca Raton, Florida 2000.

# Chapter 4

## Problem-Prevention

Based upon the previous chapter of this book, although many of the same activities are shared between problem-solving and problem-prevention, there are also distinct differences between the two. In this chapter, we will focus on how to prevent problems, but remember that many of the activities are shared with problem solving.

It seems that we spend an inordinate amount of time working on solving problems that already exist when, in reality, many of our problems could have been avoided if we had simply taken the time up front to work on preventing them. Fundamentally, prevention involves identifying potential areas of vulnerability, and the problems that could occur within these areas, and then developing and implementing actions aimed at either preventing them, reducing the probability that they will occur, or even lessening their effects, in the event that our prevention plans didn't work as we had envisioned they would.

If you think about it, doesn't it make much more sense to tie up resources working on preventing negative performance than it does spending time trying to understand why the negative performance happened in the first place? Being a *preventive organization* has so many more advantages than a *reactive organization* does. Just think about how negative performance affects your organization for a moment. Problems create things like scrap and rework, late shipments and missed deliveries, higher inventory levels, and the list goes on and on. Imagine how things might look in your company or organization if you minimized the number of problems you had by being preventive, instead of reactive. Would your job be more stressful or less stressful? Would your customers be more content or less content? Would

DOI: 10.4324/9781003462385-4

your market share be shrinking or growing? Being a preventive organization will place your company at a distinct advantage with margins moving in the right direction.

Making changes to processes, systems, and even strategies is very common in every organization, but thinking about the future isn't so commonplace. Whenever a change or modification is being planned or considered, it is critical not only to consider the positive effects but also to think about the potential negative effects or potential consequences of the change being considered. Blindly making changes can be disastrous or even catastrophic, if the change isn't thought through with respect to potential outcomes, so take the time to look into the future. Prevention is a positive mindset, with your focus being to create a positive future and minimizing the unexpected. Prevention is being proactive rather than reactive. As the old adage goes, *"An ounce of prevention is worth a pound of cure."*

## Becoming Proactive Rather Than Reactive

In this chapter, we will explore basic ways to prevent problems, rather than trying to solve them after they appear. We will look at ways to look into the future, predict what could happen, and then return to the present to develop ways to prevent any potential future problems. We will, in effect, look at ways to take control of the future, rather than having the future control us. In doing so, I will demonstrate several tools that can be used to predict what could happen. Since we can never be certain of future events, we will speak in terms of simple probabilities and look at ways to predict the future with a relative degree of certainty. Just always remember that we are attempting to become proactive and positive, rather than reactive and negative.

## Probability and Risk

Before I begin our discussion on problem prevention, I need to speak just a bit about simple probability and risk analysis. At one time or another, all of us have used a coin flip to make a decision. It's used in football games to determine who kicks off and who receives the football first. With a coin flip, there are only two possible outcomes. The coin will either be heads or tails, so the probability of guessing right is one out of two, or 50%. If you were to flip the coin one hundred times, you would most likely have approximately fifty heads and fifty tails, give or take a few.

In cards, if we want to know the probability of randomly selecting a four of any suit, for example, we know that there are fifty-two cards in a deck and four of each type card, so the odds of drawing a four randomly from a deck of cards is one in thirteen. A bit more complicated than a simple coin flip, but still easy to understand. If we were to calculate the odds of drawing a four of hearts, then the odds would be one in fifty-two. And if you play the lottery, you already know by the number of non-paying tickets, that the odds are astronomical against you selecting the right numbers. In each of these examples, you are able to calculate the odds of winning.

Calculating probabilities is another way of measuring risk and we all know that every decision involves a certain amount of risk. When we operate in a preventive environment, we are attempting to minimize this risk. The difference between solving a problem and preventing a problem is simply one of timing. In problem-solving, we are in a reactive mode, after the fact, trying to determine why something *did happen*. In problem prevention, we are in a proactive mode, trying to determine what *could happen*. Unlike games of chance, like the coin flip or the card draws, trying to predict or estimate the odds of something specific happening, requires that we use primarily our past experience, or maybe some data we have collected in a similar experience.

## The Problem Prevention Roadmap

Like problem-solving, there are a series of steps, or a roadmap, that can be followed to successfully analyze and hopefully prevent future potential problems. Figure 4.1 is such a roadmap that I developed years ago, *The Problem Prevention Roadmap*.

The Problem Prevention Roadmap contains six major sections and a total of seventeen individual steps. If you diligently follow this roadmap, I am convinced that you will significantly improve your chances of becoming a more proactive organization, anticipating problems, rather than reacting to them. So, let's now dissect my Problem Prevention Roadmap in much more detail.

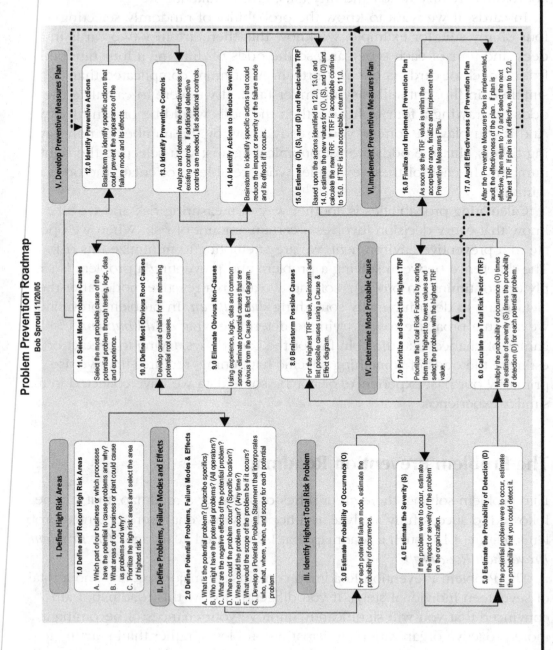

**Figure 4.1**

In this chapter I will present the roadmap, its six major sections and seventeen individual steps which need to be followed. The six major sections are as follows:

1. Defining the high-risk or vulnerable areas of your organization.
2. Defining the potential problems, failure modes, and their effects.
3. Identifying the highest total risk problems.
4. Determining the most probable cause of the highest risk problem.
5. Developing a preventive measures plan.
6. Implementing the preventive measures plan.

Each of these sections includes individual actions that are focused solely on future potential events. If you execute these actions, you will either (1) prevent the problem totally, (2) increase the probability that if the problem does occur, you will be able to detect it before any damage is done, or (3) minimize the impact or severity of the problem if it does occur. This roadmap can be used to evaluate proposed changes, equipment installations, personnel policy changes, and virtually anything that involves a future activity. Now let's look at each of the major sections and action steps more closely.

Before we look at each of these six major sections and seventeen action steps more closely, you need to understand one simple fact. In general, people have a hang-up with the future. That is to say that, typically, we are so caught up in the chaos of problems in the present and left-over problems from the past, that we rarely take the time to look into the future. People want and need to be future-oriented, to be proactive, but the pressures of problems already upon us typically preclude this from happening. Now let's look at the Problem Prevention Roadmap in more detail.

# Step 1 of Roadmap: Define and Record High-Risk Areas

In this section of the roadmap, there are three important questions and actions we must define:

1. Which parts of our business or which processes have the potential to cause problems and why could they?
2. What areas of our business or plant could cause us problems and why might they cause the problems?
3. Prioritize the high-risk areas and select the area of highest risk.

Your first action starts with the identification of areas within your organization or manufacturing facility, or a specific process, that could be at high risk or potentially vulnerable. These areas can be specific processes, systems, or even strategies or policies in place, that could have a negative impact on the long-term viability and profitability of your company. In this action, you should be asking questions like, "Which part of our business or manufacturing facility has the potential to go awry and cause us problems and why?" or "What areas within our business or plant could cause us problems in the future and why?" It's important that the questions asked be open-ended and require more than just a yes or no response. Remember, you are attempting to identify areas of *high risk*.

Some examples of high-risk areas might be something as simple as having a single supplier of raw materials, parts, or maybe even maintenance services if you contract out your maintenance. Other examples might be hourly labor or potential labor contract disputes, the pricing of your products, your customers, or any other part of your business. Remember, in this step, you are only trying to define and identify areas within your business that could go wrong, and not the actual, potential problems.

It's important to understand that identifying these high-risk areas involves openly looking at future strategies, plans, or proposed changes, and then trying to imagine what might go wrong if the plan or change isn't successful. A good technique that I recommend is to first develop a step-by-step project management plan, and then review each step or milestone for what could go wrong. You should be especially wary of new activities that your organization has never attempted before, or even things outside your current core competency. If there is a time constraint involved, it is even more important to focus on that activity. Every plan or strategy contains certain critical factors that will ultimately control the success or failure of any project. These critical factors represent the glue that holds plans together, and, if they are removed, your plans could come crashing down, so be ready to focus on them.

In this step, what we are attempting to do is to look at potential problems from ten thousand feet. That is, we are using our intuition and logic to cut our list down to a manageable size of, say, two or three potential problems. One simple way to do this is to consider two elements as follows:

1. The chances of the event going wrong.
2. The overall negative impact on the organization.

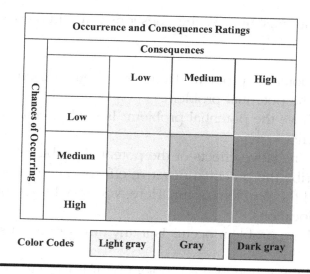

**Figure 4.2**

Figure 4.2 is a simple tool that your organization can use to help select the right area of vulnerability. You are considering the potential negative consequences facing your organization and the chances of the negative event actually happening. As described in Figure 4.2, each potential problem or negative event is rated as low, medium, or high, for both *Occurrence* and *Consequences*. As you might suspect, any potential negative event or proposed project that falls within a dark gray block should be selected first. On the other hand, any event that falls within a light gray block can now be crossed off the list. The gray blocks are borderline and represent those events that may or may not be included on your final list. Once your most important areas of vulnerability have been identified, it is now time to define the potential problems, failure modes, and potential negative effects that could occur in these areas.

# Step 2 of the Roadmap: Define Potential Problems, Failure Modes, and Effects

A *failure mode* is defined as the way or ways that a system or subsystem could *fail to perform its intended function(s)*. *Effects*, on the other hand, are the *consequences* that will occur as a result of a *failure mode*.

Once you have identified the areas of high risk, it is now time to brainstorm specific problems or failures that might occur. In order for this action to be effective, you must answer the questions listed in Step 2 of the road-map as follows:

1. What is the potential problem? Here, you should describe, in detail, the specifics of the potential problem.
2. Who might have the potential problem? Is it all operators or is it just some of them?
3. What are the negative effects of the potential problem? Here, you should describe the potential negative effects, again in detail.
4. Where could the problem occur? Here, you should describe the specific location or locations.
5. When could the problem occur? Is it any time or just in specific parts of the day?
6. What would the scope of the problem be if it were to occur? Here, you should describe each of the machines or operators that will have the problem if it occurs.
7. Develop a Potential Problem Statement that incorporates the what, the who, the where, the when, and the scope for each potential problem.

Now is the time to be as specific as possible, so avoid broad generalizations. The more detailed the description you develop, the more specific your future preventive action plan will be. In case you didn't realize this, these are the same types of questions you were asking when you were trying to define an existing problem, with the difference here being one of timing. Think about it; instead of trying to solve an existing problem, you are trying to prevent a potential problem, so keep this in mind as you go through these steps.

In this first step, suppose you have identified a single supplier of a product as being a high-risk supplier. Ask yourself what types of problems could arise, by having a single source supplier. In this case, the answer to "What?" might be the inability of the supplier to ship specific parts or materials on time without adequate advanced notification. Because, in this case, you have no backup supplier, a delayed shipment of parts or a shortage of a material might last for some time. The answer to "Where?" is the location of this supplier and where in your production plant you might be affected. The answer to "When?" would be an alarming, "At any time in the future!" The scope of the problem would be clearly dependent on how many of your own products require the parts or materials from the supplier in question. Any part or material received from that supplier, used in any of your product lines, could be at risk. We've just completed the first two steps in our roadmap. Just to refresh your memory, here is the roadmap again (Figure 4.3).

## Step 3 of the Roadmap: Estimate the Probability of Occurrence for Each Problem

Any time you are asked to "estimate" something, you typically rely on a similar past experience that might fit into a specific condition or situation. Hopefully, you may also be able to utilize data in some form to help you predict a potential problem. By knowing how some similar problem reacted, you usually go with your best estimate. For example, if you are comparing a similar defect, then use the same defect rate. But what if you don't have data or even a past experience that fits this situation? What do you do then? As appalling as this may sound to you, sometimes you just have to go with your gut instinct but, when you do, make certain that you err on the conservative side. If you make a mistake, what's the worst thing that could happen to you? You would have overestimated the probability, and that's all, with no damage done!

You may be wondering how do you go about estimating the probability that a particular event will actually happen. Believe it or not, there is actually a very simple and uncomplicated way to estimate simple probabilities. Using a scale of 1 to 10, consider each problem by itself, and then rate each problem as to how certain or uncertain you are that it will occur. A rating of 10 would translate into a 100% confidence decision that the problem will occur, under certain conditions. On the other end of the scale, a rating of 1 might mean that there is no possible way the problem will occur. The numbers between 1 and 10 will be used to estimate how certain or uncertain you are, but, remember, always be conservative when you rate each one. Logically, if you have no idea whether the problem will occur, then you might rate the problem as a 5.

Table 4.1, of unknown origin, is frequently used in the auto industry to estimate the probability of occurrence. The table contains three columns, with each one providing a different piece of information that will assist you as you estimate each one. The first column is the actual numerical ranking from 10 to 1 that we just discussed. The second column is an actual probability value, and the third column is a brief description that corresponds to the level of probability.

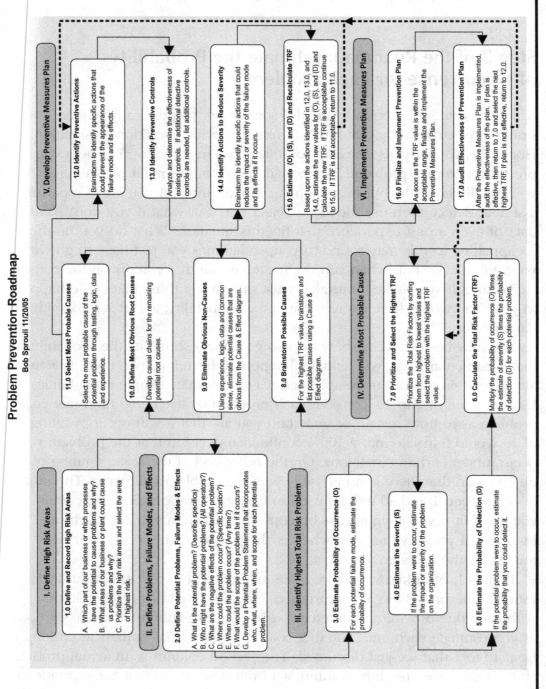

**Figure 4.3**

**Table 4.1**

| Ranking | Probability of Occurrence (O) | Probability of Failure |
|---|---|---|
| 10 | ≥1 in 2 | Almost certain to occur. |
| 9 | 1 in 3 | Very high chance of occurring. |
| 8 | 1 in 8 | High chance of occurring. |
| 7 | 1 in 20 | Moderately high chance of occurring. |
| 6 | 1 in 80 | Moderate chance of occurring. |
| 5 | 1 in 400 | Low chance of occurring. |
| 4 | 1 in 2,000 | Slight chance of occurring. |
| 3 | 1 in 15,000 | Very slight chance of occurring. |
| 2 | 1 in 150,000 | Remote chance of occurring. |
| 1 | 1 in 1,500,000 | Almost impossible to occur. |

Putting these ranking in perspective, a ranking of 10 suggests that the failure mode is almost certain to occur, while a ranking of 1 translates as the failure being a virtual impossibility. The other numbers between 10 and 1 each have discrete probabilities that are dependent upon your beliefs, experiences from the past, and level of confidence. The innate value of this table is that, if you aren't particularly comfortable or confident that you can accurately estimate the numerical probability of the failure, then you can still use the descriptive column to estimate and assign a ranking. No matter what, it's very important that you consider your own personal experiences and those of your team, and then discuss them thoroughly before assigning a ranking number.

# Step 4 of the Roadmap: Estimate the Potential Severity of the Problem

Here again, you are asked to estimate something, but this time it is not a probability, but rather an estimate of how severe or serious the problem might be, if it were to arise. There are numerous references on ways to estimate severity but, again, I want to keep it simple. Once again, a simple 1 to 10 rating scale is the most straightforward way to estimate severity. Although I am not certain of the origin of the table below, I find it to be most helpful when assigning a severity ranking. You will notice from the descriptions in Table 4.2, that it was probably developed somewhere within the auto industry, but it would be relatively simple for you to modify it to meet your needs in your industry.

In this table, there are columns for ranking the interpretation of severity and severity criteria. A ranking of 10 is labeled as "hazardous," and the criteria include things like "without warning," "safety," and "regulatory non-compliance." On the other end of the scale, a ranking of 1 means that it is totally safe, with no negative effects anticipated. The numbers between 10 and 1 are just progressive changes in severity. As with the probability of occurrence table, you should use past similar experiences and discuss the ranking with your team before you make the final ranking selection.

**Table 4.2**

| Ranking | Severity (S) | Severity Criteria |
| --- | --- | --- |
| 10 | Hazardous | Hazardous effect without warning. Safety related. Regulatory non-compliant. |
| 9 | Serious | Potential hazardous effect. Able to stop without mishap. Regulatory compliance in jeopardy. |
| 8 | Extreme | Item inoperable but safe. Customer very dissatisfied. |
| 7 | Major | Performance severely affected but functional and safe. Customer dissatisfied. |
| 6 | Significant | Performance degraded but operable and safe. Non-vital part inoperable. Customer experiences discomfort. |
| 5 | Moderate | Performance moderately affected. Fault on non-vital part requires repair. Customer experiences some dissatisfaction. |
| 4 | Minor | Minor effect on performance. Fault does not require repair. Non-vital fault always noticed. Customer experiences minor nuisance. |
| 3 | Slight | Slight effect on performance. Non-vital fault noticed most of the time. Customer is slightly annoyed. |
| 2 | Very slight | Very slight effect on performance. Non-vital fault may be noticed. Customer is not annoyed. |
| 1 | None | No effect |

# Step 5 of the Roadmap: Estimate the Probability of Detection

Curiously absent from many books and articles on the subject of potential problems is the concept of being able to detect the problem or failure either before it begins or immediately after it occurs. In my way of thinking, this is a crucial and essential part of potential problem analysis, and I am at a loss as to why it isn't discussed. The first point to take into account, when considering how we might be able to detect a failure, is to look at and consider the current controls that are in place. The current controls (either design or process) are the methods or testing already in place that notify or alert you that the cause of the failure mode could be present. Once you have identified the controls, you must turn your attention to evaluating the effectiveness of the control and then make a determination as to whether or not you must add additional controls. Remember that the important step here is that you want to be able to recognize the occurrence of the potential failure. If you aren't comfortable with the current controls, then you must develop and add additional controls, that improve the probability of detection. Each of these controls should be assessed on their ability to detect the presence of the failure mode in question.

Table 4.3, like the tables for occurrence and severity, provides a grading for the probability that you will be able to detect the presence of the effects of the failure mode. The scale is the same, ranked 1 to 10, but, this time, the order is reversed from the way you might expect. That is, the ranking of 10, in this case, is interpreted as meaning that we are certain that the controls in place will *not detect* the effects of the potential failure mode if it occurs. On the other hand, a ranking of 1 means that you are almost certain that the controls that are in place *will* detect the effects of the potential failure mode. This is done because it would be very risky if you were not able to detect the presence of the failure.

# Step 6 of the Roadmap: Calculate and Prioritize the Total Risk Factor for Each Problem

The next step in my roadmap is to calculate what I refer to as the *Total Risk Factor (TRF)* for each of the potential failure modes. The total risk factor is simply the product of the Occurrence (O), Severity (S) and Detection (D) rankings. The formula then for the Total Risk Factor (TRF) is:

$$TRF = O \times S \times D$$

**Table 4.3**

| Ranking | Detection (D) | Likelihood of Detection by Design Control |
|---------|---------------|--------------------------------------------|
| 10 | Absolute uncertainty | No controls in place to detect the presence of the effects of the potential failure mode. |
| 9 | Very remote | Very remote chance that the controls in place will detect the presence of the effects of the potential failure mode. |
| 8 | Remote | Remote chance that the controls in place will detect the presence of the effects of the potential failure mode. |
| 7 | Very low | Very low chance that the controls in place will detect the presence of the effects of the potential failure mode |
| 6 | Low | Low chance that the controls in place will detect the presence of the effects of the potential failure mode. |
| 5 | Moderate | Moderate chance that the controls in place will detect the presence of the effects of the potential failure mode. |
| 4 | Moderately high | Moderately high chance that the controls in place will detect the presence of the effects of the potential failure mode. |
| 3 | High | High chance that the controls in place will detect the presence of the effects of the potential failure mode. |
| 2 | Very high | Very high chance that the controls in place will detect the presence of the effects of the potential failure mode. |
| 1 | Almost certain | Almost certain that the controls in place will detect the presence of the effects of the potential failure mode. |

For example, suppose our ranking for occurrence was 9, our severity ranking was 5, and our detection ranking was 10. The Total Risk Factor would be 9 times 5 times 10 or 450.

Next, we simply calculate and prioritize each of the calculated TRF values, by arranging them in numerical order from the highest to the lowest value. If you were wondering why I recommend a scale of 1 to 10 for ranking the risk factors (i.e., occurrence, severity, and detection), as opposed to, say, a scale of 1 to 5, the answer is really quite simple. By using the larger range of numbers (i.e., 1 to 10), there will be a wider range of TRF values, making it much easier to differentiate or separate the really important potential failure modes from the less important ones. By doing this, we will facilitate their prioritization.

So, the question now, with multiple potential failure modes, is how would you know which TRF values to act upon first? Clearly, you want to be able to develop preventive action plans for the most important potential problems first. So, you need some way of differentiating or discriminating the truly important ones from those less important ones. It would make very little sense to act upon less important areas of risk before you acted on obvious ones. Table 4.4 below is a guide that should assist you with your ranking decision. Like the other tables for estimation of risk factors, Table 4.4 originated in the auto industry.

The way to use this table is actually pretty straightforward. All values of TRF that fall above 700 must be acted upon first, then values of 125–700, then 11–125, and finally, 1–10 values. My recommendation is that any value that is 500 or greater should be considered a candidate for inclusion in the preventive action plan. Even though you will most likely have multiple potential problems, don't be surprised if there are one or two TRF values that are conspicuous, or more prominent, than all the others. These clearly are the ones that you must act on first.

**Table 4.4**

| TRF Value | Impact | Action |
|---|---|---|
| 1–10 | Minor impact/risk | Minor design changes, process improvements, or increased controls are needed. |
| 11–125 | Moderate impact/risk | Moderate design changes, process improvements, or increased controls are needed. |
| 125–700 | Major impact/risk | Major design changes, process improvements, and 100% inspection are needed. Production may have to be stopped. |
| >700 | Catastrophic impact/risk | If in production, stop and redesign product or process, 100% improved inspection, etc., until problem is resolved |

## Step 7 of the Roadmap: Prioritize and Select the Highest Total Risk Factor

Now that you have all of your Total Risk Factors, for all of the potential problems, you must now select the highest priority one. Assuming you have done a good job of accurately estimating your three risk factors (i.e., occurrence, severity, and detection), the selection process is really quite easy. Simply arrange the TRF values from highest to lowest, and you now have your priority order. If you have two TRFs with the same value, I recommend that you select the one that has the highest severity potential, simply because that one could have the most negative effect on your organization.

## Step 8 of the Roadmap: Brainstorm Possible Causes

Now that you have identified all of your potential problems, the corresponding failure modes, and the potential harmful effects, and then prioritized them according to TRF values, you are now ready to look for potential explanations that could be the cause of the potential problem to become your current reality. The good news is that you should already know how to do this. The exact same tools that were used to develop potential causes for existing problems can be used to create a list of potential causes for the potential problems. Although the Cause-and-Effect Diagram is generally recognized as the preferred tool or technique used to create this list, it is my belief that the Causal Chain is the superior tool. Why do I say this? Because the Causal Chain lays out the chain of events that will lead to the potential problem. The directions on how to create a causal chain, which were provided earlier in this book, apply here as well. Instead of brainstorming to find potential causes of a present-day problem, we are simply looking proactively into the future at each of the potential problems and generating a list of potential causes and an associated chain of events. Don't misunderstand my comments here, as I am a huge fan of the Cause-and-Effect Diagram. In fact, I recommend that you create one as a high-level view of potential causes of potential problems.

## Step 9 of the Roadmap: Eliminate Obvious Non-Causes

One of the key points here is that not all of the possible causes listed on your Cause-and-Effect Diagram will survive the testing, logic, scrutiny, experience, and data to be retained on your list of potential causes. Some will become casualties. Eliminating possible causes from the Cause-and-Effect Diagram will only happen as a result of thoroughly analyzing data, uncovering facts, having discussions, developing Causal Chains for the most likely causes, and then achieving a consensus among your team members. Beware, I didn't say for you to eliminate a possible cause, because everyone on the team must agree on its removal. When one or two of the team members don't agree with the majority of the team, what can be done is to agree to rethink the point later, if the team fails to solve the problem. We certainly don't ever want to alienate any of the team members, so my suggestion is to seek an amicable agreement and then move on with the process.

## Step 10 of the Roadmap: Identify the Most Likely Potential Root Causes

Just like we identified potential root causes of existing problems, we will do the same for potential problems. We employ exactly the same tools and techniques used for an existing problem to identify root causes for potential problems. The Causal Chain is, once again, the best tool of all for this exercise. Let's look at this tool in a bit more depth.

When problems occur, we know that a chain of events has taken place to alter the performance of the process. We aren't always certain as to what happened, so we need some kind of tool or technique that will help us develop a theory as to what did happen. One of the most effective tools available for accomplishing this is the Causal Chain. Causal Chains are stepwise evolutions of problem causes. Figure 4.4 is a simple example of a causal chain.

Each step in the causal chain represents an object in either a normal or abnormal state. The object is placed on the line to the far right of the chain,

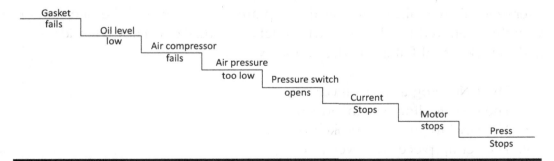

**Figure 4.4**

with the state it is listed in directly beneath it. So, in the above figure, the *object* in distress is the *press* and its *state* is that it has *stopped*. Although we might use a Cause-and-Effect Diagram to list the variety of reasons why the press stopped, it does not explain the causal mechanism that actually caused it.

In Figure 4.4 we see that a press has stopped, and we ask the question "why?". The press stopped because the motor stopped. "Why?" did the motor stop? Because the current had stopped flowing. We continue asking "Why?" until we reach the end of our chain, and find that the press stopped because the motor stopped, because the current stopped, because the pressure switch opened, because the air pressure was too low, because the air compressor failed, because the oil level was too low, because a gasket failed. We have now developed a potential theory as to why the press stopped, and, along the way, we have identified objects or items (e.g., current, oil level, etc.) that we can test to prove or disprove our theory. Each step is the cause of the next step and the effect of the preceding step. That is, the information on the step to the left is always the cause of the information on the step to the right.

What if we have more than one potential cause? How do we handle that situation? The answer is simple: we just create additional individual chains like the one in Figure 4.5 and place them along the y-axis as in Figure 4.5.

## Multiple Chain Causal Chains

Figure 4.5 is an example of a Multiple Chain Causal Chain. Here, we start with a simple statement of the problem, with the object (Ball Diameter) on top of the line, and the state that it's in directly beneath it (Oversized). This is from an actual problem-solving event that I facilitated for a manufacturer of cold-formed components, fasteners, and other related products.

In this example, the team met to determine why the ball diameter was oversized. They brainstormed as a group and then answered the question of why they believed this ball diameter might be oversized. They team identified four potential failure modes as follows:

1. The CNC program was incorrect.
2. The CNC tooling was incorrect.
3. The CNC tooling was broken or worn.
4. The set-up piece was oversized.

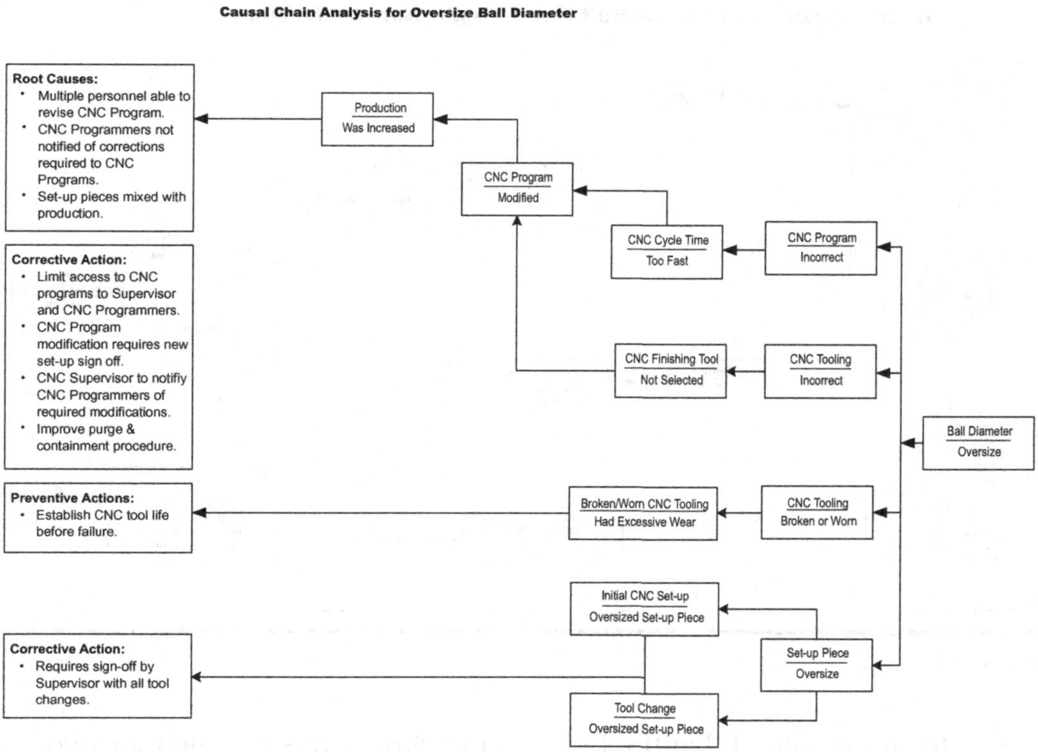

**Causal Chain Analysis for Oversize Ball Diameter**

**Root Causes:**
- Multiple personnel able to revise CNC Program.
- CNC Programmers not notified of corrections required to CNC Programs.
- Set-up pieces mixed with production.

**Corrective Action:**
- Limit access to CNC programs to Supervisor and CNC Programmers.
- CNC Program modification requires new set-up sign off.
- CNC Supervisor to notifiy CNC Programmers of required modifications.
- Improve purge & containment procedure.

**Preventive Actions:**
- Establish CNC tool life before failure.

**Corrective Action:**
- Requires sign-off by Supervisor with all tool changes.

Production Was Increased

CNC Program Modified

CNC Cycle Time Too Fast

CNC Program Incorrect

CNC Finishing Tool Not Selected

CNC Tooling Incorrect

Ball Diameter Oversize

Broken/Worn CNC Tooling Had Excessive Wear

CNC Tooling Broken or Worn

Initial CNC Set-up Oversized Set-up Piece

Set-up Piece Oversize

Tool Change Oversized Set-up Piece

**Figure 4.5**

For each of the four potential failure modes (i.e., cause-and-effect relation-ships), the team continued asking "why?" until they arrived at what they believed were the root causes of this problem. The team then developed cor-rective actions for all of the identified causes as failure modes, as well as one preventive action. The corrective and preventive actions are listed on the left side of Figure 4.5. The Multiple Chain Causal Chain worked well and the good news is that the team was able to resolve this problem and did so quickly.

## Another Example

Figure 4.6 is another example of a multiple chain causal chain. In this causal chain, we start with a simple statement of the problem, with the object (Bolt Head Thickness) on top of the line and the state that it's in directly beneath it (Too High). Like my last causal chain, this example is from an actual problem-solving event that I facilitated for a manufacturer of cold-formed components, fasteners, and other related products.

**Causal Chain Analysis for Bolt Head Height Non-Conformance**

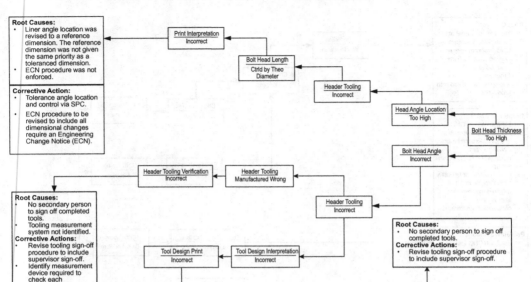

**Figure 4.6**

The team concluded that the bolt head thickness was too high for two primary reasons. The first reason was that they believed that the bolt head angle location was too high; whereas, the second reason was that the bolt head angle location wasn't correct. The team then asked why the bolt head angle location was too high and believed that the header tooling was incorrect. They then asked why this was happening and concluded that the bolt head length was controlled by the theoretical diameter. When they checked the print, they found that the print information was incorrect. The team repeated this exercise for the bolt head angle being incorrect and decided that there were two possible reasons as to why this was the case, as follows:

1. The header tooling was manufactured incorrectly.
2. The tool design interpretation was incorrect.

When they checked the header tooling, the team found that it was indeed incorrect, and, when they examined the tool design print, they found it also to be incorrect. As can be seen in Figure 4.6, the team identified the root causes for each of the chains, developed corrective actions, and implemented them with much success. Remember: the primary purpose of a causal chain, is to develop a stepwise chain of events that explains why a particular performance shortfall exists or will happen in the future. Once this is complete, hypotheses or theories can be formulated as to why a problem exists or could exist.

Figure 4.7 is a more complicated example of a causal chain with ten separate chains. You may be wondering why I am presenting so many examples of causal chains. The underlying reason is that I happen to believe that, for most problems you will encounter or anticipate that could occur, the causal

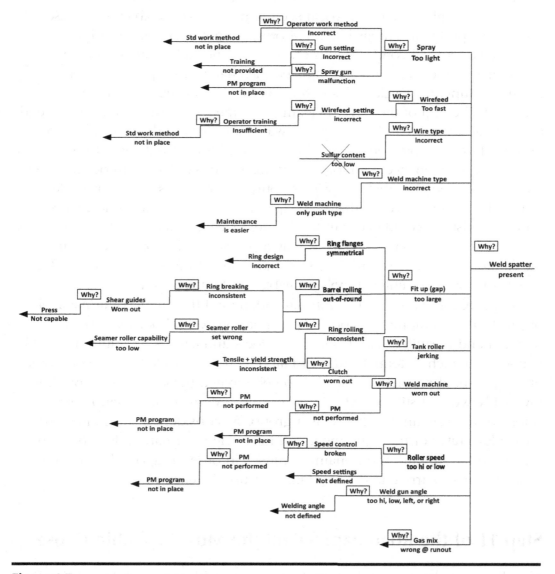

**Figure 4.7**

chain will "speed up" your ability to locate the cause or causes of the problem or potential problem in question.

Figure 4.7 is an example from a team that was working on a weld spatter problem. Here, the team brainstormed and came up with ten different chains. Each individual chain is, in reality, a brief potential step-by-step possibility as to the cause of the weld spatter problem. We always ask "why?" something is happening and then continue on with more "whys" until we eventually discover the root cause or causes. Figure 4.7 represents a complicated problem, meaning that you don't usually see this many individual chains. Follow the arrows, from right to left, and you'll see the numerous possibilities for resolution of this problem. Things like a PM program not in place, a welding angle not defined, etc., all conceivably contributed to the weld spatter problem.

Ultimately, the team either eliminated the chain(s) as a potential cause(s), through testing, or developed action items for each of the potential root causes. At the end of the day, the team performed all of the actions at the end of each causal chain and the problem was not only solved, but it was also improved from its previous state. The team used this causal chain to develop a preventive maintenance plan to prevent this same problem from occurring in the future. Remember that the primary purpose of a causal chain is to develop a stepwise chain of events, that will explain why a particular performance problem exists or could occur in the future. Once this is complete, hypotheses or theories can be formulated as to why a problem exists or could occur in the future. Causal chains are, in my opinion, one of the simplest, most effective, yet most under-utilized tools available for the team to use.

Suppose, for example, that you have identified the failure of a major piece of production equipment to be the potential problem. Your team brainstormed and created a list of potential effects and causes of failure. How do you know which potential cause of failure is the most likely to occur? Some of the potential problem causes can be eliminated through discussion, but invariably we will still be left with a short list. My recommendation is to prioritize the remaining causes, as a group, by considering things like current failure rates of the equipment and historical information. Based upon this information, rank the remaining causes in order and, one-by-one, create causal chains to arrive at the most likely cause for each one.

## Step 11 of the Roadmap: Select the Most Probable Cause

The difference between selecting the most probable cause of an existing problem, compared with a potential problem that might occur sometime in the future, is your inability to perform tests to rule out a potential problem. You would love to be able to test every potential cause, but reality tells us it is not always possible. The complete elimination of potential problems typically requires the use of things like logic, reasoning, intuition, and, whenever possible, your past experiences relating to a similar situation. Sometimes you will be lucky enough to have had experiences involving the same or a similar kind of problem. So, it is absolutely imperative that your team use methodical and logical reasoning when selecting the most probable potential cause of the problem.

Because you will be examining circumstances well into the future, many times it is difficult to agree on a single, most probable cause, and invariably your team will be left with two or three options for the most probable causes. Although some people believe you should have your team vote to reach a consensus, I believe this method is flawed. Clearly you don't want to take a chance on something that one or two members feel strongly about, but if you can't agree on a single most probable cause, then so be it. In the next step on the roadmap, you will be developing a Preventive Measures Plan, so, if you can't agree on a single most probable cause, then my advice is to build your plan around multiple, potential root causes. My advice is that if you have more than three potential probable causes, then you should look for ways to reduce the number.

At the risk of being redundant, I want to summarize the purpose and value of the Preventive Measures Plan. The plan in its finished form will have three essential components. The first part involves identifying *specific actions* that are intended to prevent the problem and its effects from occurring. The second, and equally important component, is focused on *limiting the damage*, in the event that our preventive actions don't deliver the expected results. The third part of the plan involves the development and use of *detective controls*, that should let us know that the problem is present. All three components are important and integral parts of the Preventive Measures Plan.

# Step 12 of the Roadmap: Identify Preventive Actions

Creating preventive actions for a future, potential root cause is really the same thing you would do if you were attempting to solve an existing problem. Your focus so far has been aimed at identifying potential root causes, and, hopefully, your team has agreed upon a single, most probable root cause, but often this just isn't the case. Once you have determined the potential cause of the future potential problem, you must now search for ways to prevent the problem from occurring. In doing so, your team must be creative and imaginative. Your team may or may not be able to test your proposed actions ahead of time, in an effort to ensure that your actions will prevent the problem from occurring. My advice to your team is to use the causal chains they developed earlier in an effort to better understand the potential causes of the potential problem. Simply put, use these causal chains to identify actions aimed at preventing the problem.

## Step 13 of the Roadmap: Identify Preventive Controls

As I explained earlier, the purpose of identifying preventive controls is to provide some assurance that any potential failure modes, and their related effects, are detected early enough in the process to be able to act on them, prior to the onset of the potential problem. Detective controls can be things like failsafe devices, which provide both maximum detection and protection, manual measurements on the process that could be plotted on a control chart, or even audits of the process under consideration.

When your team is attempting to identify an appropriate control, it is very important to consider which type might be best for the situation at hand. Your team must consider how severe the effect or effects might be, but they should also look at the cost to implement the control against the impact of the effect. If the effect isn't considered to be very detrimental, it would not make sense to spend much time or money developing a comprehensive, technical control. On the other hand, if the impact on the organization is considered to be extreme, then it would absolutely make sense to spend the extra time and money.

Having said all of this, the most important consideration here is to assess the apparent control and containment needs, and then compare these needs to the effectiveness of the existing controls. If there is a mismatch, then definitive action must be taken to close the gap.

## Step 14 of the Roadmap: Identify Actions to Reduce Severity

Now that you have identified the most probable cause of the problem and effective preventive actions, you must now focus on the estimated seriousness or severity of the potential failure and its potential harmful effects. As you develop actions aimed at reducing the potential severity of the potential problem, you will be assuming that there is a likelihood that the problem will not be prevented. Because of this possibility, you must now search for ways to minimize the effects of the failure that you were unable to prevent. Remember that not all potential problems will be avoidable, so your plan must include provisions to counter the possible negative effects.

Consider the example introduced earlier, where you had a single source supplier of parts or materials. One action might be to develop a secondary supplier to fill the void, in the event that the primary supplier isn't able to supply parts and materials. Another possibility might be to redesign the part in question so that it will perform the same function. Another part of the plan might be to create a safety-net of stock of the critical parts, that would keep your processes running until the problem was corrected at the supplier location. If the probability of occurrence is extremely high, then the plan might even include replacing your current supplier. Whichever the case, this is the time for the team to be imaginative and inventive, as the plan is developed.

## Step 15 of the Roadmap: Estimate Occurrence (O), Severity (S), and Detection (D), and Recalculate TRF

Once you have articulated the actions aimed at preventing, detecting, and reducing the severity of the potential problem, it is now time to recalculate the Total Risk Factor (TRF). This involves estimating the probability that the problem will occur, the severity of the problem if it does occur, and the probability that you will be able to detect it. Evaluate the planned actions and then recalculate the TRF. If the TRF falls within an acceptable range, as dictated in Table 4.5, then the plan is probably sound and sensible. If the TRF doesn't fall within an acceptable range, then more creative actions have to be developed.

A word of caution for you as you re-evaluate each risk factor. Make certain that your team is unbiased and objective as they consider the three areas of risk! If you sense that your team isn't being unbiased, it is always a good idea to get a sanity check from someone outside the group who is not vested in the outcome of the evaluation.

**Table 4.5**

| TRF Value | Impact | Action |
|---|---|---|
| 1–10 | Minor impact/risk | Minor design changes, process improvements, or increased controls are needed. |
| 11–125 | Moderate impact/risk | Moderate design changes, process improvements, or increased controls are needed. |
| 125–700 | Major impact/risk | Major design changes, process improvements, and 100% inspection are needed. Production may have to be stopped. |
| >700 | Catastrophic impact/risk | If in production, stop and redesign product or process, 100% improved inspection, etc., until problem is resolved |

## Step 16 of the Roadmap: Finalize and Implement the Preventive Measures Plan

As soon as you feel comfortable with the Preventive Measures Plan that your team has developed and re-evaluated for risk, it is now time to execute the finalized plan. You have double-checked the plan for its effectiveness, with respect to predicting the chances that the problem will occur, plus your ability to detect it, if it does occur. Your team has developed actions that are intended to counteract or neutralize the effects of the potential problem, were it to occur. Now, it is time to communicate the plan to everyone. It's always good practice to hold meetings with key personnel closest to the potential problem and review the purpose and specific actions of the plan, before it is actually implemented. If you want the plan to be executed flawlessly, then take the time to make sure that everyone involved, especially your shop floor workers, clearly understand their roles, tasks, and responsibilities.

After you are sure that everyone understands the planned actions, my advice is to simply implement your plan and then "live in the process," until you are confident that your team's plan is working effectively. When I say, "live in the process," I simply mean that you should personally manage the details and minutiae of the plan. My experiences have demonstrated the importance of this action over and over. Many times, I have witnessed good plans gone awry, simply because of how the plan was communicated to the masses. Take the time to methodically and meticulously communicate your team's plan and then be actively involved during the implementation.

If your control is a measurement or audit, again be certain that all who perform the control testing know first how to accurately make the measurement and then measure or audit often in the early stages of implementation. As mentioned earlier, *an ounce of prevention is worth a pound of cure!*

## Step 17 of the Roadmap: Audit the Effectiveness of the Prevention Plan

Soon after you have executed the Preventive Measures Plan in its entirety, you should know whether or not the plan is effective and results in the kind of results you expected. But what about the longer-term effectiveness? How can you guarantee that the new methods will continue as planned? There are no guarantees, of course, but it is always a good idea to follow up with periodic audits of the key ingredients and components of the plan. You must do this to be certain that the plan was implemented in the manner you had intended, and that the implementation continues long after the fact.

It is my recommendation that, first, you make sure that the detection methods are being performed appropriately so that the feedback you are receiving is accurate and reliable. Without high-quality feedback, your reaction to erroneous information may stimulate unjustified actions. Now is the time to be totally anal and overly cautious of everything in the plan. Being observant, alert, and watchful during and after the implementation will help ensure the plan's success.

So, these are the seventeen steps from my Problem Prevention Roadmap. It is my absolute belief that, if you follow the steps outlined in this chapter, the number of future problems will decrease dramatically! Because there will be many decisions to make along the way, my next chapter will focus on another roadmap aimed at how to make more effective decisions.

# Chapter 5

# Effective Decision-Making

Every day in life, whether we like it or not, we are called upon to make choices between different alternatives. We start each weekday with simple decisions, trying to decide whether or not we will get up and go to work, what we will wear, what we will eat for breakfast, and when to leave for work. As I said, these decisions are simple, instinctive decisions and, as such, are very simple and straightforward. But as we move through our day at our jobs, the decisions and choices we make become more complex and complicated. These decisions involve deciding what it is that we need and want, picturing alternatives, and evaluating any risks and consequences that might arise from our choices, and then we make a choice. Soon after we choose, it's not unusual for us to begin wondering if the choice we made was the right one. We continue worrying until the results of our decisions become our current reality. We find out right away if the decisions we made were the right ones or the wrong ones.

Decisions can be somewhat stressful, but do they really have to be? The answer is, no, they do not have to be. Making difficult decisions can actually be made with little or no worry if we simply follow an organized and systematic approach to making decisions. I'm sure by now you've noticed that in both problem prevention and problem-solving, there were decisions that needed to be made. Deciding on which solution for a problem or choosing which area of your company is the highest-risk area can be stressful, but, as I said, they don't have to be. Just like the roadmaps for problem-solving and prevention, effective decision-making will result if we simply follow the structured and systematic approach like the one presented in Figure 5.1, the *Decision-Making Roadmap.*

DOI: 10.4324/9781003462385-5

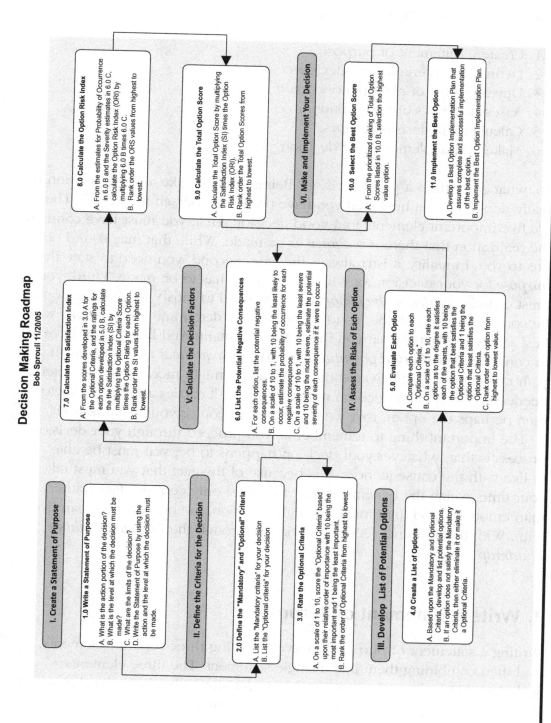

## Decision Making Roadmap
### Bob Sproull 11/20/05

**I. Create a Statement of Purpose**

**1.0 Write a Statement of Purpose**

A. What is the action portion of the decision?
B. What is the level at which the decision must be made?
C. What are the limits of the decision?
D. Write the Statement of Purpose by using the action and the level at which the decision must be made.

**II. Define the Criteria for the Decision**

**2.0 Define the "Mandatory" and "Optional" Criteria**

A. List the "Mandatory criteria" for your decision
B. List the "Optional criteria" for your decision

**3.0 Rate the Optional Criteria**

A. On a scale of 1 to 10, score the "Optional Criteria" based upon their relative order of importance with 10 being the most important and 1 being the least important.
B. Rank the order of Optional Criteria from highest to lowest.

**III. Develop List of Potential Options**

**4.0 Create a List of Options**

A. Based upon the Mandatory and Optional Criteria, develop and list potential options.
B. If an option does not satisfy the Mandatory Criteria, then either eliminate it or make it a Optional Criteria.

**IV. Assess the Risks of Each Option**

**5.0 Evaluate Each Option**

A. Compare each option to each "Optional Criteria."
B. On a scale of 1 to 10, rate each option as to the degree it satisfies each of the wants, with 10 being the option that best satisfies the Optional Criteria and 1 being the option that least satisfies the Optional Criteria.
C. Rank order each option from highest to lowest value.

**V. Calculate the Decision Factors**

**6.0 List the Potential Negative Consequences**

A. For each option, list the potential negative consequences.
B. On a scale of 10 to 1, with 10 being the least likely to occur, estimate the probability of occurrence for each negative consequence.
C. On a scale of 10 to 1, with 10 being the least severe and 10 being the most severe, estimate the potential severity of each consequence if it were to occur.

**7.0 Calculate the Satisfaction Index**

A. From the scores developed in 3.0 A for the Optional Criteria, and the ratings for each option developed in 5.0 B, calculate the Satisfaction Index (SI) by multiplying the Optional Criteria Score times the Option Rating for each Option.
B. Rank order the SI values from highest to lowest.

**8.0 Calculate the Option Risk Index**

A. From the estimates for Probability of Occurrence in 6.0 B and the Severity estimates in 6.0 C, calculate the Option Risk Index (ORI) by multiplying 6.0 B times 6.0 C.
B. Rank order the ORS values from highest to lowest.

**9.0 Calculate the Total Option Score**

A. Calculate the Total Option Score by multiplying the Satisfaction Index (SI) times the Option Risk Index (ORI).
B. Rank order the Total Option Scores from highest to lowest.

**VI. Make and Implement Your Decision**

**10.0 Select the Best Option Score**

A. From the prioritized ranking of Total Option Scores listed in 10.0 B, selection the highest value option.

**11.0 Implement the Best Option**

A. Develop a Best Option Implementation Plan that assures complete and successful implementation of the best option.
B. Implement the Best Option Implementation Plan.

**Figure 5.1**

There are six major sections in the roadmap, all signifying a separate purpose and function. The six sections of the roadmap are:

1. Create a statement of purpose.
2. Define the criteria for the decision.
3. Develop a list of potential options.
4. Assess the risks of each option.
5. Calculate the decision factors.
6. Make and implement your decision.

So, what constitutes a good decision? Being able to make a good decision is really dependent on how well you have prepared yourself to make it. There are five important elements in a good decision. First, you must have come to the realization that there is a *choice* to be made. While that may sound obvious to you, in reality, it isn't always the case. Second, you need to state the *purpose* for your decision, or why this decision has to be made. Third, you must completely *define the factors* that you need to satisfy for the decision to be considered a good one. Fourth, you have to determine what *actions* will best satisfy the factors that you think are important. And finally, you have to consider *the risks and potential negative consequences* associated with your choice of options. Even though an option might meet all of the criteria needed to satisfy your decision requirements, if it carries a large risk factor, then perhaps the option isn't worth the risk to you or your organization.

The important thing to remember as you proceed through your decision process is that, whatever your decision happens to be, you must be able to live with the consequences. It is because of this fact that you must take your time, weigh the benefits against the risks, only consider facts rather than emotions, and then make the right decision, the one that you can live with. With this in mind, let's now proceed through the *Decision-Making Roadmap*.

# 1. Write a Statement of Purpose

Writing a statement of purpose involves defining three separate elements, and then combining them into a single statement. The three elements include: what is the action portion of the decision, what is the level at which the decision must be made, and what are the limits of the decision?

Each decision you make must always be made with a specific purpose or intention in mind. A good statement of purpose includes any action you are intending to take and the results that you hope to achieve by taking this action. The statement of purpose sets the stage for everything that follows in the decision process, so it must be comprehensive enough to provide direction, and include a defined set of limits, especially if there is a team involved in making the decision. If your statement of purpose, for example, was simply to improve the shipping of products to your customers, it might provide some sense of direction, but it would hardly set any limits. A better statement of purpose, in this case, might be something like, "to improve your on-time delivery from 80% to 95% to customer "X," within six months or less." This statement provides a clear sense of direction and has well-defined limits.

Creating your statement of purpose is an important first step because it sets the stage for all of the actions that follow. The action portion of the decision is to state what actions you are contemplating that require a decision. The level at which the decision must be made is simply "who" in your organization has the final say on the contemplated action. In terms of limits, ask yourself if this decision is strictly within the confines of your company, or would it be appropriate to include customers and/or suppliers in the final decision? When these questions are answered correctly, you then simply create your statement of purpose.

## 2. Define the "Mandatory" and "Optional" Criteria for the Decision

There are two distinctly different types of criteria involved in all decisions. First, there are things that you must have, or that are *mandatory*, in order to guarantee that your final decision will be successful. The second type is everything else that falls into the *optional* criterion category. When we consider options later on in this process, which are intended to deliver your statement of purpose, an option either satisfies the mandatory criteria or it does not. If the option doesn't meet all of the mandatory criteria, then we must either eliminate it or move it to our list of optional criteria. All mandatory criteria must be measurable and clearly defined and have no ambiguity.

On the other hand, optional criteria are those things that aren't mandatory, but they would be really good to have. A simple example of an optional criterion, if you were buying a car, might be that the price must be under $30,000. Any car that is over this price would not be considered and would automatically be rejected. However, if you wanted a red car, but would buy a car that was a different color, then the color red would be an optional criterion. The options that you will be considering will be judged on their relative performance against the optional criteria. Remember, we are simply comparing options against each other, and optional criteria help us draw this comparison.

## 3. Rate the Optional Criteria

Now that you have developed your list of optional criteria, you must now rate them by giving each of them an individual score on a scale of 1 to 10, based upon their relative order of importance to each other. First, when you decide which of the optional criteria is the most important to your team, rate it as a 10. All other optional criteria are then rated in comparison to this most important one. It should be obvious that a rating of 10 would be the most important, whereas a rating of 1 is the least important. Keep in mind that there could be more than one of the optional criteria rated as a 10, but you must be totally honest and objective when rating these criteria. When this step is completed, simply rank them in order from the highest to the lowest rating. Your intention here will be to do this to provide a visual display of all of the criteria compared with each other. So, if the final ranking of these criteria might appear to be out of order in some way, now is the time to discuss and re-order them, if necessary.

## 4. Create a List of Options

Based on the mandatory and optional criteria, you must now develop and list potential options. If an option does not satisfy the mandatory criteria, then either eliminate it or make it one of the optional criteria. The ultimate option would be one that satisfies all of the mandatory and optional criteria but, unfortunately, these typeS of options are few and far between, so use your evaluative skills to make an informed decision. In some cases, there may only be one option to consider, so your decision now is whether or not the results it is intended to deliver are adequate to meet your needs. It is important to remember that the way we are currently doing things should always be considered as an option, even though we aren't happy with the results.

# 5. Evaluate Each Option

Now that we have our final list of potential options, you must now evaluate each option for how well it satisfies the mandatory and optional criteria. For the mandatory criteria, the option either satisfies them or it doesn't. If it doesn't, then eliminate it immediately or make it optional. For each of the optional criteria, we need to compare each possible option with each of the other optional criteria and then give each one a rating of 1 to 10. A rating of 10 means that the option satisfies all of the optional criteria. At the other end of the rating scale, a rating of 1 means that it in no way satisfies it. When you have finished scoring all of the options, rank the options from the highest score to the lowest to provide a visual comparison of all the options. By rating each option against its ability to satisfy the mandatory and optional criteria, we are evaluating each option's quality of fit.

# 6. List the Potential Negative Consequences

Just like you did in the Problem Prevention Roadmap, you now need to assess the risks or potential negative consequences of each option. So, how do you do this? First, you brainstorm, discuss, and list any potential negative consequences associated with each of the individual options on the final list. Once you have completed this step, you must then estimate the probability that each of these potential negative consequences might occur. Here, you need to rely on things like your past experiences in a similar situation, research information, or, as a last resort, your own intuition. Again, you will apply a rating of 10 to 1, with 1, in this case, meaning that the consequence is likely to occur, and 10 meaning that it will probably not occur. In this case, you are not rating one consequence against the others, but rather each one individually.

Here, not only are you concerned about whether or not a negative consequence will occur, but you are also interested in the impact or severity on the organization if it were to occur. Again, you will use a scale of 10 to 1, with 1 interpreted as being catastrophic to your organization, and 10 meaning there will be little or no impact if the consequence were to occur. The numbers between 10 and 1 are indicative of increasing or decreasing severity on the organization. When you complete this rating, once again arrange the consequences from highest to lowest, based on their individual ratings.

## 7. Calculate the Satisfaction Index

Now that you have completed the hard work of assigning rankings to the optional criteria and the options, it is now time to make an initial calculation known as the Satisfaction Index. This index is simply a measure of how well each option stacks up against each optional criterion. You perform this task by multiplying the optional criteria score you assigned in Step 3 of this *Decision-Making Roadmap* by the rating you have assigned for each option that you assigned in Step 5 of the Roadmap. The formula for the Satisfaction Index (SI) is:

$$SI = \text{Optional Criteria Score} \times \text{Option Score}$$

For example, suppose we rated an optional criterion as a 9, and an option as a 6, then the satisfaction index for this criterion and option combination would be:

$$SI = 9 \times 6 = 54$$

Once you have completed the math for all options and all optional criteria, arrange them in numerical order from highest to lowest. The results you get may surprise you.

## 8. Calculate the Option Risk Index

It is now time to assess the risk associated with each individual option. Even though an option might have scored highest on the Satisfaction Index, this does not guarantee that it will be your final selection. It is now time to calculate the Option Risk Index in Step 8 of our Roadmap. This is done by simply multiplying the estimate for the probability of occurrence from Step 6 in the Roadmap for each option by the corresponding severity estimates that you assigned earlier. The formula for the Option Risk Index (ORI) is:

$$ORI = \text{Probability of Occurrence Rating (O)} \times \text{Severity Rating (S)}$$

Or

$$ORI = O \times S$$

Suppose we had rated Occurrence (O) for an option as an 8, and Severity (S) as a 9, then the ORI would be equal to 9 × 8 = 72.

Once the ORI has been calculated for each option being considered, you should then rank the ORI values from highest to lowest. Does the order of the ORI look the same as the SI list? If it doesn't, then the risks may dictate a new best option.

## 9. Calculate the Total Option Score

Now that you have calculated the Satisfaction Index and the Option Risk Index, it is now time to calculate one more measure, the Total Option Score. The Total Option Score is used to separate and rank all of the available options, from best to worst, which sets the stage for your decision-making. The Total Option Score is calculated by multiplying the Satisfaction Index by the Option Risk Index as follows:

$$\text{Total Option Score (TOS)} = \text{Satisfaction Index (SI)} \times \text{Option Risk Index (ORI)}$$

Or

$$\text{TOS} = \text{SI} \times \text{ORI}$$

Suppose we had calculated the SI to be 54 and the ORI to be 72, then the TOS would be:

$$\text{TOS} = 54 \times 72 = 3888$$

Calculate the Total Option Score for each of the options, and then rank them in order from the highest to the lowest.

## 10. Select the Best Option Score

From the rankings for the Total Option Scores, you should now select the option at the top of the list. If you have done everything correctly and kept your emotions out of the scoring or rankings for each option and each optional criterion, then the option with the highest score should be your best option for your decision-making. Most of the time, if you have done everything according to the *Decision-Making Roadmap*, your decision-making ability should improve dramatically.

# 11. Implement the Best Option

Just like any implementation, you should carefully consider what should be in your implementation plan and then create a plan that ensures the complete and successful implementation of the best option. The best option for an implementation plan is that it must include a detailed list of items that must be implemented, as well as the order in which they are carried out. I have seen several good decisions made, that were implemented without thought, and the results were disastrous. Take your time, like you would with any other implementation.

For those of you who may be confused about which roadmap should be used, in the next chapter, I will be presenting a very simple roadmap, or rather, a flow chart, that will make your roadmap selection much easier.

# Chapter 6

# Needs Assessment

In the past three chapters, you have learned how to best solve problems, prevent problems, and how to make more effective decisions. I have provided roadmaps to follow for each of the three actions that you or your organization will be faced with, as you do your jobs. When or where to use each of these roadmaps will be obvious to most of you, but for some, it won't be. It is for these people that this brief chapter will focus on an assessment of your organization's needs.

Before we discuss assessing your needs, I want everyone to understand the full intentions of these three roadmaps. I want you to think for a minute about what you do before you leave for a new destination in your car. Most people do one of two things. Either they log onto their GPS, or some other internet location finder, and get specific directions to where they're going, or, if this location is one that they visit frequently, then, after several trips, they no longer need the GPS for directions, because they now know how to get to where they want to go.

So, too, is the intention of each of these individual roadmaps. Use them, and learn them, and they will become committed to memory. The old adage of "practice makes perfect" really is true. The point is, as you become more familiar and comfortable with each of the three roadmaps, you will no longer need them because you will know exactly what to do next. You will have put it all together and it will eventually become a habit.

DOI: 10.4324/9781003462385-6

# Assessing Your Needs

As I just explained, some of you will understand automatically, when to use each of the three individual roadmaps, but some of you will not. For those of you who won't understand what to do next, I have developed what I refer to as a *Needs Assessment Roadmap*, as shown in Figure 6.1.

The *Needs Assessment Roadmap* is simply a series of straightforward questions for you to answer as the circumstance you are faced with presents itself. The first two questions are, "Is there a problem to be solved?", followed by the question, "Does the problem already exist?". If the problem already exists, then you can proceed immediately to the *Problem-Solving Roadmap*. Once there, you will now be able to guide yourself through all of the individual steps until you have reached the root cause of the problem. Once you have the root cause, you will then be guided through developing a solution to the problem.

If the answer to the second question is no, then you must answer this question, "Is there a problem to be prevented?". Since this indicates that you are contemplating that a problem could arise, then you will proceed to the *Problem Prevention Roadmap*. Once there, you will again follow the individual steps to identify the high-risk areas, the potential failure modes and effects, and the potential root cause, followed by the development and implementation of a Preventive Measures Plan.

The next question on this roadmap is, "Is there a decision involved?". If the decision has already been made, then it is a good idea to follow the *Problem Prevention Roadmap*, to be certain that you have considered all of the potential problems and risks, relative to your decision. If the decision has not been made, then you can proceed to the *Decision-Making Roadmap*. There, you will be guided through all of the steps to first develop a Statement of Purpose, that includes the reason for the decision, the actions to be taken, and the level and limits of the decision. You will then develop the mandatory and optional criteria to be satisfied by the decision, develop options, assess the risks, and then select the best options.

I am hopeful that the *Needs Assessment Roadmap* will help those of you that are having trouble deciding which of these three roadmaps to follow. I think I have kept it simple and straightforward for you.

## Needs Assessment Roadmap
### Bob Sproull

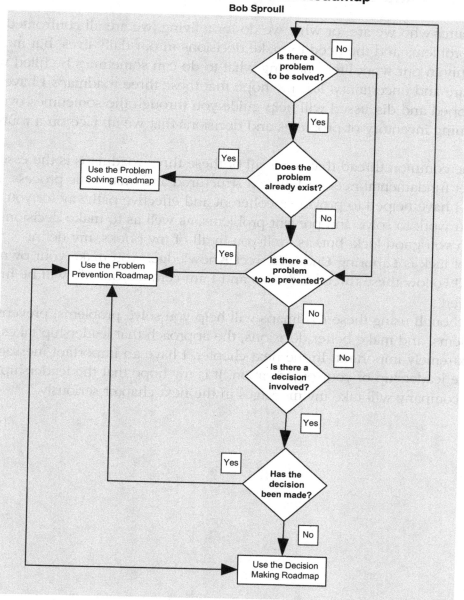

**Figure 6.1**

# Problems and Decisions: Conclusion

No matter who we are, or what we do for a living, we are all confronted with problems and the need to make decisions in our daily lives, but most certainly in our work life. Knowing what to do can sometimes be filled with pressure and uncertainty. It is my hope that these three roadmaps I have developed and discussed will help guide you through the sometimes-overwhelming inventory of problems and decisions that we all face on a routine basis.

The common thread that binds all of these three roadmaps is the essential yet fundamental need to follow a structured and systematic process. I hope I have helped to provide a coherent and effective pathway for you as you work to solve and prevent problems, as well as to make decisions. I wish you good luck, but, as I tell you in all of my books, my definition of luck is **L**aboring **U**nder **C**orrect **K**nowledge…you make your own LUCK! Follow these three roadmaps and I am certain your life will be much "luckier!".

Although using these roadmaps will help you solve problems, prevent problems, and make better decisions, the approach that leadership takes will be extremely important. In the next chapter, I have an important message for the leadership of your organization. It is my hope that the leadership of your company will take my messages in the next chapter seriously.

# Chapter 7

## A Message for Leadership of Systems

### What is Leadership?

Before I present, as the chapter title states, my message to leadership, I think it might be meaningful to put some kind of definition on the term "Leadership." [1] Bill Dettmer, one of the foremost authorities on systems thinking, in one of his white papers, defines leadership as, "The exercise of power to influence people to do willingly, in a coordinated way, what they may not be under any obligation to do."

In this same white paper [1], Dettmer introduces us to the elements of leadership as depicted in Figure 7.1. To quote Dettmer, "Expertise and charisma normally inspire people. Legitimacy formally conferred, rewards dispensed, and coercion applied (in the form of punishment) tend to compel expected behavior. This figure illustrates the necessary condition relationships among these elements." Figure 7.1 is actually in the form of a Goal Tree (which I will discuss in Chapter 9), with the Goal being "Leadership." The Goal Tree uses necessity-based logic and uses the syntax, *In order to have "x" I must have "y."* So, based on Figure 7.1, it would be read as, "In order to have Leadership (The Goal), I must have *Followers, Power,* and *Action.*" The remaining entities in Figure 7.1 follow the same necessity-based logic.

So, based on the contents of Figure 7.1, Dettmer redefines leadership as, "Leadership is the exercise of power to influence people to do willingly, in a coordinated way, what they may not be under any obligation to do."

DOI: 10.4324/9781003462385-7

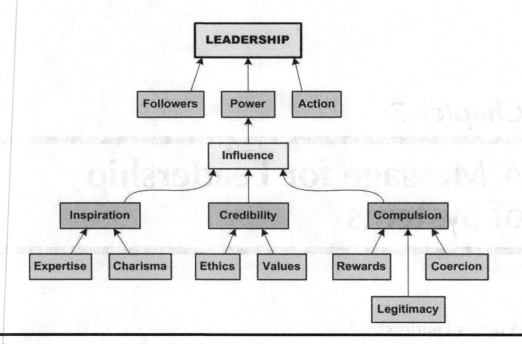

**Figure 7.1**

Dettmer goes on to say, "There's a subtle characteristic of this definition that warrants emphasis – it is completely neutral to value judgments about purposes, ends, or results. The determination of good versus bad leaders can only be made with reference to those purposes or results, not the activity of leading itself. But the interesting thing is that this definition applies to the activity of leadership at all levels of any system. Whether you're leading a team of volunteers or a country, leadership involves the art of motivating and focusing other people's efforts toward a desired end." For me, Dettmer hit the proverbial nail on the head with his definition of leadership!

Next, Dettmer asks the question, "What should a leader's function be? If we remember our definition of leadership – the exercise of power to influence people to do willingly, in a coordinated way, what they may not be under any obligation to do – and if we accept the idea that organizations must be agile, maneuverable, and flexible, then we're forced to conclude that:

1. Centralized, top-down control is not going to be helpful.
2. Authority, and the responsibility that goes with it, must be deployed to subordinate leaders.
3. Senior leaders must safeguard the positional security of their subordinates.

4. Leaders must provide a clear, unequivocal vision of the goal and the general strategy for attaining it.

Dettmer ends this paper with a quote from Dwight David Eisenhower:

> In order to be a leader, a man must have followers. And to have followers, a man must have their confidence. Hence the supreme quality for a leader is unquestionably integrity. Without it, no real success is possible, no matter whether it is on a section gang, on a football field, in an army, or in an office. If a man's associates find him guilty of phoniness, if they find that he lacks forthright integrity, he will fail. His teachings and actions must square with each other. The first great need, therefore, is integrity and high purpose.
>
> **—Dwight D. Eisenhower**

If you haven't read this series of papers by Bill Dettmer, I highly recommend that you do! In this next section of this chapter, I recommend ten questions that Leadership should answer.

## The Questions of a Leader

I once had a Vice President of Operations for a company ask me what he needed to do to get his people to use a structured approach to problem-solving. He had spent money on consultants (not me) teaching problem-solving in the past, but his staff's ability to solve problems hadn't changed or improved. They had continued to be reactive and seemingly disinterested in applying what they had learned. My answer to him was simple. I told him that, since he was the leader of the organization, it was up to him to force this behavioral change. Not change by brute force, but rather by setting the appropriate expectations and by setting the right example. I told him that, if the leader of an organization doesn't expect, be adamant about, and personally use a structured approach to solving problems, then why should he expect anything different from the rest of his organization? This VP assured me that he did expect this to happen, but he admitted he did not use it himself.

I prepared a list of ten simple questions for him to ask of his people each time they were presenting a problem to him. If the person did not have an appropriate answer for the question asked, then the VP was to instruct him or her to go get the answers and come back to him when they did. Here are the questions I gave him.

## Ten Questions from a Leader on Problem-Solving

- What is the problem? (Specifically describe the problem.)
- Where is the problem occurring? (Where is it in the plant and where is it on the object?)
- When is the problem occurring? (When did it start and when does it recur? Trend chart.)
- Who has the problem? (Is it one operator or multiple operators? Pareto chart.)
- What is the scope of the problem? (How many product types have the problem? Or how many machines have the problem?)
- What is the trend? (Is the problem increasing, decreasing, or remaining constant? Trend chart.)
- What is your problem statement? (Incorporates all of the above.)
- Is it a change-related problem? A launch problem (distinctions)? or a hybrid problem (a combination of a change and a launch problem)?
- Have you formed a team? (Is it a diverse group including at least one operator and one non-production member?)
- When can I expect a solution to the problem?

Sadly, this VP did not use these questions on a regular basis, and the results of problem-solving actions remained as they had been. If he had used them, a noticeable change in his and his management team's approach to problems would have become obvious, and so would have the results. The leader of the organization is the one who sets the tone and expectations for how things get done and how problems are solved. So, if you want your team to use a structured approach to solving problems, you had better set the right expectations and lead by example.

## Why Teams Fail

Even though a team might be conscientious and diligent in following a structured approach, not all problems get solved the first time for a variety of different reasons. [2] Kepner and Tregoe remind us that it is important to remember that you may fail! If you do fail, then Kepner and Tregoe tell us that there are two primary reasons:

■ The team has achieved insufficient identification of key distinctions and changes.
■ The team has allowed assumptions to distort their judgment during the testing step.

The two reasons for failure just listed are very specific and do not adequately explain the failures of many teams. Here is a more comprehensive list.

■ *Failure to select the right team members*: One of the reasons why teams are more effective than individuals at solving problems is the synergy that should be demonstrated but isn't always. So, what would block this synergy? One of the most common reasons why teams fail is the basic member selection process. It's really no different from a professional sports franchise buying superstars in the free-agent market. Having a collection of superstars is no guarantee that a championship will follow. When teams are selected, care should be taken to select known "team players" that are more interested in solving the problem rather than their own self interests. The membership should be selected based upon a particular skill that they can bring to the team.
■ *Failure to define or understand the real problem*: Defining the problem is absolutely a critical first step in resolving the problem. Without the focus provided by the problem definition, not everyone is properly focused and aligned and having the entire team aligned is critical to the success of the team. Otherwise, people will go off in different directions and the team will most likely fail. What typically happens when a problem isn't thoroughly defined is that problem-solving team members attempt to solve world hunger.
■ *Treatment of symptoms instead of the root cause*: Sometimes, people get confused and mistake symptoms of the problem for the problem itself. When this happens, temporary, short term "fixes" or relief actions are applied to problems based on what worked in the past, instead of performing a rigorous problem analysis. It's no different to going to a hospital for severe abdominal pain and, rather than determining the source of the pain, the doctor gives you pain pills. The pain medication might

give you relief, but the problem is still there when the effects of the medication (i.e., the short-term fix) subside. Based on my experience, treating symptoms rather than finding and eliminating the root cause is a very common occurrence when people are trying to solve problems.

■ *People lack the basic skills necessary for problem-solving*: Because many people don't understand the nature of problems and because they have never really had any formal training in problem analysis, they tend to apply the "change something and see what happens" approach. All this does is complicate the situation, because if you aren't careful, you can lose track of the changes you make and probably worsen the problem. This lack of basic skills is one of the most significant reasons or causes of failed problem-solving initiatives. It's not your fault since you have probably never been provided with any form of effective problem-solving training. Many of you might have received training on specific tools or techniques, like cause-and-effect diagrams, or Pareto charts, or maybe even trend charts. But how many of you have learned how and when to use these tools to define a problem, search for a change, identify a defect-free configuration, or clarify a distinction? Solving problems requires a systematic approach and it's my bet many of you have never had this kind of training.

■ *Failure to look at problems holistically*: Many times, people only focus on the symptoms of the problem and fail to look at the causal mechanism that created the conditions for the problem to occur. Remember, we are looking for cause-and-effect relationships here. I absolutely agree with Kepner and Tregoe in this aspect, but, again, it all comes down to the level of problem-solving training people have received and the expectations of leadership to follow a structured approach.

■ *Failure to use a structured and systematic approach*: The number one cause of failure to solve problems is the failure to follow a logical and systematic process. When problem-solving teams don't follow a systematic approach, there is a tendency to wander aimlessly, and usually problems do not get solved! It is only through being disciplined enough to use a structured approach that most problems actually get solved. Although this, again, is a training issue, the reality is that the fault lies with the leader of the organization. The leader must set expectations that structured approaches to problem-solving will be used.

■ *Tendency to prematurely jump to solutions*: Successful problem-solving is not the result of putting a team together, brainstorming causes, and then picking out one to try from an extensive laundry list of opportunities. Success is achieved by first carefully thinking through the problem, identifying what kind of problem it is, relating things like symptoms or changes to the problem, developing causal chains and theories of what the root causes are, and then *cautiously* developing solutions.

■ *No support or expectations from leadership*: Support and expectations from the leadership in any organization are not just important, they are critical pieces of the problem-solving pie. If the problem-solvers do not get the support they need, and if the expectation of leadership isn't to use a structured approach to solving problems, then, quite simply, problems won't get solved effectively!

My message to leadership then is clear. If you want problems solved, then set high expectations. Expect a structured approach to be used and expect problems to be solved. And, once again, set an example by using the same approach yourself. In addition, give your people a chance, by making sure they receive the right training. But even by setting expectations, you must establish a culture for problem-solving.

## The Culture of Problem-Solving

"It is not uncommon at all for people to rush from one crisis to another, leaving behind a trail littered with the carcasses of unsolved or partially solved problems. In many cases, they never really seem to fix problems, but rather, they just stop them from getting any worse." Roger Bohn writes, in what I consider a classic business article, [3] *Stop Fighting Fires*, "In business organizations, there are invariably more problems than people have the time to deal with. At best, this leads to situations where minor problems are ignored. At worst, chronic firefighting consumes an operation's resources. Managers and engineers rush from task to task, not completing one before another interrupts them. Serious problem-solving efforts degenerate into quick-and-dirty patching. Productivity suffers and managing becomes a constant juggling act of deciding where to allocate overworked people and which incipient crisis to ignore for the moment." In effect, the culture exhibits classic firefighting behaviors. Does this sound familiar to you? If it does, don't be alarmed because many organizations are in the same boat.

In my travels throughout the world, I have been fortunate (or maybe I should say unfortunate) enough to see many examples of firefighting first-hand and it's not a pretty sight at all. [3] Bohn and Jaikumar observed firefighting behaviors in many manufacturing and new-product development settings and have actually developed a list of *"fire-fighting symptoms."* These are to be used as a guide to determine if an organization is a victim of fire-fighting. Their claim is that, if your organization exhibits three or more of the following symptoms, then you are a victim of firefighting:

1. *There isn't enough time to solve all the problems.* The number of problems out-numbers the number of problem solvers. (*I have seen this symptom many times.*)
2. *Solutions are incomplete.* Many problems are simply patched and never really solved. That is, the superficial effects (symptoms) are treated, but the root causes are never found and eliminated. (*Based on my experiences, this is the most common behavior.*)
3. *Problems recur and cascade.* Incomplete or haphazard solutions usually cause old problems to recur and sometimes create new problems. (*Directly tied to 2.*)
4. *Urgency supersedes importance.* The "squeaky wheel gets oiled first" syndrome is usually at work. Problem-solving efforts never really continue to fruition because of constant interruptions due to "fires" that must be extinguished. (*Usually happens because priorities aren't realized.*)
5. *Performance drops.* Because of the ineffective problem-solving that always occurs, overall performance usually drops dramatically. (*This is a natural cause-and-effect relationship.*)
6. *Many problems become crises.* Problems smolder until they flare up, often just before a deadline, and then they require heroic efforts to solve. (*Thompson's Law, which tells us that Murphy was an optimist.*)

These symptoms pretty much sum up what I have typically seen in companies that exhibit firefighting. Please understand that there are ways to get out of this mess and we will get to this a bit later.

## Crisis and Failure

On this last observation (i.e., *many problems become crises*), [4] Robert Hayes hypothesized that one reason why American factories are more chaotic than Japanese factories was differences in culture. He wrote, "American managers actually *enjoy* crises. They often get their greatest personal satisfaction, the most recognition, and their biggest rewards from solving crises. Crises are part of what makes work fun. To Japanese managers, however, a crisis is evidence of failure."

I totally concur with Hayes, but I would add that this realization of failure extends beyond just Japanese managers to include organizations (even American) that have developed strong problem-solving cultures. That is, most successful organizations recognize the need to be proactive in their approach to problems and simply won't tolerate chronic crises. Great organizations don't reward people for solving problems that shouldn't have occurred in the first place.

[3] Bohn tells us that, firefighting isn't necessarily disastrous, and, whereas it clearly hampers performance, there are worse alternatives. "Rigid bureaucratic rules can help a company avoid firefighting altogether but at the price of almost no problems getting solved. Also, sometimes even a well-managed organization slips into a firefighting mode temporarily, without creating long-term problems. The danger is that the more intense firefighting becomes, the more difficult it is to escape from." Truer words have never been said!

But why is it that some companies almost never fight fires, even though they have the same amount of work and the same amount of resources? How is it that these companies are able to avoid the fire-fighting trap? Based upon my experiences (and that of [3] Bohn), it is because of the existence of their strong problem-solving cultures, cultures that are committed to finding root causes and genuine solutions to problems, instead of just patching them with temporary fixes and moving on to new ones. Or, as Bohn tells us, "they perform triage." Bohn claims that the key to success for these companies is that they refuse to reward firefighting! Let me say that again. *They refuse to reward firefighting!!* They insist upon a rigid analysis of the problem, a discovery of the true root cause(s) of the problem, and then, and only then, do they implement solutions that work. They don't permit their problem-solvers to ride in on white horses and save the day. As a matter of fact, successful companies either shoot all their white horses or put them out to pasture.

# Traffic Intensity

[3] Bohn introduces what he refers to as *traffic intensity* or the number of problems relative to the resources devoted to problem-solving. Bohn presents the following equation:

$$\text{Traffic intensity} = \frac{(\text{Days to solve}) \times (\text{Number of new problems/day})}{\text{Number of problem-solvers}}$$

By simple math, we see that traffic intensity will increase when either the number of problems or days required to solve the problems increases, and/or the number of problem-solvers available decreases. Conversely, the traffic intensity decreases when the number of problems to be solved and/or the time required to solve problems decreases and/or the number of available problem-solvers increases. So, what does this equation mean? Bohn explains that, as long as the traffic intensity stays below 80%, then the system seems to work well. But when the value nears or exceeds 100%, that is, when there are more problems than can be solved, organizations get into real trouble and firefighting exists. If, for example, three problems arise each day and four problem-solvers take an average of two days to solve each problem, then, by the end of the third week, 15 problems are waiting in queue. As this queue grows, the problem-solvers and their managers feel pressure (i.e., the self-imposed internal pressure of knowing they are behind, and external pressure from customers, senior managers, etc.) and the severity of firefighting increases until the system breaks down.

Problems also by-pass the queue because of political reasons and the problem-solvers find themselves spending less and less time actually working on the problem and more and more time in meetings or preparing documentation in response to irate inquiries. The problem-solving effort becomes less efficient precisely when the most work needs to get done. In general, what these companies are dealing with is information overload. But, even worse, the problems are not only solved inefficiently, but badly as well. "Gut feel" solutions to problems become the norm until finally the system simply shuts down.

## The Effects of Firefighting

The important lesson Bohn reinforces for us is this. Although structured and systematic problem-solving appears to take longer than "gut feel" techniques, in reality the exact opposite is true. Patching not only takes more time than systematic problem-solving, it also fails to fix problems! As [3] Bohn points out, "Haphazardly introduced changes raise an even more serious issue; they can easily create new problems elsewhere in the process." With few exceptions, firefighting and patching are destructive because solution rates fall, and the number of hidden problems increases.

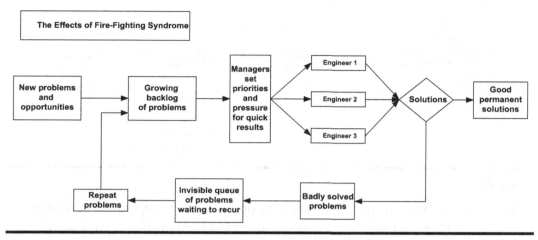

**Figure 7.2**

[3] Bohn characterizes this phenomenon in Figure 7.2. Here, we see the new flow of problems through an organization. Bohn tells us that new problems and opportunities continue entering the organization as before, but now, because of the number of badly solved problems, an invisible queue of unresolved problems will develop and re-enter the system in the form of repeat problems, and overload the system. Now, the organization has the new problems that patching has created, the old ones that patching has failed to solve, and the new problems that are normally present. In effect, firefighting has tripled the opportunity for problems to flow into the organization.

The problem-solvers' environment becomes increasingly chaotic because there is less and less time to study problems the correct way, and, in some cases, the organization's ability to solve problems will collapse completely and, of course, the performance of the organization will rapidly deteriorate. This deterioration then calls for drastic action to be taken, such as outsourcing or bringing in a costly massive infusion of outside help.

# Escaping Firefighting

So, the obvious question is, "How do some companies escape from or avoid the evil clutches of firefighting whereas others can't?" Like all good problem-solving methodologies, before we can correct or reduce the impact of firefighting, we really need to understand the underlying causes of it. Again, we turn to [3] Bohn, who developed a simple firefighting model (see Figure 7.3) that helps us understand the flow of problems through organizations.

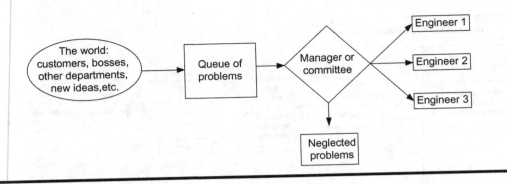

**Figure 7.3**

Bohn used an example of a factory engineering group in the midst of a new product ramp-up. As problems arise from customer complaints, special orders, quality issues, supplier problems, etc., they are sent into a queue until they are assigned to an engineer (doesn't have to be an engineer) by a manager or a committee. As the engineer finishes his problem, the manager presiding over the queue decides which problems are the most urgent and selects the best-qualified engineer to work on them. Because of the nature of problems (i.e., differences in size, shape, complexity, etc.), allocation of problems to problem-solvers is not always a simple task. Different people have different knowledge bases, experience levels, etc., so matching the right person to the right problem isn't necessarily straightforward.

So, if your organization is mired in firefighting, what can you do to resolve this situation? Again, Bohn tells us that firefighting can be eliminated, but it requires a level of commitment that did not exist before the situation escalated to where it is. [3] Bohn suggests that there are primarily three approaches for eliminating firefighting:

1. Tactical methods
2. Strategic methods
3. Cultural methods

Let's look at each of these approaches in a bit more detail.

## Tactical methods

When the backlog of problems becomes overwhelming, and the organization is on the verge of collapsing, one approach is to bring in temporary help to work on problems. Although this can be effective, it should be viewed as a short-term option until a better one is realized. The key to this approach is finding help that has a specific field of expertise, and sometimes this can be difficult. For example, if you are in the business of producing gears, then your help would obviously need a background in this area. Because you are hiring someone for their specific expertise, the cost of this outside help can sometimes be excessive.

## Strategic methods

This method is more of a long-term option, simply because it involves modifying the basic design of the product. The good news is, the longer-term payoff can be very significant, but again the length of time that passes before results are seen can be long. Although this approach usually results in a striking increase in the number of problems solved, the commitment required is much higher. Because you are focusing on design issues, the strategic method of developing design solutions is typically adaptable to other product lines which can accelerate elimination of the overall backlog of problems.

[3] Bohn explains that the key to success for all organizations is the development of more problem-solvers who learn the correct method for root cause analysis, which is a structured and systematic method. When this happens, the resource base for problem-solving expands, and problems are addressed correctly in much shorter times. So, if you're going to spend money on outside help, this approach clearly has the highest return on your investment dollars; it may take longer, but the longer-term payback can be very significant.

## Cultural methods

As I stated earlier, change requires both a shift in the mindset of the entire organization and a behavioral change of senior management. The organization's problem-solving culture must be top-down-driven and the expectation of senior and middle leadership must be one that will not accept firefighting. Bohn provides us with some guidelines on how to change the culture to escape the devastating effects of firefighting. Here are some of the guidelines:

- *Don't tolerate patching.* I cannot overemphasize this point, but enforcing this requires the support, commitment, and persistence of management at all levels. If lower-level employees see that patching is no longer acceptable from an organizational perspective, they will no longer do so.
- *Don't push to meet deadlines at all costs.* One of the reasons why you are in a firefighting mode is the unreasonable and uncompromising deadlines you as leaders have set. Problems aren't solved immediately, so you must give your problem-solvers sufficient time to (1) define the problem, (2) analyze it, (3) determine potential root causes, (4) develop meaningful solutions, (5) adequately test the solutions, (6) implement the best solutions, and (7) develop and implement appropriate preventive controls.
- *Don't ever reward firefighting.* I cannot emphasize enough how critical this is if you want to experience a cultural change! This is a slippery slope to climb because, on the one hand, you're happy the problem has been solved, but, on the other hand, the people that should be rewarded are the managers who don't have fires to put out! It's a challenge for you, but if you want your culture to change, then be very careful of when and why you give praise.

I have added two additional guidelines that should help you escape the evil clutches of firefighting:

- *Lead by example.* If you want your organization to truly embrace a new way of solving and preventing problems, then you must lead this transformation by publicly and privately learning and using the same problem-solving and prevention approach that you expect from your organization. Without doing this, your efforts will be seen as mere rhetoric.
- *Set irrefutable and unquestionable expectations.* The organization needs to be given clear and concise expectations on solving and preventing problems. This includes a mandate that only the use of a structured and systematic method for problem-solving and problem-prevention will be tolerated. It won't take long before the organization will "get it," and effective problem-solving and -prevention will become a vital part of the new culture.

Before we leave these chapters on problems and decisions, it's important to understand that, when there are problems to be solved and prevented, and decisions to be made, conflicts can arise: conflicts in the way we approach problems, as well as conflicts as we work to make effective decisions. For many people, being able to resolve these conflicts is not a simple task. In the next chapter, I want to introduce you to a method that will help you resolve these conflicts as they appear.

## References

1. H. William Dettmer, *Leadership in Complex Systems* Part 10 in a series of 12 articles on systems thinking, Goal Systems International, 2006.
2. Kepner and Tregoe, *The New Rational Manager: A Systematic Approach to Problem Solving and Decision Making*, 2013.
3. Roger Bohn, Stop Fighting Fires, *Harvard Business Review*, August 2000 Issue.
4. Robert Hayes, Why Japanese Factories Work, *Harvard Business Review*, July–August, 1981.

# Chapter 8

# Resolving Conflicts

With every problem that arises, there are conflicts that seem to get in the way of our ideas on how best to solve and prevent these problems. "When introverts are in *conflict* with each other...it may require a *map* in order to follow all the silences, non-verbal cues, and passive-aggressive behaviors!" so said [1] Adam S. McHugh. Conflicts are inevitable in life and part of our everyday work life in manufacturing. We've all seen situations where people with the same objective and desires have clashed, and we've all witnessed the often-intense personal hostility that can result. But does it have to be this way? I happen to agree with Mr. McHugh in that, many times, it does require a map of sorts to resolve our conflicts.

With every problem, there are conflicts that seem to get in the way of our ideas on how best to solve a problem. There are, basically, three primary types of conflict that we must deal with as we work to resolve problems. The first conflict is one where one force is pulling us to do one thing, but an equal and opposite force pulls us in the opposite direction. The second type of conflict is one in which we are forced to choose between different alternatives. The third type of conflict is what I refer to as *the hidden agenda* conflict. In a hidden agenda conflict, generally, a personality is involved and typically is manifested in a desire or inherent need to hold onto some kind of power.

In attempting to resolve conflicts, it is important to recognize that there are three types of resolution that can be achieved: a *win–win*; a *win–lose*; or a *compromise*. Of the three possibilities, we should always attempt to achieve a win-win solution, but sometimes it just isn't practical or even possible. In a win-lose situation, one side typically gets just about everything

DOI: 10.4324/9781003462385-8

it wants, while the other side gets very little. This type of solution serves to create antagonistic or hostile attitudes and your chances of success are diminished because the losing side might attempt to sabotage your solution. Not openly, mind you, but rather covertly or stealthily. In the case of a compromise, generally, the solution ends up being sub-optimal, because you are attempting to satisfy most of the requirements of both parties engaged in the conflict. But having said this, a compromise is better than a win-lose or imposed solution, but remember, it generally results in a sub-optimal solution. The solution for a hidden agenda conflict is much like what happens in a win-lose conflict, in that someone works against you behind the scenes in the hope of holding on to their apparent power. So, how do we resolve conflicts?

[2] Dr Eliyahu Goldratt introduced us to a Thinking Process tool that he aptly named the *evaporating cloud*. The evaporating cloud (aka conflict resolution diagram (CRD)) identifies and demonstrates the relationship between the key elements of a conflict and then suggests ways to resolve it. (Note: For a detailed description of how to create and use a CRD, read William Dettmer's, [3] *Breaking the Constraints to World-Class Performance*). The diagram includes a common objective, the necessary conditions that lead to it, and the prerequisites needed to satisfy them. Figure 8.1 is the basic structure of the evaporating cloud.

The conflict resolution diagram was developed by Goldratt to achieve at least eight different purposes:

■ To *confirm* that the conflict exists and that it is *real*.
■ To *identify* the conflict associated with the problem.
■ To identify all of the *assumptions* between the problem and conflict.

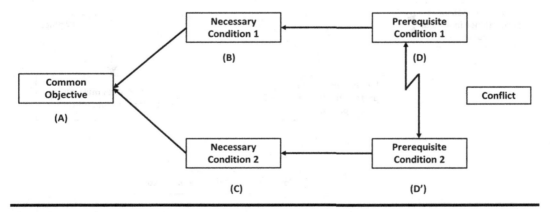

**Figure 8.1**

- To provide a comprehensive *answer* as to why the problem is present.
- To *create solutions* that could result in win-win situations.
- To *create innovative solutions* to problems.
- To provide a *resolution* of the conflict.
- To *avoid* compromising situations.

Figure 8.2 is an example of such a cloud, as presented by [4] Debra Smith in her breakthrough book, *The Measurement Nightmare*. The conflict cloud is a logic diagram of a conflict that is designed to help us sort through and develop a breakthrough solution to our conflict. In Figure 8.2, we start with the manager's objective (A), followed by a necessary condition (B) for the production manager to realize the objective. The specific action, required by the production manager to achieve the necessary condition (B), is called the prerequisite. The operation's portion of the cloud would then be read as follows. In order to maximize the performance measures (A), the plant must ship on time (B). In order for the plant to ship on time, all resources must operate at the same pace as the constraint (D). The assumption that connects B and D is that, by running non-constraints at the same pace as the constraint, will result in maximum throughput in the shortest cycle time.

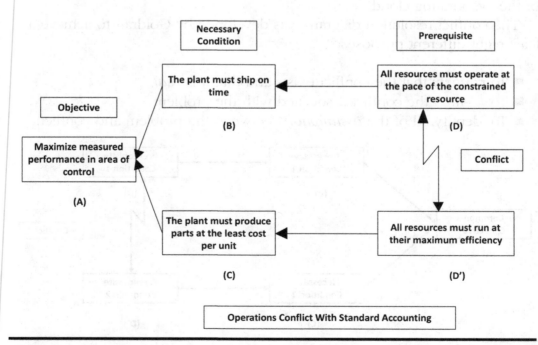

**Figure 8.2**

The same sequence is then repeated on the bottom of the cloud. According to Cost Accounting, in order to maximize performance measures (A), the plant must produce parts at the lowest cost per unit (C). In order to produce parts at the lowest cost per unit, all resources must operate at maximum efficiency (D'). The assumption connecting C to D' is that maximizing all individual processes will result in minimum product cost. This assumption is fatally flawed and is the source of enormous amounts of waste and therefore excess costs. But, for now, if the plant cannot create a faster throughput rate than the constraint, then maximizing the output at non-constraints will only serve to (1) create excess work-in-process (WIP), (2) increase the overall cycle time, and (3) decrease cash flow. The conflict arises between the two prerequisites, D and D'. This is a real conflict that exists in many companies today. The requirements (necessary conditions) are not in conflict with each other, but the prerequisites certainly are.

As [4] Debra Smith rightfully explains, "Assumptions are the glue holding logic together." She further tells us, "Our conclusions are only as good as the assumptions on which they are based." Understanding the assumptions allows the logic of the desired actions to be challenged openly. In Figure 8.2, the assumption behind the B–D arrow is that, in order to ship on time, we must have all resources operating at the pace of the constraint. Key to breaking conflicts are the assumptions surrounding the conflict, so it's imperative that we understand what they are. We must operate at the same pace as the constraint because:

■ Outpacing the constraint drives up the WIP inventory.
■ Excess WIP ties up cash and lengthens the overall cycle time.
■ Lengthening the cycle time of the product through the process negatively impacts on-time delivery.
■ Late shipments hurt future sales.

Without future sales, profitability is negatively impacted.

The assumption underlying the C–D' arrow is that, to produce parts at the lowest cost per unit, we must have all resources running at their maximum efficiency. We must have all resources operating at maximum efficiency because:

■ Maximum efficiency guarantees parts are produced at the lowest cost per unit.
■ Lowest cost per unit ensures maximum profitability.

The conflict arises between D and D', so we must look at the assumptions for both and determine which are correct and which are incorrect. If you are a traditional Cost Accounting proponent, then you believe the assumptions (the "because" statements) associated with D'. And, if you are a proponent of the Theory of Constraints and Throughput Accounting, then you believe the assumptions associated with D. In this example, the assumptions behind the C–D' arrow were found to be faulty and the conflict was broken.

Managers are faced with many conflicts as they attempt to solve and prevent problems and make effective decisions while doing their jobs. But conflicts like this one always seem to get in the way of making the right decisions. Let's look at examples of some of these conflicts. [4] Smith presents what she calls a *Spiderweb Conflict Cloud*. In Figure 8.3, below, Smith articulates many of the basic conflicts that production and plant managers are confronted with every single day and, as you can see, many are a direct result of our outdated Cost Accounting systems. Is it any wonder that managers are confused about how they should be doing their jobs? Let's look at a couple of these conflicts to better understand why things might be so confusing for managers.

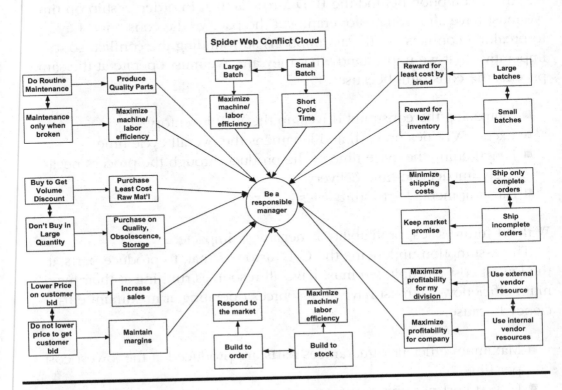

**Figure 8.3**

One thing we know to be true is that shorter cycle times are an essential part of the way we should be doing business, and one sure way to accomplish this is to generate product in smaller batch sizes. But Cost Accounting measures tell us that we must maximize machine and labor efficiencies, and the way to do this is to generate product in large batch sizes, in order to avoid equipment changeovers. So, here, we have an example of a manager wanting to do a good job, but, because of a Cost Accounting measure, with flawed assumptions, a conflict arises. Should the manager do what's holistically best for the company, at the expense of the performance measure, or should he conform to what the measures are telling him to do and protect himself? Unfortunately, since his and his department's performance are measured on the basis of optimizing local efficiencies, the decision will most likely be to produce in large batches, even though he or she knows it's better to produce in small batches. Let's look at another conflict.

Managers know that one of the best ways to produce quality parts is to routinely shut down equipment to perform preventive maintenance. But, once again, we are told by Cost Accounting, that we must maximize individual efficiencies on operators and equipment. In order to maximize efficiencies, the assumption is that we need to keep the equipment running longer, which is in direct conflict with our need to shut the equipment down for maintenance. What do we end up doing? We probably run the equipment until it eventually breaks down! Again, the right decision would be to do what's best to achieve better quality, but we can't (or won't) because it's in direct conflict with Cost Accounting's need to maximize local efficiencies which is, again, based upon a flawed assumption!

As you can see in Figure 8.3, the Spider Web Conflict Cloud, managers are routinely caught in a sort of "Catch-22" situation: a "damned if we do and damned if we don't" scenario. The question is, how in the world did we ever get to the point where our managers must choose between doing the right things for the overall organization against satisfying a Cost Accounting policy and protecting their own jobs? More importantly, why has Accounting failed to recognize that traditional Cost Accounting practices force managers to make such illogical decisions?

The reality is that most managers are caught in the middle and end up trying to satisfy both the organization's holistic needs and the needs of Cost Accounting. Managers end up compromising both sets of necessary conditions and end up sub-optimizing the system. They do a little bit of one, one day, and a little bit of the other, the next day. Smith further tells us that "The variance reporting generated at the end of every month, purportedly to control costs, is not useful or timely and actually puts departments into conflict with each other and with the overall goal of maximizing throughput at a maximum cash flow."

In addition to the above conflicts, the use of standard Cost Accounting principles, and specifically the need to maximize local efficiencies, typically pits departments against departments. In one company I was consulting for, one department (a cutting center) in this company cut fabric for another department (an assembly operation). The performance of both departments was measured using standard labor efficiencies. On one particular day, the cutting center was in the midst of one of their typical long production runs, producing a particular type of fabric. The assembly operation was about to run out of a different type of fabric and asked the cutting center to stop and cut what they needed. The cutting center refused to do so and, as a result, the assembly operation ran out of the needed fabric and subsequently had to shut down until the cutting center completed their run, changed over, and cut the fabric needed. When the cutting center manager was asked why he hadn't stopped and produced the fabric needed by the assembly operation, he explained that the changeover would have negatively impacted his efficiencies! So, at the end of the day, although one department had great efficiencies for this day, the other department lost a significant amount of throughput, all because of a standard Cost Accounting performance metric!

In all fairness to Cost Accounting, they are bound by law to externally report financial information (GAAP) to the Internal Revenue Service, the Securities and Exchange Commission, investors, creditors, and other regulatory agencies, and I would never question this. But the fact is, this information is generally historical and does very little to help managers make *real-time* production decisions. Since this information is reported externally, the question becomes, "Why is it that we can't have a separate report that is published for internal use, that focuses on real-time events, as well as an external report that satisfies legal reporting needs?" The answer is that we can!

In Chapter 8 of [4] Smith's book, she presents the how-tos of creating a *bridge* between throughput and GAAP financial statements. Smith points out that there is a misconception that a company needs to maintain two sets of books for Throughput Accounting and GAAP reporting, a belief which has contributed to the reluctance to adopt Throughput Accounting as the primary internal format. I would fervently recommend that all company leaders, especially those responsible for the Accounting function, read Smith's book and begin to make the transformation to Throughput Accounting. [4]

Smith explains that "Any attempt to run a Theory of Constraints operation, while using traditional accounting measures, controls, and incentives, is doomed to failure. Integral to the new measurement system is the need to create a total shift away from the ingrained 'cost/efficiency' mentality. Unless this is done, the company will continue to send conflicting signals and take conflicting actions."

The fact is that, if you are unwilling to do so, then you are doomed to continue what you're doing now! On the other hand, if you are willing to make the change, then you will be able to see returns that will simply "blow you away!" We all know that change is inevitable, but the question is, do you want to continue reacting to change or do you want to manage it? You, as the leadership within your company, are at a business crossroads. You can choose to maintain the status quo, replete with all of its internal conflicts, or you can choose a new direction. If you opt for the new direction, then you have the opportunity to maximize your return on investment and significantly improve your bottom line. The choice is yours!

Being able to develop an effective improvement plan is not always an easy task for many companies. In order to be effective, your plan needs to be developed after a thorough examination of your company's current state. In the next chapter, I'm going to present a very simple, yet comprehensive method for doing just that. The method I am referring to is something referred to as The Goal Tree.

# References

1. Adam S. McHugh, *The Listening Life*, Intervarsity Press, 2015.
2. Eliyahu M. Goldratt, *The Goal*, North River Press, 1986.
3. H. William Dettmer, *Breaking the Constraints to World Class Performance*, Quality Press, 1998.
4. Debra Smith, *The Measurement Nightmare – How the Theory of Constraints Can Resolve Conflicting Strategies, Policies, and Measures*, CRC Press, 2000.

## Chapter 9

# The Goal Tree – A New Way to Make and Use It

One thing I haven't yet touched on is the power of combining Lean, Six Sigma, and the Theory of Constraints. I will do that in a future chapter, but, in this chapter, I want to introduce you to a simple planning tool known as the Goal Tree. I began using the Goal Tree quite a few years ago, back when it was known as the Intermediate Objectives Map (IO Map), but, since then, I have modified it on numerous occasions so that it has become a very powerful planning tool for me.

The Goal Tree is something I have written about numerous times on my personal blog, and, as a matter of fact, in one of my blog post series, I introduced you to a book I had been reading, [1] *The Four Disciplines of Execution: Achieving Your Wildly Important Goals*, by Chris McChesney, Sean Covey, and Jim Huling. As I mentioned in that series of posts, I saw the teachings within that book as a way to enhance the Goal Tree. So, in this chapter, I want to share how I believe the Goal Tree can be improved upon, by including the teachings in that wonderful book. For those of you who have never used a Goal Tree, I will start with a description of this tool and what a well-conceived Goal Tree can do for your organization. As I am presenting the new version of the Goal Tree, I will include and describe how I plan to improve it, using the teachings within this book. So, let me start with some background on the Goal Tree.

Many people who have gone through a Theory of Constraints (TOC) Jonah training session have come away somewhat overwhelmed and sometimes feeling like they are unable to apply what they have just learned. Let's

DOI: 10.4324/9781003462385-9

face it, the TOC Thinking Process tools are just not easy for some people to grasp and apply, so they kind of put them on the back burner, rather than taking a chance of doing something wrong. Well, for everyone who fits into this category, I have hope for you and this hope is referred to as the Goal Tree. The Goal Tree is a logic diagram that is actually simple to construct and, unlike the TOC Thinking Process tools, it is one that I think you will feel very confident using. So, let's review both the history and basics of the Goal Tree.

Bill Dettmer, who is generally credited as being the man who developed the current version of the Goal Tree, tells us of his first exposure to the Goal Tree back in 1995 during a management skills workshop conducted by Oded Cohen at the Goldratt Institute. As I mentioned earlier, back then, the Goal Tree was referred to as an IO Map, but, in recent years, Bill Dettmer has recommended that the IO Map should now be referred to as a Goal Tree. In fact, Bill now believes that it should be the first step in a full Thinking Process analysis. He believes this because it defines the standard for goal attainment and its prerequisites in a much more efficient manner. I believe that the Goal Tree is a great focusing tool to better demonstrate why an organization is not meeting its goal.

Bill Dettmer tells us that other advantages of using a Goal Tree first are that, by including it, there is a better integration of the rest of the Thinking Process tools that will accelerate the completion of Current Reality Trees, Conflict Clouds, and Future Reality Trees. The other thing I like about the Goal Tree is that it can be used as a stand-alone tool which results in a much faster analysis of the organization's weak points. In this chapter, I will discuss the Goal Tree as a stand-alone tool.

When using the logic-based TOC Thinking Process tools, there are two distinctly different types of logic at play: *sufficiency-type* logic and *necessity-type* logic. Sufficiency-type logic is quite simply a series of *if-then* statements: if I have "this," then I have "that." Necessity-based logic trees use the syntax, *"in order to have 'this'.......I must have 'that'."* The Goal Tree falls into the necessity-based category. For example, *in order to have a fire, I must have a fuel source, a spark, and a source of air.* If the goal is to have a fire, I must have all three components. The fuel source, spark, and air are referred to as *Critical Success Factors* (CSFs). Take away even one of the CSFs and you won't have a fire.

The hierarchical structure of the Goal Tree consists of a single Goal, several CSFs which must be in place to achieve the goal, and a series of *Necessary Conditions* (NCs) that must be in place to achieve each CSF. The

Goal and CSFs are written as terminal outcomes, as though they are already in place. The NCs are written more as activities that must be completed in order to achieve each of the CSFs. Let's look at an example of what a completed Goal Tree might look like.

Suppose that you were working with an organization that is profitable but wants to become a highly profitable one. You assemble the CEO and key members of his or her staff to develop an effective plan to achieve this goal. In the Goal Tree drawing below (Figure 9.1), after much discussion, you agree on your Goal as "Highly Profitable Company" and place it inside the Goal box. This goal statement, which is the desired end-state, is written as a terminal outcome, as though it's already been achieved. You think to yourself, "What must I have in place for our goal to be realized?" You think, "I know that we must have highly satisfied customers for sure and that our throughput must be high and growing," so you place both of these in separate CSF boxes. One by one, you continue listing those things that must be in place to achieve your goal and place them into separate CSF boxes, as in Figure 9.1 below. In a Goal Tree, Bill Dettmer recommends that you should have no more than three to five CSFs.

Because the Goal Tree uses necessity-based logic, it is read in the following way: "In order to have a highly profitable company, I must have highly satisfied customers as well as the other four CSFs." Directly beneath the CSFs are NCs, that must also be in place to achieve each of the CSFs.

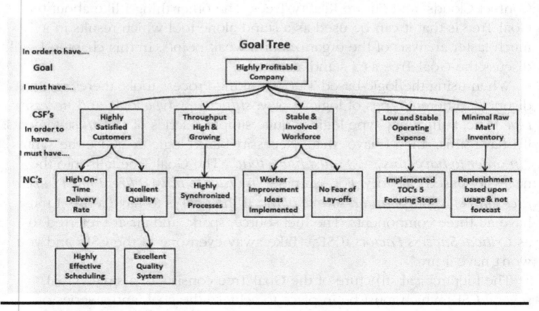

**Figure 9.1**

So, continuing to read downward, "In order to have highly satisfied customers, I must have two NCs, high on-time delivery rates, and excellent quality." Remember: the CSFs are written as terminal outcomes, as though they're already in place.

You continue reading downward: in order to have, for example, a high on-time delivery rate, I must have a highly effective scheduling system in place and functioning well. The Necessary Conditions represent actions that must be completed to achieve each individual CSF, so they form the basis for your improvement plan. Similarly, your team completes all of the NCs until you are satisfied that what you have in place in the Goal Tree will ultimately deliver the goal of the organization. Typically, in a Goal Tree, there are three to five CSFs and no more than two to three layers of NCs. OK, so what happens next?

Earlier in this chapter, I indicated that I would lay out the first change I am making in how I will be developing and using the Goal Tree going forward. I indicated that this is a subtle change but one that is very important. This change has to do with how the Goal and Critical Success Factors (and some of the NCs) are worded. One of the key learnings in [1], *The Four Disciplines of Execution: Achieving Your Wildly Important Goals,* the author presented the concept of Lead and Lag Measures. The lag measure has to do with Goal achievement and should be written in such a way that there is a clear measurement of Goal units, with a well-defined target. So, for example, instead of the Goal being written as "A highly profitable company," like we have in our Goal Tree example, let's word it as though it were a performance measure with a target. Let's say that this company's current profit margins are around 3%. What if we re-wrote the Goal as follows: profit margins above 15%? Written this way, we can measure it and it has a clear target, just like a finish line in a race. In this way, everyone knows what the company wants to achieve and how to measure success.

Now, let's look at the CSFs. The first CSF in our example is written as Highly Satisfied Customers. Can you now see how vague this CSF was as it was originally written? Written in this manner, it is neither measurable nor does it have a target for the improvement team to shoot for. If we re-worded this CSF, an example might be something like, "Customer Satisfaction Index greater than 96%." By writing it this way, it becomes measurable and has a clear target or measure of success to attain. What I'm suggesting is that the CSFs should be written as Lead Measures that tie directly to the Lag Measure. In other words, if we were able to move the lead measures in a positive direction, then the lag measure would eventually improve as well.

Let's look at the original Goal Tree, with the remaining CSFs written using these simple guidelines.

As you can see in Figure 9.2, each of the CSFs are now measurable and display a clear success target. For example, one of the CSFs is written as, "Operating Expenses less than 6% of Revenue." Clearly, Operating Expenses are measurable and the target to reach has been set as less than 6%. Now, let's look at the NCs.

As written in the Goal Tree above, some of the NCs are written with the same clarity as the CSFs. I chose to do so because when they are measurable, and have a target as some of them do, it becomes much easier for the improvement team to define activities that will move these lead measures. If these lower-level lead measures move in a positive direction, they will move the upper-level lead measures in a similar manner. For example, one of the lower-level NCs is stated as "Schedule Compliance greater than 96%." If this is achieved, then the assumption is that on-time delivery will also be met. If this CSF is met, then it should move the Goal, Profit Margin "Above 15%," closer to the targeted level. As we know, each CSF contributes to the achievement of the Goal. The improvement team concluded that, if they

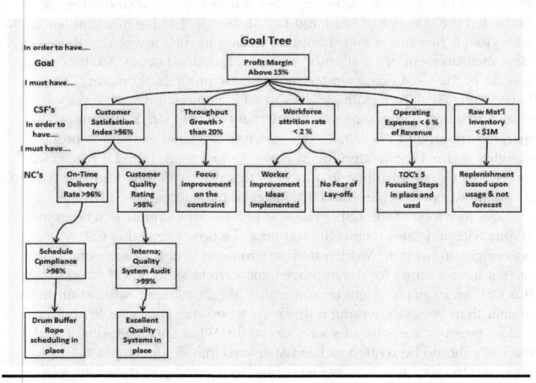

**Figure 9.2**

implement Drum Buffer Rope, then their target of 96% schedule compliance would most likely be achieved. OK, so what's next?

Here's where I've departed from the traditional Thinking Process (TP) tools in that, as Bill Dettmer recommends, the next step would be to use the Goal Tree to construct a Current Reality Tree. Although I totally support Bill Dettmer's approach, when time is not a factor, I continue on with the Goal Tree in the way that Bill recommends. But, when time is a factor, my immediate next step is to facilitate a critical discussion with the improvement team on the real-time status or current state of the Goal, CSFs, and NCs. I use a simple light gray, gray, and dark gray coding system to describe how each of the Goal Tree entities exists in our current reality. With this new approach, the status of each entity becomes much easier. I might add that the coding system I will now describe is a departure from the way I had been using the Goal Tree in the past.

Notice the key on the bottom right-hand side of the Goal Tree in Figure 9.3 and you'll see that a box shaded in light gray indicates that the measure is at or above the target level. Light gray can also be used to describe

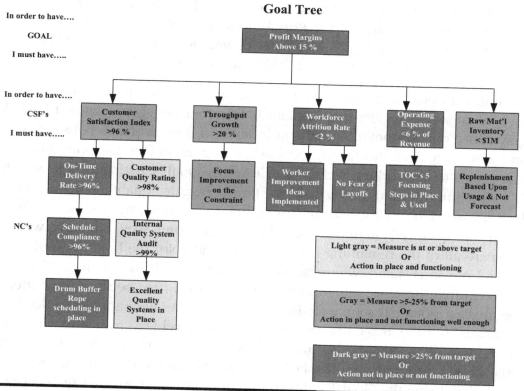

**Figure 9.3**

actions that we plan to take to drive the lead measures in a positive direction. In this case, the required action is in place and functioning, so no changes need to be made. Likewise, a gray box indicates that a lead measure is greater than 5%, but less than 25% away from the defined target; or if it's a required action, then it means that there is something in place, but that it needs improvement. A box shaded in dark gray means that the lead measure is greater than 25% away from its target, or, if it's a required action, then the entity is either not in place or that something is in place, but it isn't functioning. (Note: it should be obvious that any entity shaded in dark gray has a higher priority than one shaded in gray.) Please understand that these guidelines that I've established are mine, so they are not hard-and-fast rules taken from some textbook. I encourage those using the Goal Tree in this manner to develop their own guidelines. Let's look at our Goal Tree and see how this fictitious company made out.

The following were the values assigned to the current lag measure (i.e., the Goal) and all of the lead measures (i.e., all of the CSFs and some of the NCs):

> *Profit margin = 3% (Lag Measure); Customer Satisfaction Index = 89%; Throughput Growth = 2%; Workforce Attrition Rate = 10%; Operating Expenses = 13%; Raw Material Inventory = $1.1 M; On-Time Delivery = 75%; Customer Quality Rating = 97%; Schedule Compliance = 71%; Internal Quality System Audit = 99.2%.*

Starting with our lag measure for the Goal, we see that it is currently at 3% and, because it is greater than 25% away from our target, we shade it in dark gray. Since our Customer Satisfaction Index is at 89%, which is between 5% and 25% away from our target, we shade it in gray. In fact, the only thing that seems to be working well is our Customer Quality Rating at 97%, which is well within the limit of 5% from the target. Because quality is not a problem, it is shaded in light gray, meaning that if this company continues with its current Quality System, they should continue doing well. Similarly, we compare all of the remaining lead measures and color the boxes accordingly.

As I previous stated, where we observe dark gray boxes, it should be apparent that these are the areas we must focus on first, because they offer the greatest potential source for improved results. As we improve the lead measures in these areas, improvement in upper-level lead measures will take place until, ultimately, the lag measure (i.e., the Goal of Profit Margins Above 15%) should also improve. The key, then, for creating a focused improvement plan, using the Goal Tree, is to first develop the required Lag and Lead Measures, and then to set realistic targets to achieve each one of them. The key though is to make sure there is a "correlatable" relationship between the lead and lag measures.

So, here it is, a different way to utilize a Goal Tree, which is easy both to understand and construct, and which permits the development of a very focused improvement plan in very short order. In my experience using this approach, the team that develops it will embrace it because it is their plan. The good news is, from start to finish, it only takes less than a day, rather than days or weeks to develop.

When I started this chapter, I introduced you to a book I have been reading called *The Four Disciplines of Execution: Achieving Your Wildly Important Goals*, by Chris McChesney, Sean Covey, and Jim Huling. I want to thank these authors for "enlightening" me with their book. Once again, I encourage everyone to go get this book, read it, and apply it, especially if they're involved in improvement efforts. The authors also describe why many improvement efforts fail and how to overcome barriers to success.

But, before I move on, I want to add one additional change to the new Goal Tree. In this new version, I have included Lead and Lag Measures, but one important fact is not in the equation......the "when" of these metrics. That is, I will now add a "time piece" to the Lead and Lag measures. In Figure 9.4 below, I have inserted completion dates into the Goal Tree and, as you can see, each layer in the hierarchy displays an earlier date as you progress down the tree. By adding dates to the Goal Tree, the improvement team now has a sense of timing so that priorities on what to work on are clearly visible to them.

This nested hierarchy of dates and actions provides the team with a road-map, if you will, on what to work on first, then next, and so on. For example, if we look at "Schedule Compliance Greater Than 96% by 12/15/2013," it is clear to the team that Drum Buffer Rope must be implemented well in advance of that date. That is to say, in order to achieve the Necessary Condition of "On Time Delivery Rate Greater Than 96% by 12/30/2013," then schedule compliance must be completed first. In a sense, the upper-level lead measures are both lead and lag measures. Improvements to the upper-level lead measures only occur when the lower-level lead measures are achieved. In the case of action steps, each too should have completion dates associated with it, even though I haven't depicted any dates in the Goal Tree figure (Figure 9.4). For example, in the case of "Throughput Growth Greater Than 20% by 1/15/2014," it is clear that the associated NC (Focus Improvement on the Constraint) must be in place in advance of that date.

So, now you have the complete list of changes I will be using on the Goal Tree going forward. I want to make one point though, as it applies to

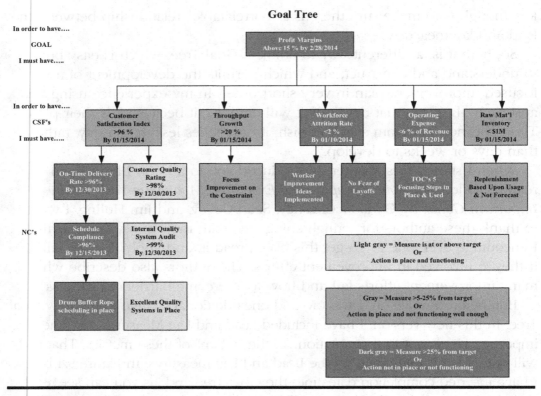

**Figure 9.4**

how I create the initial Goal Tree. I will probably still create the initial Goal Tree as I always have, prior to adding the lead and lag measures and completion dates. I think it's important to do that prior to inserting the measures and dates. I say this because I have found that the flow of ideas should move forward in an unencumbered way, and, by waiting until later to introduce the lead and lag measures and the completion dates, this will happen.

As you progress through the Goal Tree, problems will most likely be uncovered that require a structured approach to finding solutions to these problems. In Chapter 2, we discussed the nature of problems and how to go about determining the best solution to these problems.

Change of any kind is not always an easy thing to do. One of the primary reasons for this difficulty is this thing called variability. Variability can be a very difficult thing to overcome, especially if you don't understand the type of variability you are dealing with. In the next chapter, we will dive into the concept of variability in more detail.

One other thing before I complete my discussion on the Goal Tree. When I'm creating a Goal Tree, you'll notice in my figures that the connecting arrows are facing downward. In reality, when I've finished completing my Goal Tree, I reverse the direction of the arrows so that they face upward. This is because, in order to use necessity-based logic (i.e., in order to have this (the entity at the tip of the arrow), I must have that (the entity at the base of the arrow). Figure 9.5 is the actual finished Goal Tree with the arrows pointing upward.

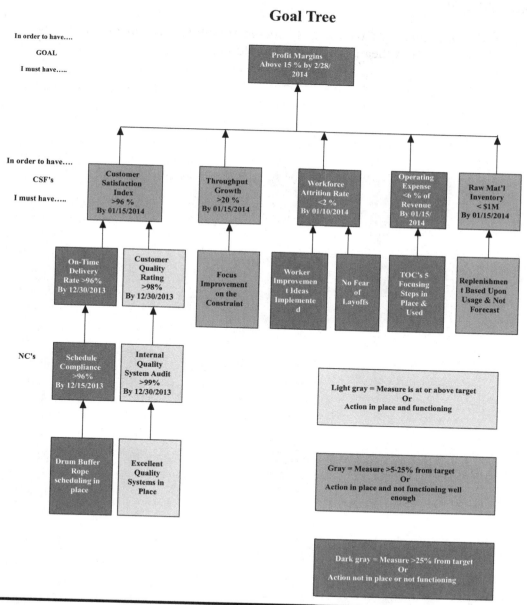

**Figure 9.5**

This completes my discussion on the Goal Tree and how it can be used to develop an improvement plan. In my next chapter, I want to turn our attention to the subject of variation and how devastating excessive amounts of variation can be for a company.

# Reference

1. *The 4 Disciplines of Execution: Achieving Your Wildly Important Goals*, by Chris McChesney, Sean Covey and Jim Huling.

# Chapter 10

# Paths of Variation

For years, people and organizations have dedicated considerable time and effort to identifying, reducing, and controlling the variation that exists within their systems. Since the days of Walter Shewart and his creation of the control chart, the goal has always been to remove as much variation as possible from the system and then bring the remaining variation under control, making it more predictable. No matter how much planning is done, no matter how much effort is expended, it's important to understand that some amount of variation will still remain within your system!

If you were asked the question of how long it takes you to get to work every day, your response might be something like, "about thirty minutes." The instant you answer with the word "about," you have introduced variation into the system. You know that, historically speaking, some days you can get to work in twenty-five minutes, and yet, on other days, it can take thirty-five or forty minutes. In your "get to work" system, things can happen that will either speed up the process or slow it down. And the bad news is, the actual time is not predictable.

Variation exists in everything, but especially within a system. It's important for you to understand that some processes will produce at a faster or slower rate than others, and this is the basic premise behind variation. Because of variation, the output from a system will not be predictable, but rather it will operate within a range that changes on a regular basis. This variable range is known as statistical fluctuation, and it is present within every system. It's very important to understand that, no matter how hard you try to reduce variation, you simply cannot eliminate all variation. You can reduce it, and then bring the remaining variation under control to make

DOI: 10.4324/9781003462385-10

it somewhat predictable, but you can't eliminate all of it. With the arrival of Six Sigma, the effort to reduce variation entered the scene. But even with the most heroic of efforts, involving the spending of much time and money, not all variation can be removed.

Once you understand and accept that variation is a constant variable in any system, it's easier to understand that, at some point, you will reach the minimum variation that is controllable in the system and any efforts to reduce variation beyond that point are generally fruitless. Perhaps, instead of spending so much time and effort on techniques to remove variation, the focus should really be on techniques that will help you manage variation.

We're all familiar with the positive effects of implementing Cellular Manufacturing (CM) in our workplaces, such as the improved flow through the process, overall cycle time reduction, and throughput gains, as well as other benefits. But there is one other positive effect that can result from implementing CM that isn't discussed much. This potential positive impact is what CM can do to reduce variation. But before we reveal how this works, let's first discuss the concept of paths of variation.

When multiple machines performing the same function are used to produce identical products, there are potentially multiple paths that parts can take from beginning to end as we progress through the entire process. There are, therefore, potential multiple *paths of variation*. These multiple paths of variation can significantly increase the overall variability of the process.

Even with focused reductions in variation, real improvement might not be achieved because of the number of paths of variation that exist within a process. Paths of variation, in this context, are simply the number of potential opportunities for variation to occur within a process because of multiple machines processing the parts. And the paths of variation of a process are increased by the number of individual process steps and/or the complexity of the steps (i.e., number of sub-processes within a process).

The answer to reducing the effects of paths of variation should lie in the process and product design stage of manufacturing processes. That is, processes should be designed with reduced complexity and products should be designed that are more robust. The payback for reducing the number of paths of variation is an overall reduction in the amount of process variation and ultimately the generation of more consistent and robust products. Let's look at a real case study.

Many years ago, I had the opportunity to consult for a French pinion manufacturer located in Southern France. For those of you who are not familiar with pinions (i.e., *pignons* in French), a pinion is a round gear, usually the smaller gear in a gear drive train, which has several applications. Figure 10.1 is a drawing of what a pinion might look like and, as you might suspect, pinions require a complicated process to fabricate.

When our team arrived at this company, based on our initial observations, it was very clear that this plant was being run according to a mass production mindset. I say this because there were many very large containers of various-sized pinions stacked everywhere. The actual process for making one particular size and shape of pinion was a series of integrated steps from beginning to end as depicted in Figure 10.2. The company received metal blanks from an outside supplier which were fabricated in the general shape of the final product. The blanks were then passed through a series of turning, drilling, hobbing, etc., process steps to finally achieve the finished product.

The process for this particular pinion was highly automated, with two basic process paths, one on each side of this piece of equipment. There was an automated gating operation that directed each pinion to the next available process step as it traversed the entire process, which consisted of fourteen (14) steps. It was not unusual for a pinion to start its path on one side of the machine, move to the other side and then move back again which meant that the pinion being produced was free to move from side to side in a random fashion. Because of this configuration, the number of possible

**Figure 10.1**

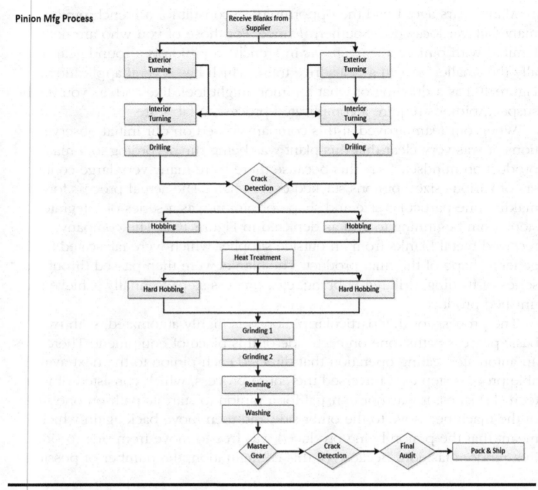

**Figure 10.2**

combinations of individual process steps, or paths of variation, used to make these pinions was very high.

Let's now take a look at the number of paths of variation that existed on this machine as seen in Figure 10.3.

The first step in the process for making this style of pinion was an exterior turning operation with two exterior turning machines available to perform this function (labeled A1 on one side of the machine and A2 on the other side of the machine, as shown in Figure 10.3). The purpose of this first step, like the others to follow, was to shave metal off of the blank to ultimately achieve its final shape and critical dimensions.

The next step in the process is referred to as interior turning and, again, there are two interior turning machines labeled B1 and B2, one on each

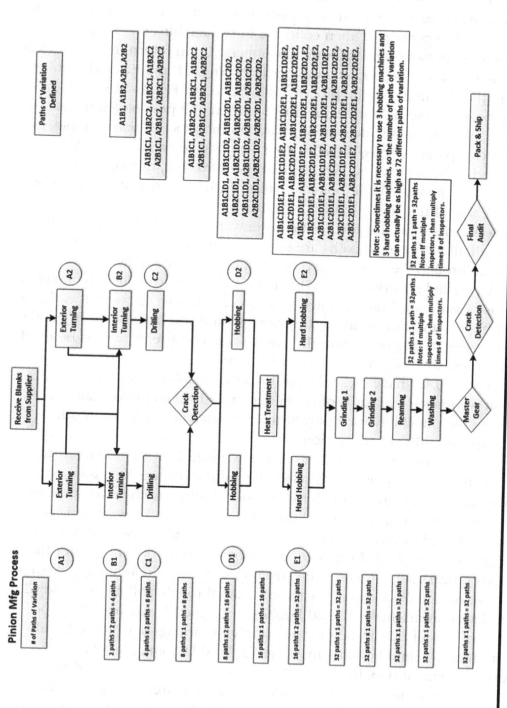

**Figure 10.3**

side. In the third step, there were two possible choices for drilling, C1 and C2. After the pinion was automatically inspected for cracks (with one common automated gauge), it then progressed to one of two hobbing machines, D1 and D2. The parts were then collected in storage bins and sent as large batches to an outside vendor for heat treatment. Upon return from heat treatment the pinions then proceeded to hard hobbing, E1 and E2, and then on through the remainder of the process as indicated in Figure 10.3.

The boxes to the right in Figure 10.3 represent the possible paths that the pinion could take as it makes its way through the process. For example, for the first two process steps, there are four (4) possible paths: A1B1, A1B2, A2B1, and A2B2. The parts then move to the third step, drilling, where you now see that there are eight possible paths of variation which are listed on the right side of the above drawing.

As you can see, as the part continues onward, the possible paths continue until all 32 potential paths are seen. Do you think that the pinions produced through these multiple paths will be the same dimensions or will you have multiple distributions? What if we were able to reduce the number of paths of variation from 32 down to 2, do you believe the overall variation would be less and how many distributions would you have now? In another way of saying it, do you believe the part-to-part consistency would be much better if there are only two paths of variation?

In Figure 10.4, I have created what I refer to as a "virtual cell," meaning that we limited the paths of travel that an individual pinion can take by removing the possibility for a part to traverse back and forth from side to side of this machine configuration.

In simple terms, the part either went down side 1 or side 2, rather than allowing the gating operation to select the path. In Figure 10.4, you can see that pinions passing through the exterior turning machine A1 are permitted to proceed only to internal turning machine B1. Those that pass through internal turning machine A2 are permitted to proceed only to turning machine B2. In doing so, the number of paths of variation for the first two process steps was reduced from four to two. Continuing, the parts that were turned on A1 and B1 can only pass through drilling machine C1, crack detection machine D1, and hobbing machine E1, whereas those produced on A2 and B2 can be processed only on drilling machine C2, drilling machine D2, and hobbing machine E2. To this point, the total paths of variation remain at two, instead of the original number of paths of 16.

The part continues to hard-hobbing where there are, once again, two machines available. The parts produced on A1B1C1D1E1 proceed only to the

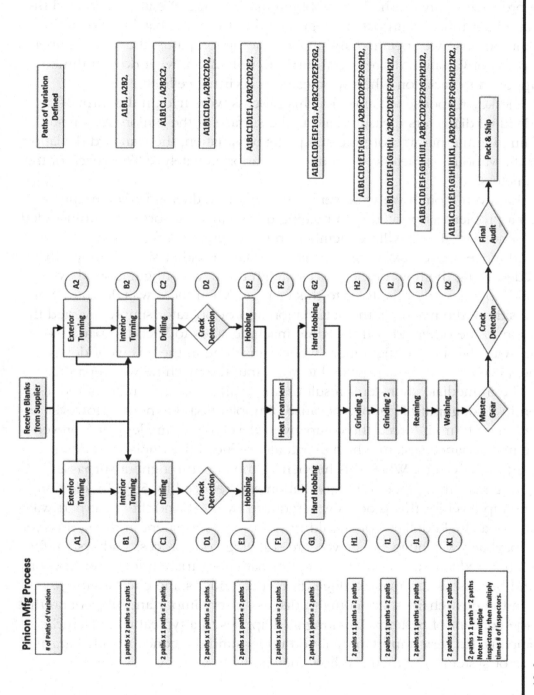

**Figure 10.4**

G1 hard-hobbing machine, whereas those produced on A2B2C2D2E2 can be processed only on the hard-hobbing machine G2. We also instructed the heat-treater to maintain batch integrity and not mix the batches. So, at this point, because we specified and limited the pinion paths, the total number of paths of variation decreased from 32 to only 2! So, what do you think happened to variation when we created our virtual cell?

The key response variables for this process were five, in the form of individual diameters measured along the surface of the pinion. As a result of limiting the number of potential paths of variation, the standard deviation for the various diameters was reduced by approximately 50% on each of the diameters!

But, even though we were very successful in reducing variation, there was a problem associated with making this change…a sort of an unintended consequence, if you will. Remember, in the original configuration, pinions could move to the next available machine (i.e, on either side) as they proceeded along the flow of the process. With the new configuration, they could no longer do this. Prior to this change, when there was downtime on one side of the machine, the automation and/or operator simply diverted the pinion to the other side on the same machine so as to keep the parts moving. With the new configuration, when a machine in the cell went down unexpectedly, the parts now had to wait until the machine was repaired.

The immediate short-term result of this change was a significant reduction in throughput of pinions because of unplanned downtime. However, in the longer term, it forced the company to develop and implement a preventive maintenance system which eventually reduced the unplanned downtime to nearly zero. When this happened, the new throughput surpassed the original throughput and the variation was reduced by 50%! In addition, the scrap level for this process was reduced by 40%! And the great part was that not a single dollar – or should I say, euro? – was spent in doing this, yet the payback was huge. So, as you are studying your process and system for variation reduction, keep the concept of paths of variation foremost in your mind because it can make a huge difference under some circumstances.

In the next chapter, I'm going to discuss a very important subject and that is the concept of Systems Thinking as it applies to a typical manufacturing company. It's very important that you understand the concept and characteristics of systems and then see how they apply to your own system.

# Chapter 11

# Systems Thinking in Manufacturing

One of the keys to success in manufacturing is to understand that your company should be viewed and thought of in the context of a system, rather than just a collection of interrelated parts. So, you may be wondering, just what is a system? In its most basic form, a system is a group of interrelated, interdependent, and interacting parts that combine to achieve a specific purpose. A system takes inputs in some form and acts on them in some way to produce outputs. In reality, the outputs should have a greater value than the sum total of the inputs. In other words, the system should add value to these inputs as it works to change them into outputs.

In 2015, [1] Arnold and Wade presented a paper entitled, *A Definition of Systems Thinking: A Systems Approach*. In this paper, they presented what they referred to as, "The System Test." The System Test, as described in Figure 11.1, was devised as a means by which to test a system's thinking definition. The test, as presented by Arnold and Wade, is relatively simple to follow and understand. Although the intention of Arnold and Wade was to use this test to verify the requirements for a system's thinking definition, my use will be to outline the basic structure of a manufacturing system and the thinking that goes along with it. As such, I have slightly changed the wording originally presented by Arnold and Wade to describe the three characteristics (or Items) of a manufacturing system, namely its *purpose*, the *elements* within a system, and the *interconnectedness* of the system's elements. I happen to fully support the three parts of a system described by Arnold and

DOI: 10.4324/9781003462385-11

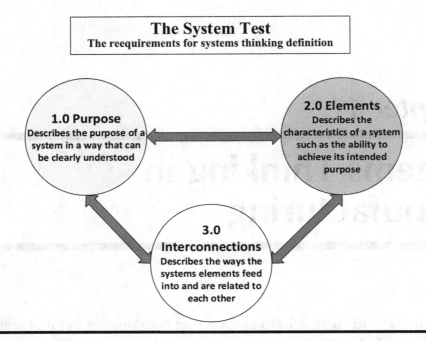

**Figure 11.1**

Wade. If you haven't read their paper, I highly recommend that you download a copy and read it!

1.0 *Purpose*. The purpose or goal should describe the purpose of systems thinking in a way that can be clearly understood and relates to everyday life in manufacturing.

2.0 *Elements*. The elements will manifest the characteristics of systems thinking as they apply to a manufacturing environment.

3.0 *Interconnections*. This is the way the elements or characteristics feed into and relate to each other within a manufacturing setting.

Arnold and Wade tell us that "there have been numerous attempts to define "systems thinking" over the years." The originator of the term "systems thinking," Barry Richmond, in 1994 defined systems thinking as "the art and science of making reliable inferences about behavior by developing an increasingly deep understanding of underlying structure." [2] Richmond emphasizes that people embracing systems thinking position themselves such that they can see both the forest and the trees: one eye on each." [1] Arnold and Wade explain that this definition is broad but useful, especially the notion of "seeing both the forest and the trees," but it fails Item 3.0 of the System Test because it does not adequately explain the interconnections between the elements of systems thinking.

[1] Arnold and Wade then introduce us to [3] Peter Senge, another leader in the field. The authors explain that,

> Senge defines systems thinking as a discipline for seeing wholes and a framework for seeing interrelationships rather than things, for seeing patterns of change rather than static snapshots. Senge also asserts that people who succeed in handling complexity are working in an intuitive domain we don't even consider in our educational theories, underscoring an intuitive property of systems thinking.

[1] Arnold and Wade also explain that,

> Senge's definition, although interesting, is also vague. The definition does describe several highly critical elements of systems thinking, but it does not provide a purpose for systems thinking. It could be argued that this lack of purpose makes the definition difficult to understand. Also, the interconnections between elements are not specified or recognized. Therefore, it does not pass the System Test. However, the way that Senge defines systems thinking, by describing it as a discipline and a framework, seems to evoke a certain understanding of its deeper meaning, hinting at its nature as a system.

In this same paper, Arnold and Wade explain that [4] Linda Sweeney and John Sterman, authors and researchers in the field of systems thinking, list specific systems-thinking skills as including the ability to:

1. Understand how the behavior of a system arises from the interaction of its agents over time (i.e., dynamic complexity).
2. Discover and represent feedback processes (both positive and negative) hypothesized to underlie observed patterns of system behavior.
3. Identify stock and flow relationships.
4. Recognize delays and understand their impact.
5. Identify non-linearities.
6. Recognize and challenge the boundaries of mental (and formal) models.

The authors [1] then move on to Sweeney and Sterman, who attempt to define systems thinking in terms of a purpose, to represent and assess dynamic complexity, but they don't explain what the purpose of assessing dynamic complexity is (to aid in solving systemic problems). They then break this definition down into parts. It seems that [4] Sweeney and Sterman's high-level definition can immediately be reduced to this simpler statement: *The art of systems thinking involves the ability to represent and assess dynamic complexity.* This idea is then followed by their six specific systems-thinking skills.

[1] Arnold and Wade tell us that,

> Overall, this definition is extremely useful, as it lists actual skills agreed upon by many advocates of systems thinking. However, this definition fails the System Test because it does not clearly define Item 1.0 (Purpose or goal) in their System Test. Also, interconnections between 2.0 (Elements) are not addressed. The definition fails to capture the overall nature of systems thinking – Item 3.0 (Interconnections), or parts interacting to form a whole system.

The authors then explain that [5] Hopper and Stave draw upon Richmond, Senge, Sweeney, and Sterman in their definition, along with many others. However, their definition does not contain interconnections or a statement of purpose for systems thinking and thus fails the System Test. Their definition is simply a set of characteristics and not a system.

[1] Arnold and Wade present numerous other authors who have attempted to define systems thinking. They explain that

> in all of these definitions, common elements tend to include interconnections, the understanding of dynamic behavior, systems structure as a cause of that behavior, and the idea of seeing systems as wholes rather than parts.

This is especially true if extra consideration is given to the comprehensive literature review provided by Hopper and Stave, which covers a vast arena of literature on the topic, and to Peter Senge and Barry Richmond, well-respected gurus in the field.

As shown above, the definitions of systems thinking proposed by many other authors have focused on the elements of which systems thinking is made, by defining its components (which has been accomplished quite thoroughly), but have neglected to detail what systems thinking actually is, and perhaps even more importantly, what systems thinking does; the "essence" of what makes the system what it is. These characteristics seem to lack some abstract, but important elements. This element is the system aspect of systems thinking. Following Richmond's principle to focus on both the forest and the trees, it appears that many of these definitions may have focused on either the forest or the trees. Some define systems thinking too vaguely, whereas others have simplified systems thinking too much, and, in doing so, both approaches have failed to capture the systemic essence of systems thinking.

Therefore, a new definition is proposed by the [1] authors – to define systems thinking as a system by identifying its goal, and then elaborating upon both its elements and the interconnections between these elements. The authors then provide their own definition of systems thinking as:

> *Systems thinking is a set of synergistic analytic skills used to improve the capability of identifying and understanding systems, predicting their behaviors, and devising modifications to them in order to produce desired effects. These skills work together as a system.*

Finally, the proposed definition must be subjected to the System Test. It passes Item 1.0 of the test, as it contains a clearly defined, understandable, and relatable goal. It also passes Item 2.0: its elements are described in detail. It also passes Item 3.0, decribing interconnections and dependencies between the elements. Therefore, this definition is the first that passes the author's System Test and successfully defines systems thinking as a system. The definition includes a clear goal, elements of systems thinking, and descriptions of interconnections between these elements.

In conclusion, the [1] authors state that "The ability of our world's citizens to perform effective systems thinking is extremely important to the world's future. The use of systems thinking transcends many disciplines, supporting and connecting them in unintuitive but highly impactful ways. Thus far, the systems thinking skill set has remained on educational margins for a variety of reasons. One of these reasons is the absence of a widely accepted, complete definition of systems thinking. Proposed in this paper is such a definition.

Continuing, [1] the authors then explain that,

> The proposed definition passes a System Test, confirming its systemic fidelity. The definition includes a clear goal, elements of

systems thinking, and descriptions of interconnections between these elements. The definition synthesizes the most common and critical systems thinking competencies discussed in the literature. Moving forward, this definition can be used for systems thinking educational efforts, systems science, and a myriad of other disciplines, including *manufacturing systems*, which all require the use of critical systems understanding and intuition.

Now that we have a clear and concise definition of systems thinking, let's now look into the characteristics of a manufacturing system, which expand on the authors' [1] definition just presented. Those characteristics of a manufacturing system include:

1. All systems exist to achieve a specific *purpose*, and one of the keys to understanding a system is to fully understand its intended purpose. As an example, ask yourself what the purpose of a manufacturing system is. The basic purpose of a manufacturing system is to produce manufactured parts to satisfy customers' requirements. If all steps in the process are not functioning as they should, then the purpose will not be achieved.
2. Every manufacturing system contains multiple *elements* and has at least one constraining factor that controls the output of the system. If the system's purpose is to produce a product, then it is critical to locate the constraining factor, exploit it, and then subordinate the other parts of the system to it.
3. The distinct order in which a manufacturing system is arranged and *interconnected* affects the performance of the system. In other words, if the individual steps are not arranged in the correct order, then parts cannot be produced according to specified requirements.
4. All steps in the process must be present in order for a system to achieve its intended purpose. If, for example, one step experiences downtime, then the system will not function for its intended purpose.
5. In order for manufacturing systems to maintain stability, there must be a feedback mechanism in place to transmit information. Without a mechanism to provide feedback, systems will not function to achieve their intended purpose. Selecting the right performance metrics, for example, is critical for systems to operate effectively.

## Understanding a System's Purpose

To fully understand a manufacturing system, understanding its purpose is critical. This fact is true whether it's a separate entity or part of an even larger system. For most systems the intended purpose is clear, but it is important for everyone interacting within the system to fully understand its purpose. I say this because it's important to understand that the output of a system is not the sum total of each of the individual components of the system, but rather the impact of the interconnected elements. Systems always exist to realize a specific purpose and, in reality, the purpose should be viewed as the goal of the system or the objective toward which all effort should be directed. If we are attempting to improve our current system, then we must do so with our goal in mind.

Improvement implies that change will be required from the system's current status, but, because changes to our system can be either good or bad, we must do so with the ultimate system goal clearly to the forefront. Let's now consider a very simple example. This example is one I use when teaching the concept of the system constraint and why it must be identified and then exploited in order to improve the system. Just as Arnold and Wade have explained, the system must have a well-defined purpose, with inter-connected elements!

In Figure 11.2, we see the cross-section of a simple piping system used to transport water (i.e., its *purpose*) starting from Section A. Each of the different pipe diameters represents the basic *elements* of this *interconnected* piping system. This system is gravity fed, with water entering Section A, then flowing into Section B and continuing until the water reaches a receptacle directly beneath Section I. Suppose there was an increasing demand for water, and you have been assigned the responsibility to satisfy this increased demand. What would you do and why would you do it?

Applying what we learned through the "System Test," it should be apparent that, if the *purpose* is more water is required, then you must first identify that part of the system (i.e., the *element* and the *interconnections*) that could be limiting or constraining the output of water through this piping system. In Figure 11.2, we see that the constraining factor is Section E's diameter. It should be evident that, in order to increase the output of water through this system, Section E's diameter must be enlarged. The new diameter must be

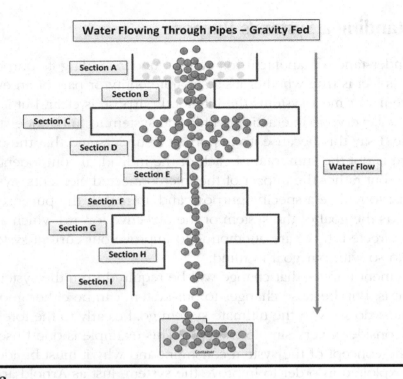

**Figure 11.2**

completely dependent upon the demand requirement being placed on this system. In other words, how much more water is required?

Figure 11.3 is this same piping system but with Section E's diameter enlarged to allow more water to flow through the system. The new output of water has clearly increased but is now limited by a new constraining factor, Section B. If there was a further surge in demand for water, then our focal point would now be Section B. So how does this simple piping system relate to a typical manufacturing system?

Figure 11.4 is a simple, linear manufacturing system with individual cycle times listed for each interconnected step. Parts, or raw materials, enter Step 1, are processed for 30 minutes, and are then passed on to Step 2. In Step 2, the semi-finished product is processed for 45 minutes and passed on to Step 3. Step 3 requires 90 minutes to process the semi-finished product and then passes it on to Step 4, which requires 30 minutes to process. When Step 4 is completed, the finished product is sent directly to either shipping, to direct sales, or is stored in racks to satisfy future orders.

If the purpose was to increase the output rate of product through this manufacturing system, the first thing we must do is to locate that part of the system that is the limiting or constraining factor (i.e., its element). Just like

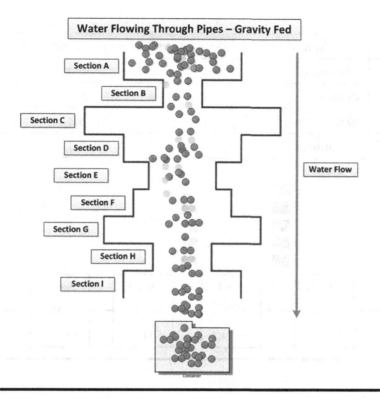

**Figure 11.3**

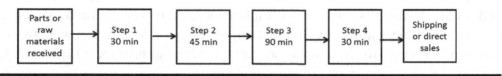

**Figure 11.4**

we identified Section E in our piping system as the constraint, we must do the same thing for this manufacturing system. Whereas, in our piping system, in order to identify the constraint, we simply looked at the volume of water passing through each pipe, which was proportional to its diameter, as well as looking for a "backup" of water waiting to pass to the next section. In our manufacturing system, we must identify which step has the longest cycle time. Here, we see that Step 3, at 90 minutes, is clearly the longest cycle time, so it is labeled as the system constraint. If our purpose was to increase the output of this manufacturing system, we would undoubtedly need to reduce the time required at Step 3.

**Table 11.1**

| Step # | Cycle Time | Output Rate (No. of Products) in 8 Hours |
|--------|------------|------------------------------------------|
| 1 | 30 minutes | 16.0 |
| 2 | 45 minutes | 10.7 |
| 3 | 90 minutes | 5.3 |
| 4 | 30 minutes | 5.3 |

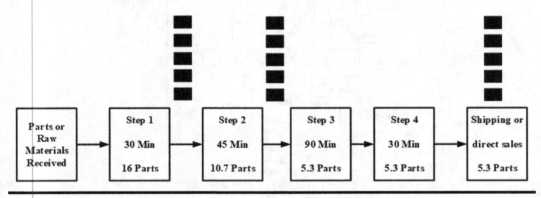

| Parts or Raw Materials Received | Step 1<br>30 Min<br>16 Parts | Step 2<br>45 Min<br>10.7 Parts | Step 3<br>90 Min<br>5.3 Parts | Step 4<br>30 Min<br>5.3 Parts | Shipping or direct sales<br>5.3 Parts |

**Figure 11.5**

This system, in its current state, can produce one part every 90 minutes, because that is the rate of the system constraint. Even though Steps 1, 2, and 4 can produce parts at much higher rates than Step 3, the total system is limited or constrained by Step 3's output rate. Table 11.1 is a step-by-step summary of cycle times and output rates for this system for a typical eight-hour day.

Clearly, Step 1's output capacity is dominant at 16 parts every eight hours, while Step 2's rate is approximately 11 parts every eight hours. The system constraint (Step 3) can produce product at only about five parts in eight hours, which then limits what Step 4 can produce. That is, Step 4 can only produce what Step 3 delivers to it. The question now becomes, in its current state, how fast should Steps 1 and 2 be running? If they continue to produce semi-finished product according to their current capacities, then clearly an accumulation of work-in-process (WIP) inventory will be the result, as is demonstrated in Figure 11.5, which represents the state of this system after one eight-hour day; if Steps 1 and 2 continue to produce product at their current capacities, then WIP inventory will simply continue to accumulate within this process. This is a prime example of the interconnectedness

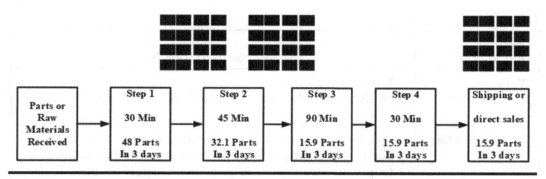

| Parts or Raw Materials Received | Step 1<br><br>30 Min<br><br>48 Parts In 3 days | Step 2<br><br>45 Min<br><br>32.1 Parts In 3 days | Step 3<br><br>90 Min<br><br>15.9 Parts In 3 days | Step 4<br><br>30 Min<br><br>15.9 Parts In 3 days | Shipping or<br><br>direct sales<br><br>15.9 Parts In 3 days |

**Figure 11.6**

within this manufacturing system. The purpose is not to build excessive WIP but rather to satisfy orders from customers.

Figure 11.6 represents the state of this system after three eight-hour work days with all steps producing to their current capacities. It makes no sense for this system to continue producing product at these rates, simply because the net result is increased WIP inventory, which needlessly ties up cash, causes delayed deliveries to customers, and generates a host of other negative effects. Again, I ask, how fast should each step be running to avoid this explosion of WIP?

Earlier, I introduced the characteristics of a system and explained that every system contains elements and has at least one constraining factor that controls its output. In our manufacturing system, we identified Step 3 as our constraining factor. The fact is, in order to avoid the explosion of WIP inventory, and all of the other negative consequences associated with it, Steps 1 and 2 should be producing product at the same rate as the constraining factor, which, in our example, is 1 part every 90 minutes. Again, if we want to increase the output of this manufacturing system, we must reduce the time required to process material in Step 3.

The most effective way to reduce the cycle time of our system constraint is by looking at it through the lens of both waste and variation. There are many different forms of waste that exist within all manufacturing systems. Table 11.2 is a tool I have successfully used many times to search for sources of waste within manufacturing systems.

You will notice that I have listed ten different sources of waste, and symptoms of their existence, instead of the traditional eight forms of waste. I do this to be as specific as possible in our search for waste. For example, I have listed over-production and inventory separately, because the negative impact of over-production exhibits symptoms completely different to those

**Table 11.2**

| Waste Description | Symptoms to Look For |
|---|---|
| Waste of Transportation | 1. Too many forklifts<br>2. Product has to be moved, stacked and moved gain<br>3. Process steps are far apart |
| Waste of Waitig | 1. Frequent/chronic equipment breakdowns<br>2. Equipment changeovers taking hours rather than minutes<br>3. Oeperators waiting for inspectors to inspect product |
| Waste of Organization and Space | 1. Operators looking for tools, materials, supplies, parts, etc.<br>2. Large distances between process steps<br>3. Not able to determine process status in 15 seconds<br>4. Many different work methods for same process<br>5. Poor lightning or dirty environment |
| Waste of Over-processing | 1. Rework levels are high<br>2. Trying to produce perfect quaity that isn't required by customer<br>3. No documented quality standards |
| Waste of Motion | 1. Process steps located as functional islands with no uniform flow<br>2. Excessive turning, walking, bending, stooping, etc. within the process |
| Waster of Inventory | 1. Product being made withour orders<br>2. Obsolete incentory<br>3. Racks full of product |
| Waster of Defective Product | 1. Problems never seem to get solved and just keep coming back<br>2. Independent rework areas have become just another step in the process<br>3. Excessive repairs |
| Waste of Overproduction | 1. Long production runs of the same part to avoid changeovers and set-up time<br>2. Pockets of excess inventory around the plant<br>3. Making excess or products earlier or in greater quantities than the customer wants or needs |
| Waste of Underutilization | 1. No operator involvement on problem-solving teams<br>2. No regular stand-up meetings with operators to get new ideas<br>3. No suggestion system in place to collect inprovement ideas<br>4. Not recording delays and reasons for the delays |
| Waste of Storage and Handling | 1. Many storage racks full of product<br>2. Damaged parts in inventory<br>3. Storing product away from the point of use |

of waste of inventory and will require different actions to correct. It helps us to focus better.

It's very important to understand that both waste and variation reduction efforts are not effective if they aren't carried out with a systematic plan that ties both steps together. You want waste and variation to be attacked simultaneously to ensure that any changes made in the name of waste reduction aren't negatively impacting variation, and vice versa. Remember that, for now, because the constraint dictates throughout, and increasing throughput yields the highest potential for significant profitability improvement, you are focusing your waste and variation reduction efforts only on the constraint. The exceptions to this would be upstream process steps causing the constraint to be starved or downstream process steps causing product scrapping or excessive rework. You cannot ignore these two exceptions, but, primarily, you will be focusing your improvement efforts on the system constraint.

Let's now take a look at several of these wastes and see how we might be able to use them to reduce the cycle time in our system constraint. For example, let's explore the "waste of inventory." Here, the symptoms observed will be product being made without orders, obsolete inventory, and racks full of product waiting to be sold. Why is it that companies make product without having orders to fill? When this happens, the result could be racks full of inventory, which could also result in the condition of obsolete inventory. Doesn't it make sense to produce product to fill orders?

Another waste we might consider is waste of overproduction, with the symptoms being long production runs of the same part (in order to avoid changeover and set-up time), pockets of excess inventory around the plant, and making excess product or product earlier or in greater quantities than the customer wants or needs. Although this is similar to our waste of inventory, the impact is clearly different.

Another waste to look for is waste of waiting, with the symptoms to look for being things like frequent and chronic equipment breakdowns, equipment changeovers taking hours rather than minutes, and operators waiting for inspectors to inspect product. The important thing to remember as we work to reduce key constraint cycle times is that waste does exist.

An important factor that must be considered is that, as we reduce the cycle time of our current system constraint, we must be on the lookout for our new constraint, once the existing one has been "broken." Suppose, in our example, we are able to reduce the cycle time from 90 minutes down to 35 minutes. Ask yourself where your new constraint would be located? Clearly, the new system constraint would be Step 2 with a cycle time of 45 minutes, as demonstrated in Figure 11.7. The good news is that, by reducing Step 3's cycle time from 90 minutes to 45 minutes, we have doubled the output of this manufacturing system!

Now that we have discussed waste in our system, let's now turn our attention to variation. There are basically two types of variability that you are interested in discovering. No, we're not talking about special cause and common cause. We're talking about processing time variability (PTV) and process and product variability (PPV), which are very different from each other. Sources of PTV are those things that prolong the time required for parts to progress through each of the individual process steps. On the other hand, PPV are those variables that cause the quality characteristics of parts to vary. PPV has a profound impact on PTV, simply because PPV negatively interrupts the process flow. There are many examples of situations that disrupt processes and, therefore, create variation. Some of the more common examples include unreliable equipment (PTV and PPV), lack of standardized work procedures (PTV and PPV), defective product (PPV and PTV), late deliveries from external and internal suppliers (PTV), and many others.

Variability burdens a factory because it simply leads to congestion, excessive inventory, extended lead times, quality problems, and a host of other operational problems. There are two prominent theories on variation and how to treat it. Walter Shewart's idea was to "minimize variation so that it will be so insignificant, that it does not, in any way, affect the performance of your product." Taguchi, on the other hand, tells us to "construct (design) the product in such a way, that it will be robust to any type of variation." They're both right, of course. So, what are your options when dealing with the negative effects of variation? There are three ways to handle variation, namely eliminate it, reduce it, or adapt to it. Because it's impossible to totally eliminate variability, you must reduce it as much as possible, and then adapt to the remaining variation.

To summarize the key point in this chapter, taking into account [1] Arnold and Wade's "System Test," we have defined the *purpose* of our system in a way that can be clearly understood. That is, we defined it as attempting to produce more finished product. As far as the element portion of the System

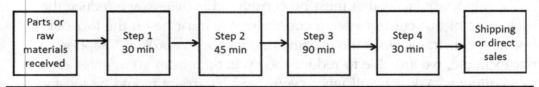

**Figure 11.7**

Test goes, we have described the characteristics of our system, whereby the system constraint controls our system output. And finally, in terms of interconnections, we have described the ways that the systems thinking elements feed into and relate to each other. Clearly, the constraint controls the ultimate output of our manufacturing system.

Now that you probably have a better idea of what a system is, let's now turn our attention to tools we can use to assess a system. Appropriately, these tools are referred to as system thinking tools.

# References

1. Ross D. Arnold and Jon P. Wade, *A Definition of Systems Thinking: A Systems Approach*, In Conference on Systems Engineering Research, 2015.
2. B. Richmond, *Systems Dynamics/Systems Thinking: Let's Just Get On With It.* In International Systems Dynamics Conference, Sterling, Scotland, 1994.
3. P. Senge, *The Fifth Discipline, the Art and Practice of the Learning Organization.* Doubleday/Currency, 1990.
4. L.B Sweeney and J.D. Sterman, Bathtub dynamics: Initial results of a systems thinking inventory, *System Dynamics Review*, 2000.
5. M. Hopper and K.A. Stave *Assessing the Effectiveness of Systems Thinking Interventions in the Classroom*, In The 26th International Conference of the System Dynamics Society (pp. 1–26). Athens, Greece, 2008.

## Chapter 12

# Theory of Constraints Systems Thinking Tools

In previous chapters, I have introduced you to the basics of the Theory of Constraints, but TOC has much more to offer. The systems thinking tools were developed and popularized by Dr Eliyahu Goldratt. These tools are basically a series of thinking processes, or, more specifically, logic trees, that can be used individually to solve problems, or they can be used in a defined sequence to conduct a full systems analysis. It is not the intention of this chapter that the reader will become proficient in using these tools, but rather the intent is to make the reader aware that such tools exist, and then present a basic discussion about what these tools can do and the basics of how they work.

## Current Reality Tree (CRT)

The Current Reality Tree (CRT) is used to determine your organization's current reality at a single point in time. It's a snapshot in time of a system as it currently exists. It is an assemblage of entity statements that are linked together using *sufficiency* logic. Sufficiency is based on "if" and "then" statements. In other words, *If I have (*Entity "A") … *then I will have* (Entity "B"). The CRT is the tool of choice for defining and logically connecting the current state of activities within your system.

The foundational structure of the CRT is comprised of entities commonly referred to as *Undesirable Effects* (UDEs), as they are commonly known. The UDE list is best populated by asking the question; "*In my current reality, it*

DOI: 10.4324/9781003462385-12

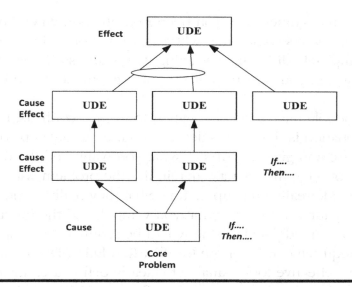

**Figure 12.1**

*bothers me that … ?"* Determine the best statement that answers this question. The UDEs become the collection of *all* the bad things (Undesirable Effects) that seem to be happening at the same time within your system. Sometimes, what may appear to be many random negative events, all happening in isolation of each other, are actually events that can be linked together using *cause–effect–cause* relationships. These different, and apparently random, events, that appear to be unrelated, can be logically connected using a CRT. As it turns out, random events are not nearly as random as we think they are. Using sufficiency logic to determine the cause–effect–cause relationships between events will provide a detailed and clear understanding of why particular events seem to be happening over and over again. Figure 12.1 demonstrates the basic structure of a CRT.

Once the CRT is completed, logically connected, and verified, it is possible that a single UDE (the core problem) at the bottom or near the bottom of the tree is often actually creating all or many of the other UDEs. With the core problem now identified, it becomes clear where to focus the improvement effort. In Figure 12.1, the ellipse between two arrows is the logical "and" statement – meaning that both entities must exist to cause the stated effect.

## Conflict Resolution Diagram (CRD)

The Conflict Resolution Diagram, often referred to as the "Evaporating Cloud", as it was originally developed, is a powerful tool for resolving conflicts. How many times have you been in a situation where, on the one hand, somebody wants something, whereas, on the other hand, you want something completely different? The thing they want is different from what you want. How can you possibly come to an agreement, if you both want different things?

For years, people have used negotiation to resolve conflicts, but the problem with negotiation is that both sides are required to give up something. You compromise and give up parts of what you want, and the other side gives up parts of what they want. Therein lies the problem with a compromise – neither side really ends up getting what they really want. What if there was a way for you to have what you wanted, and the other side to have what they wanted? Neither side would be required to compromise on their desired requirement. Enter the Conflict Resolution Diagram. This is, by far, the most effective tool available to clearly define a conflict, and then surface the assumptions that cause the conflict to continue to be a conflict. If both sides could get what they wanted, then a conflict would not exist.

The Conflict Resolution Diagram uses necessity-based logic using the statement, *In order to have entity A … I must have entity B ….* And it is constructed from these three components:

- Objective.
- Requirements.
- Prerequisites.

The objective becomes the common ground between the two parties. It's the statement about what both parties really want. It should be stated succinctly and at a high enough level to meet the needs of the two parties. The requirements are the necessary conditions that both parties must have to be able to meet the objective.

The prerequisite is an assumed condition necessary to be able to achieve the desired requirement. It is usually these two prerequisite entities that will be in conflict with each other. One entity may say, "Do something," whereas the opposite entity may proclaim, "Don't do it." One entity may say, "Change," and the other entity says, "Don't change." The battleground is now set because we've established the conflict. Figure 12.2 demonstrates one way to configure the structure of the Conflict Resolution Diagram.

With the structure in place, and the conflict precisely verbalized, you can surface the assumptions. The assumptions are located on the arrows

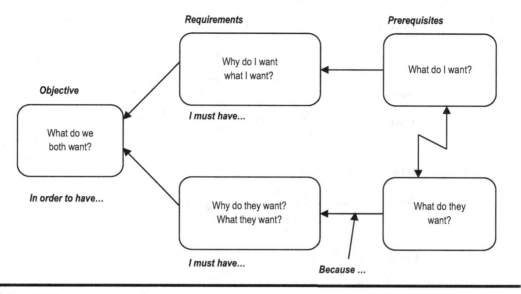

**Figure 12.2**

between the entities. These lines are solid lines because they are assumptions that exist. You can surface the assumptions by stating, *"In order to have (Objective), I must have (Requirement)... because ... assumption?"* Do this for each arrow and list the assumptions. If you can dissolve an assumption and make it go away, then the conflict can be resolved. The line is no longer solid because it no longer exists. If you are able to invalidate an assumption, then the conflict will no longer exist. If we replace the invalid assumption with a new idea, then we have an *Injection*. The injection becomes the new idea you want to pursue.

## Future Reality Tree (FRT)

How many times has it happened that we think we have a good idea, only to find out that our idea wasn't so good? You usually find out when you implement your "good" idea, and then bad things start to happen. What if there was a way to test an idea before it was implemented to determine if the idea generates the results you want to have happen? A way, if you will, to run the movie in fast forward and see if we like the ending. Such a tool does exist, and it's called the Future Reality Tree (FRT). With an FRT, you can logically test the virtues of an idea before it is implemented and look for those unwanted, undesirable effects that might happen. If you can predict

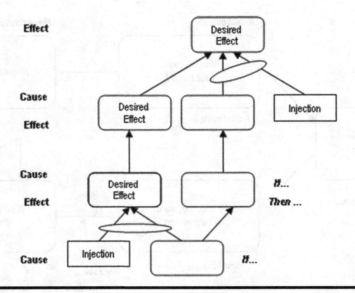

**Figure 12.3**

what might go wrong, and you have a way to overcome the negative effect, then the bad things shouldn't happen. Such is the function of an FRT. Figure 12.3 demonstrates the structure of the Future Reality Tree.

An FRT is constructed using sufficiency with the *If . . . Then . . .* statements. What you are looking for are the *Desired Effects* – the good things that happen from implementing your idea. The FRT can also provide advanced warning for the *Negative Effects* – the bad things that might happen. If you find negative effects (branches) coming from your idea, then think of an *Injection* – an idea that overcomes the negative effect and makes it positive again. The more negative effects you can overcome, the more powerful your idea is, and the greater the chance that the implementation becomes successful.

## Prerequisite Tree (PRT)

Once you have tested your idea using the FRT, and you decide your idea is worth moving forward with, then the Prerequisite Tree (PRT) becomes the tool to surface the obstacles to your idea. Ask yourself, "Why can't I do this right now?" What are the reasons or obstacles that stand between you and completing your idea? You might even try presenting your idea to someone else. They offer suggestions such as, "It's a great idea, but ..." As soon as they say "but," they will offer their opinion as to why the idea won't work.

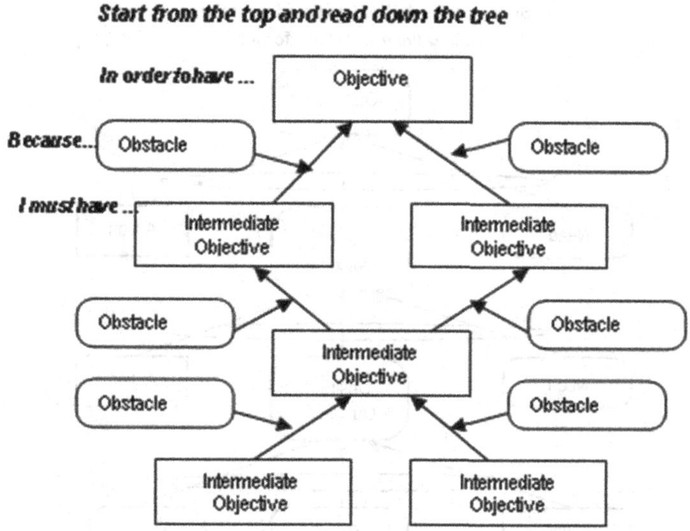

**Start from the top and read down the tree**

*In order to have ...*   Objective

*Because...*   Obstacle     Obstacle

*I must have ...*   Intermediate Objective     Intermediate Objective

Obstacle     Intermediate Objective     Obstacle

Obstacle     Obstacle

Intermediate Objective     Intermediate Objective

**Figure 12.4**

This means they have surfaced an obstacle that you might have to overcome to make your idea real. The purpose behind a PRT is to surface and overcome as many obstacles as you can so your idea will be implemented as smoothly as it possibly can. Figure 12.4 displays the basic structure of the Prerequisite Tree.

Think of as many reasons as you can as to "why" your idea won't work. What stops you right now from doing this? With each obstacle you surface, counter that thought with an *Intermediate Objective* that makes the obstacle no longer an obstacle. The PRT is read from the top down. You are looking for the logical connections between the Intermediate Objectives (IO) that make the obstacle go away. If you achieve the defined Intermediate Objective, then the obstacle is removed and is no longer a problem. Once all of the IOs are completed, the objective can be achieved.

## Transition Trees (TT)

The final tool is the Transition Tree (TT). Based on popularity, it is not a tool that is often used. However, the TT can provide an excellent logical structure for going deeper and being more fractal in your thinking. It is designed at a level that requires the definition of *actions* to be taken and *needs* to be filled.

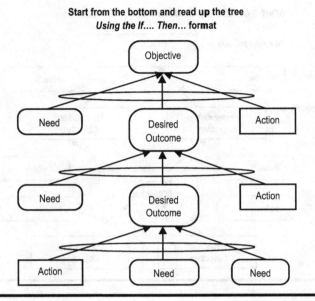

**Figure 12.5**

The basis of the TT is sufficiency, and it is read with the *If ... then ...* statements. Figure 12.5 shows the structure of the TT. If you encounter an Intermediate Objective (IO) in your Prerequisite Tree that may be particularly difficult to achieve, then the TT is an excellent tool to define the actions necessary to meet the needs to accomplish the IO.

The TT is comprised of an *Objective, Actions,* and *Needs.* The Objective can be defined as the difficult Intermediate Objective from the PRT, or any other objective you might have that benefits from planning at a detailed level. With the objective in mind, consider what need you are trying to fill and what action you can take to immediately make it happen. When you read the TT from the bottom up, the intrinsic order of the actions, desired outcomes, and needs are clearly defined. Start at the bottom, complete that action, and achieve your desired effect, then take the next action, which fills a need, and continue until the objective is accomplished. At this level of detail, actions could be equal to making phone calls, writing a paper, doing a presentation, or whatever the action is that you can start today. The trick here is: ***Take action***.

## The Full Thinking Process (TP) Analysis

The Thinking Process tools can be used on a standalone basis and can also be used in a specific sequence to drive a complete systems analysis. With the full level of analysis, you are trying to answer three questions:

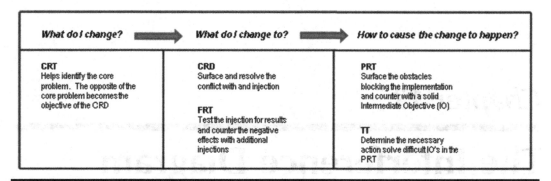

**Figure 12.6**

1. What do I change? Identifying the core problem.
2. What do I change to? Determining the best solution to solve the problem.
3. How to cause the change to happen? The steps to implement your great idea.

Figure 12.6 displays the sequence when conducting the full thinking analysis.

The full Thinking Processes analysis can be time consuming and possibly frustrating, but is certainly worth the effort to find the core problem, provide the correct injection (idea), and determine the best way to implement the new idea.

As part of every improvement effort, there are "things" that get in the way or interfere with your effort. What if there was a simple tool that would help you both identify and remove these interferences? In the next chapter, I will present a tool that hasn't gotten much attention and that tool is known as the Interference Diagram.

# Chapter 13

# The Interference Diagram

One improvement tool that hasn't gotten much coverage and attention is one referred to as the *Interference Diagram* (ID). When the interference diagram was first being developed and drawn on whiteboards, it was done so not with the intention of replacing any of the current systems thinking tools (discussed in Chapter 12), but rather to fill the void of a need to complete the analysis in less time. The Interference Diagram is a thoughtful mind-mapping tool, that can quickly point a team or individual in the right direction to solve a problem, without requiring the construction of a Current Reality Tree (CRT). In effect, the ID was able to answer the question of "What to change." In this case, the "What to change" became a list of the many interferences that stand in the way of solving a problem, and not just a single core problem. It is also a valuable tool for listing those "things" that get in the way of maximizing throughput.

[1] Bob Fox, at the Theory of Constraints (TOC) Center, New Haven, Connecticut, sometime around 1995, is generally credited with introducing the Interference Diagram. Since then, the use and structure of the ID tool *has not* been very well documented or transferred to the public at large, but rather it has been used by a limited number of practitioners within the TOC network. Unlike the other systems thinking tools, the ID is not based on any kind of logic, but rather it's based on intuition and experience. The arrows in the ID diagram are just arrows, without any link to sufficiency- or necessity-based logic. The thinking behind the ID is not to develop or isolate a single answer, but rather to list the interferences that could work to block the achievement of the desired objective.

DOI: 10.4324/9781003462385-13

Many times, it has been said that the biggest obstacle to solving a problem is the ability to adequately define the problem. If you aren't sure what the problem is that you are trying to solve, then it is very difficult to determine the correct solution. That is, if you don't know where you are going, then conceivably any path you follow will get you to where you're going. You'll just never know when you get there. The ID structure and concepts are very simple, but they can deliver very powerful results.

## Interference Diagram (ID) Types

In reality, there are essentially two different ways to apply an Interference Diagram (ID). The first way is by using the Interference Diagram as a sort of thinking tool, to exploit a known constraint. The second way involves using the ID in combination with the Goal Tree/Intermediate Objectives (IO) map. This second application offers a fast and highly effective way to develop an overall improvement strategy and then create a corresponding implementation plan.

Let's first consider the exploitation of a system constraint. When the system constraint is identified, then the question that must be answered is, "How can I get more from the constraint?" In other words, "What are the 'interferences' that stand in the way or stop the constraint from producing more?" It's possible that there could be multiple interferences that block the higher performance of the system constraint. This list of "interferences" becomes the reasons "why" the constraint is unable to do more. The best way to create this list of interference is by assembling your improvement resources that use the constraint, and then asking the operators to list and explain what these interferences are. After all, they are the true subject matter experts who can successfully define the interferences, simply because they are most familiar with the constraint and how it works or doesn't work.

When these subject matter experts are asked the question: "What gets in the way or interferes with you getting more from this operation?" the chances are good that they will be brutally honest with their answers and the answers will come quickly. What becomes important at this stage of information-gathering, is to separate the "emotional" responses from the "logical" ones. You'll need to determine whether the response is really a system problem or strictly a personal annoyance or complaint. This analysis will provide better results if the emotional responses are removed upfront before placing the statement on the list of interferences.

The entities on this list of interferences suggest that they are stopping the constraint from doing more of what it does. After all, the interferences are essentially stealing time away from the constraint. So, in order to get more from the constraint, you must reduce the negative impact of these interferences or completely remove them. Any interference that can be reduced or eliminated will free up more time for the constraint to deliver more. Let's now go through an example of how to construct an Interference Diagram. In our example, let's say that we have identified one particular machine in a production line as the constraint. We will refer to it as "the XYZ machine". Let's define the steps to construct.

## Step 1: Define the Goal/Objective

The Goal should be something that you must have but which doesn't exist in your current reality. For our example, let's say our Goal is "More parts from the XYZ machine." This can be written on a whiteboard, in the center of a piece of paper, or on a computer screen. My advice is to make sure everyone involved agrees on what the Goal should be, including the person responsible for delivering the Goal.

## Step 2: Define the Interferences

Step 2 is best accomplished by using observations of the system, plus interviews with the operators. When observing the constraint, you will be looking for those things that get in the way, either slowing it down or stopping it from producing more output. In other words, "What are the interferences that take time away from achieving more of the Goal?" If what you have identified as the system constraint is truly a system constraint, then keeping it busy all the time will be paramount to successfully achieving more system throughput. In this example, let's say our possible list of obstacles or interferences might include:

1. Parts not available to work on.
2. Operator on break/lunch.
3. Operator has to find his own parts.
4. Operator is looking for the supervisor.
5. Operator is attending training.
6. Machine is broken.

The most important element when creating an Interference Diagram is to identify those things that are currently stopping the constraint from doing more of what it does. When you take the time to observe the constraint, your observations might reveal other things that impact time at the machine, such as having to do setups for a different product. All of the observations and interview items combined equal the list of interferences that prevent the achievement of the goal of more parts from the XYZ machine. There is no set limit on the number of interferences that need to be listed, but rather you should list as many as you think are necessary to fully describe "why" the machine doesn't produce more parts.

## Step 3: Quantify the Time Component for ALL Interferences

In this step, quantifying the time component associated with each interference is extremely important, in order to fully understand the impact of each interference on the available constraint time. The time component will also help filter the important few from the trivial many, which helps identify those items that should have the greatest impact on the output of the constraint. Knowing the impact of the time component for each interference will be useful in determining the priority order in which interferences should be reduced or eliminated first. When you accurately quantify the time component for each interference, it sets the stage for a Pareto analysis. The Pareto analysis will help you determine which interference has the greatest impact, plus the fundamental order in which improvement should be conducted. Pareto analysis allows the needed *focus* to gain the most *leverage* from the actions to be implemented.

Keep in mind that it is probably unrealistic to assume that the impact of all of the interferences will be reduced or eliminated. The fact of the matter is that there will be some interferences that do not offer themselves as candidates for elimination, but rather as entities that can benefit from a reduced time impact. For example, if an interference with a time of 45 minutes can be reduced to 15 minutes, then the benefit gained for the system is 30 minutes, which represents more time for the constraint to produce more output. In another example, the time for breaks and lunch can't be removed, simply because employees must be permitted to have lunch and break times. But, as an alternative, you could gain some machine time by having another employee or crew work the machine during lunch and breaks. If you can eliminate, reduce, or offload some of these activities, then more time is available to get more product produced by the constraint, resulting in more throughput through the entire system.

## Step 4: Alternatives to the Interferences

The interference list defines all of the obstacles or interferences that stand in the way of producing more of what you want. With the interferences defined, you should now be able to counter the negative effect of the interferences with an "Injection Objective" or "Intermediate Objective (IO)." This can be accomplished by asking the question: "What must be in place for the interference to no longer exist?" Whatever your answer is, the Injection or Intermediate Objective to overcome the negative impact of the interference is now defined. Continue working your way down your list of interferences and create an Injection/Intermediate Objective for each one listed. Remember, the items on the IO list are those things that must be accomplished in order to reduce or eliminate the negative effects of each of the inferences. With the addition of IOs, the list should provide sufficient "ideas" on how to move you closer to the Goal you have set. This list answers the question of "What to change to." Table 13.1 is the completed list of IOs.

**Table 13.1**

| Interferences | Intermediate Objective/ Injections | Estimated Time |
|---|---|---|
| Parts not available to use | Parts are kitted and ready for use | 75 minutes |
| Operator is on break or lunch | Train an alternate crew or person | 60 minutes |
| Operator has to find his own parts | Parts delivered to operator | 90 minutes |
| Operator is looking for the supervisor | Supervisor notification system | 45 minutes |
| Operator is looking for paperwork | Paperwork follows job in the system | 30 minutes |
| Machine is broken | Preventive maintenance (priority #1) | Avg 30 minutes/ week |

Figure 13.1 is an example of what the completed Interference Diagram looks like from our example. The circle contains the Goal, and each of the interferences is listed around the center circle. The direction of the arrows makes no difference because these arrows are based on the ID user's intuition and not necessity or sufficiency logic. Notice in Figure 13.1, that the interference times have been added for every interference identified, which allows for a quick visual of the time impact.

When using the Pareto analysis, you should always base it on available machine time, so as to clearly demonstrate the impact of each of the interferences. If the available machine time for the XYZ machine is considered to be eight hours for one shift, then the available time is 480 minutes (60 min × 8 hours = 480 minutes) during an 8-hour period. When you use the 480 minutes as the baseline to measure the impact of the interferences, the results will show the conflict between the time available to work and the time the machine actually spends working. Table 13.2 below displays an example setup of the Excel input sheet to show the interference description, the total minutes that the interference consumes, and the percentage impact on the total minutes available. As you can see, the leading time impact comes from not having parts available at the machine to work on. Fixing this interference alone could provide an additional 90 minutes of throughput

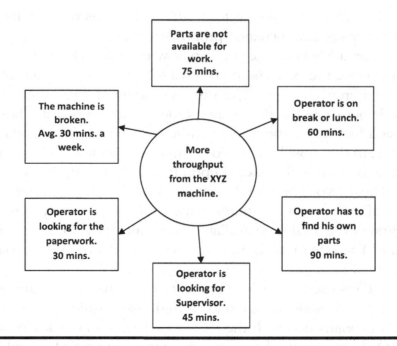

**Figure 13.1**

**Table 13.2**

| # | Description 13.3 | Daily Time (Minutes) | Percent Interference |
|---|---|---|---|
| 1 | Parts not available | 75 | 16% |
| 2 | Breaks and lunch | 60 | 13% |
| 3 | Operator finding parts | 90 | 19% |
| 4 | Looking for supervisor | 45 | 9% |
| 5 | Looking for paperwork | 30 | 6% |
| 6 | Machine is broken[1] | 6 | 1% |
| | Total Interference Minutes[2] | 306 | |
| | Available work minutes[3] | 174 | |
| | Total available minutes | 480 | |
| | Utilization Percentage | | 36% |

[1] Six minutes is calculated from weekly average of 30 minutes (30 mins/5 days)

[2] Sum of interference minutes

[3] Available minutes – interference minutes

time every day. Actually, if you factor in the 75 minutes when parts are not available, the throughput increases proportionally.

From this spreadsheet setup, you can now display a classic Pareto Chart that will help drive the point home relative to the impact of each of the individual interferences. Figure 13.2 displays the interferences in a Pareto analysis to demonstrate the descending order of improvement. Those interferences listed highest on the list should be reduced or eliminated first, if possible, to gain the most benefit. For example, Operator finding for parts, at 19% of the total, should be acted upon first, followed by Parts not available (16%). These two represent 35% of the total, which could translate into a proportional increase in constraint output! Table 13.2 clearly demonstrates that only 36% of the total time available is actually used to make parts on this machine. The other 64% of the time is consumed by the combined interferences.

When the ID is used to analyze and exploit a constraint, it can be a quick and effective tool to generate good ideas and results quickly. This method, when used in conjunction with the Pareto analysis, can quickly provide the visual tool to determine the key impactful interferences and provide the

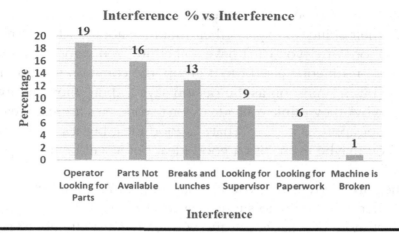

**Figure 13.2**

needed *focus* and *leverage* on those few important actions that will achieve the highest levels of improvement.

## Interference Diagram (ID) for Strategy

In the previous example, I demonstrated how to use the Interference Diagram (ID) to *exploit a constraint*. Now let's look at another application of the Interference Diagram, which is *strategy development*. When using the Interference Diagram for strategy development, it's important for you to *focus* on a higher-level Goal, especially if the input audience is considered cross-functional. Your Goal has to be at a high enough level so that it satisfies all parties concerned. When using the ID for the purpose of strategy development, it is best if it is used in conjunction with the Intermediate Objectives (IO) Map/Goal Tree that was discussed in Chapter 9. The combined thinking power of the ID/IO map is what [2] Bruce Nelson referred to as the *Simplified Strategy*. This will permit not only the development of an effective strategy but also the development of a detailed implementation plan. In this case, the Goal Tree/IO Map provides the correct sequence of the strategic actions needed to accomplish the overall strategy.

When the Interference Diagram is used for strategy development, it is not a constraint you are looking for, but rather the strategic Goal that you are trying to reach. When the Goal has been defined, you then look for those "interferences" that will obstruct the progression toward your Goal. Characteristically, there will be several key interferences that will block your pathway to achieving the Goal. If there is one thing that people are really good at, it's their ability to express their rationale about "why" something isn't working, or "why" you can't have something you want. When you present your idea to someone else or to a group, the common reaction is, "That's a great idea, but...." As soon as the person says "...but," they will interject the reason "why" they think your idea won't work. "It's a great idea but the boss will never approve it." Or, "That's a good idea, but it's not the way we do it here." Or maybe even, "It's a good idea, but it will be too expensive to implement."

What they are really telling you is what they think the interferences are that will hinder your ability to succeed at reaching your Goal. In order for you to get more of what you want, you really must attempt to reduce the *impact* of the interferences or remove them completely. Let's now go through the steps on how to construct an Interference Diagram that will be used for strategy development.

## Step 1: ID Strategy – Define the Goal

The Goal for the strategic application of the Interference Diagram is to focus on a strategic direction, rather than on a constraint. It generally answers the questions, "Where do we want to go from here?" The Goal has to be at a level high enough to include everyone. However, with that said, it's also important to understand that an effective strategy development can be done within the confines of a specific organization, such as engineering, procurement, or manufacturing. When developing your strategy, think in terms of a higher-level Goal for your company. This is especially important when dealing with a single organization or combining the objectives of many organizations into a single system strategy. The Interference Diagram can work very well in a group setting because it helps the users to surface those interferences across many different organizations.

## Step 2: Define the Obstacles and Interferences

When a group consensus is realized and the Goal has been clearly defined, you then need to look for those interferences that will characterize "why" you can't have more of what you want. Again, when using the Interference Diagram for strategy development, the interferences can, and most probably will, cross many organizational functions. There is no minimum or maximum number of interferences required, but, rather, you should be looking for a list of interferences that are comprehensive enough to surface those interferences that are standing in the way of achieving your Goal. For example, suppose that your cross-functional team listed the following interferences for achieving the Goal of "Increased Revenue."

## Obstacles and Interferences

1. Not enough sales.
2. No markets to grow into.
3. Customer has low perception of our product.
4. Products are priced too high.
5. Competitor has higher quality.
6. Production takes too long.

This list defines the key interferences that are believed to currently exist that will conceivably block achievement of your Goal. In other words, these are the "things" that currently stand in the way of being able to achieve increased revenue. This list might seem to be a bit overwhelming, but don't lose faith just yet. Let's do the rest of the steps and see if we can, in effect, "tame the beast."

## Step 3: Define the Injection/Intermediate Objectives

In Step 3, your objective is to list those Injection/Intermediate Objectives (IOs) that must exist in order to make each of the interferences disappear or at least that their impact can be significantly reduced. Ask the group this question: "What must exist in order for the interferences not to be a problem anymore?" When you think of the actions required for eliminating or reducing the size of the interferences, you must be bold. Describe, in detail, what you think is *really necessary* to counter the problem(s) to reach your stated Goal. Don't shy away from Intermediate Objectives and Injections just because you think you cannot make them happen. If they are important for achieving your Goal, then write them down, no matter how difficult they might seem to be able to accomplish. Table 13.3 is a list of some possible

**Table 13.3**

| Obstacles/Interferences | Intermediate Objectives and Injections |
| --- | --- |
| Not enough sales | Increased sales |
| No markets to grow into | Explore and find new markets |
| Customers have low perception of our product | Customers have high product perception |
| Products are priced too high | Products priced competitively |
| Competitor has higher quality | Quality higher than competitor's |
| Production takes too long (lead-time) | Lead-time reduced (increase throughput) |

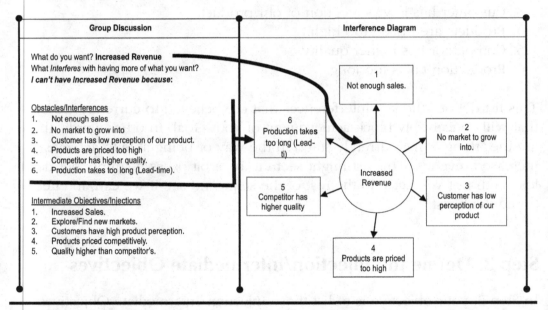

**Figure 13.3**

Intermediate Objective or Injection examples for the obstacles on the list already defined.13.3

With the Intermediate Objectives and Injections defined, you now have the list of the required actions needed to eliminate the interferences. While it may appear to be an ominous list and, seems, at first glance, to be almost impossible to achieve any of these actions, my advice is to be patient. Figure 13.3 provides an example of the basic structure and layout for using the ID for strategy development.

After completing this step, the next step is to construct the Goal Tree/ Intermediate Objective Map in order to determine the actions needed to accomplish the Goal and the development of the corresponding implementation plan. My advice to you here is, don't rush through this step as it forms the backbone of your improvement effort.

## Intermediate Objectives (IO) Map/Goal Tree

The Intermediate Objectives (IO) Map was developed by [3] Bill Dettmer, and in the spirit of combining methods within a methodology, this tool certainly fits into this criterion. In recent years, Dettmer has changed the name of the IO Map to The Goal Tree; I will use these names interchangeably throughout this chapter. The IO Map/Goal Tree has been refined over the years to become a very practical and useful organizational and thinking tool. Instead of using the full spectrum of the Thinking Process tools (presented in Chapter 12) to conduct a full analysis, the Goal Tree/IO Map combines the Prerequisite Tree (PRT) and the Conflict Diagram (CD) into a single tool. In his paper about Intermediate Objective mapping, Dettmer defined the IO Map as a PRT without any obstacles defined.

Dettmer's primary intention for this tool was to simplify the construction and accuracy of the Current Reality Tree (CRT), in order to focus the attention on a better-defined Goal, rather than a core problem. The IO Map/Goal Tree can be used to surface the *Undesirable Effects* (UDEs) and, in most cases, the UDEs can be discovered by describing the exact opposite of the desired Intermediate Objectives that are listed. These UDEs then become the building blocks for a CRT. UDEs are what exist in your current state, while the IOs are what you want to have in your current state.

Dettmer also defines an expanded function for the IO Map, indicating that it serves well the purpose of strategy development, and, as such, it provides a robust tool to do that. As discussed in Chapter 9, the Goal Tree/ IO Map, using a standalone technique, can provide the necessary clarity and direction to accomplish a needed strategy. The Goal Tree/IO Map is a very concise organizational thinking tool that is based on *necessity logic*.

The Goal Tree/IO Map allows the user to define the Intermediate Objectives and then the intrinsic order of the IO Map task completed by using necessity logic. In other words, it is read with necessity as the

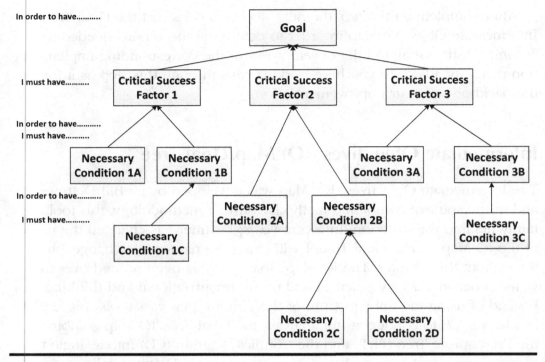

**Figure 13.4**

outcome. *In order to have... (Entity Statement at the tip of the arrow), I must have...(Entity Statement at the base of the arrow).* Necessity logic states that entity B must exist before you can have entity A. The entity cannot be there just sometimes, but rather necessity states it *must always* be there. The existence of entity B is not a causal existence simply because necessity requires that the "B entity" exists before the "A entity" can be achieved.

The structure of the Goal Tree/IO Map is really very simple, as discussed in Chapter 9. There are three primary levels, or thinking levels, required to construct the Goal Tree/IO Map. The first level is defining the *Goal.* The second level identifies the *Critical Success Factors (CSFs)* or those Intermediate Objectives that must exist prior to achieving the Goal. The third level is populated with the remaining *necessary conditions* required to achieve each of the Critical Success Factors (CSFs). Figure 13.4 provides an example of the basic structure of a Goal Tree/IO Map.13.5

Figure 13.6 is the completed Goal Tree/IO Map inserted into our strategy figure. The shaded IOs in the above diagram are the Intermediate Objectives that surfaced when constructing this IO Map. These IOs did not appear on the original IO list, but instead surfaced after construction began on the IO map.

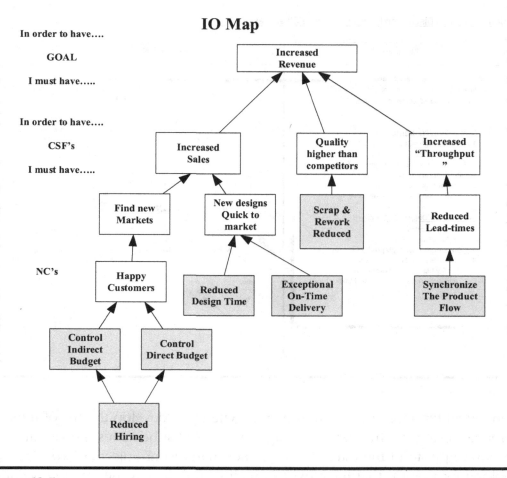

**Figure 13.5**

# The ID/IO Simplified Strategy

Now that you have an understanding of both the Interference Diagram (ID) and the Intermediate Objective (IO) Map, and how they can be used as standalone techniques to generate some impressive improvement results, let's talk about how they can be combined. The [3] Simplified Strategy, named by Bruce Nelson, who developed it, is a way to combine these two tools, depending on the situation being analyzed and the desired outcome required. It is possible that when using the ID to define the interferences, they are actually obstacles that are not necessarily time driven, but rather event driven. The ID allows you to define the interferences if they are not already well known. Sometimes, the interferences do not provide the means to implement a simple solution in isolation, but rather are collectively

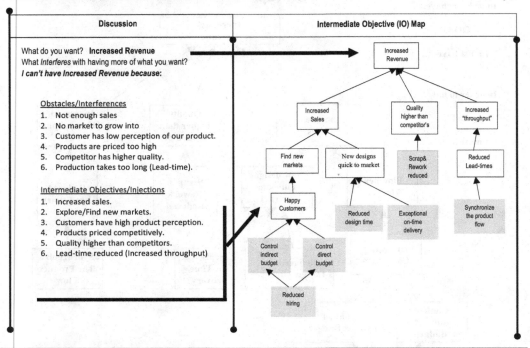

**Figure 13.6**

connected by necessity. In other words, when you develop the list of inter-ferences, using the Interference Diagram, the IO list becomes the verbal-ization opposite of the interferences rather than just an injection. You are looking for the IOs that must exist in reality, in order for the interference to no longer be a problem.

What happens next is that the listing of IOs becomes just that, a list of IOs. Now, with the IO mapping tool, you are able to establish the logical necessity between single IO events that require another predecessor event before the event can happen. In other words, there is a logical dependency and intrinsic order in the sequence. Just randomly selecting and completing the IO's will not satisfactorily achieve your Goal. When you analyze the IO list, you realize that all of the IOs need to be completed, but which one do you start with first? In this situation, the IO Map can be used to determine the sequence and order of completion. From the IO list, you can determine which events are Critical Success Factors (CSFs) and which ones are the Necessary Conditions (NCs). By using the IO Map to determine the necessity between the events, it becomes *precisely clear* which IO you need to start with in order to implement your strategy.

Each level of the Intermediate Objective Map becomes logically connected to formally outline both the "strategy" and the "tactics." In other words, your Goal is the *strategy* and the Critical Success Factors are the *tactics* needed to accomplish your Goal. At the next level, the Critical Success Factors now become the *strategy,* whereas the Necessary Conditions become the *tactics.* The same thinking applies down through the next levels of Necessary Conditions. When you reach the bottom of an IO chain, you know what action you need to take first in order to start the process moving up through the IOs. By using the IO map as a problem-solving supplement to the Interference Diagram, it provides the organization needed to logically align the IOs. The Goal Tree/IO Map will provide well-defined interferences to better focus the creation of the correct IOs to negate the interferences. Keep in mind that, most of the time, you cannot generate a good solution without first understanding what exactly the problem is.

Even though these tools can be used in combination, it might not always be necessary to do so. In fact, the power of these tools allows them to be used in reverse order, if so desired. If you already understand what you need to do, then the Goal Tree/IO Map can be your beginning tool, as discussed in Chapter 9. If, however, you are not so sure why you cannot achieve a particular Goal, then the ID helps identify the interferences that stand in the way of achieving the Goal.

Even if you begin with the IO map and you discover a particular IO that is necessary, but you're just not sure how to make it happen, then you can use the ID as a subset of the IO map to discover the interferences that stand in the way of achieving that IO. If you remove the interferences for a specific Intermediate Objective, then you can achieve the IO. When you achieve that particular IO, you can move on to the next one. Figure 13.7 shows a possible template for the combined approach.

With the completion of the ID/IO Simplified Strategy, you now have the outline necessary to prepare an effective and accurate Implementation Plan. The intent of the Goal Tree/IO Map is not to provide implementation detail at a low level but rather to provide specific milestones or markers to make sure you are traveling on the right path.

## Conclusions

In today's world, that requires "Better, faster, and cheaper", the Simplified Strategy approach of the Interference Diagram (ID) and Intermediate

ID/IO Simplified Strategy

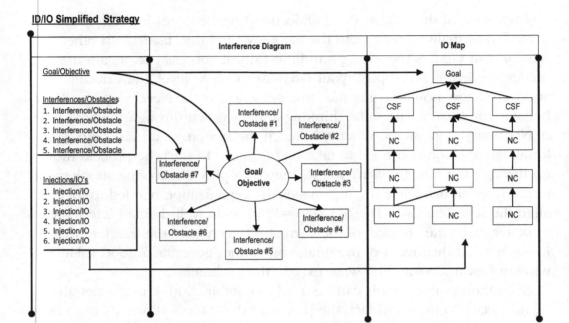

**Figure 13.7**

Objective (IO) can provide exceptional results in a relatively short period of time. By combining the power of these two thinking tools, into the [2] ID/IO Simplified Strategy, the user will benefit from an effective and complete analysis that is completed in significantly reduced time. These tools, used in either a standalone environment or a combined approach, will provide the thinking necessary to develop great results. The speed with which these tools can be used is an enormous benefit over the original Systems Thinking tools to achieve the ability to answer the three questions:

- What do I change?
- What do I change to?
- How do I cause the change to happen?

The structure and concept behind these tools make them easily adaptable and well understood and accepted in a group situation, to allow for faster collection of data and analysis of issues.

For those of you who manufacture products from raw materials, you've no doubt had problems with "stock-outs," even though you have mountains of raw material inventory. In the next chapter, I'm going to present TOC's version of a replenishment solution that will cut your on-hand raw material inventory in half, while virtually eliminating stock-outs.

# References

1. Robert Fox, TOC Center, New Haven, CT, discussions, circa 1995.
2. Bruce H. Nelson, "ID/IO Simplified Strategy", Original works, March 2011.
3. H. Wlliam Dettmer, "The Intermediate Objectives Map", http://goalsys.com/books/documents/IOMapPaper.pdf, November, 2008.

# Chapter 14

# Theory of Constraints Distribution and Replenishment Solution

Most businesses in today's business world are in some way linked to some kind of supply chain system. It really doesn't matter if your company sells, distributes, or manufactures goods because you must have stock keeping units (SKUs), parts, or raw materials from somebody else, in order to do whatever it is you do before you pass it on to the next link in the supply chain. In today's business world, many businesses typically use what's referred to as the minimum/maximum (Min/Max) model to manage their supply chain. Businesses replenish what they sell, but unfortunately many times there are periods of excessive stock-outs of parts, even though inventory levels are typically quite high. Wouldn't it be great if there was a way to eliminate stock-outs and reduce on-hand inventory levels to a much more manageable level? Well, for everyone who experiences these annoying stock-outs, even though inventory levels are much higher than desired, there is hope for you.

The Theory of Constraints (TOC) Distribution and Replenishment Model reaches both backward and forward in the supply chain to significantly reduce inventories, while virtually eliminating stock-outs. The impact of implementing this model in your business will be dramatic improvements in flow which drives revenue upward, as well as significant improvements to responses to customers' ever-changing needs. In this chapter, I will demonstrate how the Theory of Constraint's Distribution and Replenishment

DOI: 10.4324/9781003462385-14

Model can be used to reduce your inventories by 50% or more, while simultaneously eliminating these troublesome stock-outs. But before I explain this model, let's first review both the basics of the Theory of Constraints and what method most companies are using to replenish their parts and materials.

Consider this simple piping system used to transport water in Figure 14.1. The system is gravity fed, whereby water flows into Section A, then flows through Section B, then Section C and so forth until, ultimately, the water is collected in a receptacle immediately below Section I. Suppose it has been determined that the rate of water flow is inadequate to satisfy current demand and you have been called in to fix this problem. Think about what you would do and why you would do it.

If you're like most people, you will immediately see that water is backing up in front of Section E. You will probably also recognize that, if more water is needed to flow through the operation, then Section E's diameter needs to be enlarged. You will also think that enlarging the diameter of any other section of the piping system will not result in more flow of water through this system. In order to determine what the new diameter of Section E must be to satisfy the new demand, you will need to know how much more water is needed. In other words, in order to answer this question, you

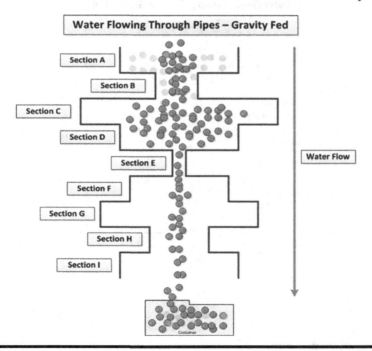

**Figure 14.1**

need to know what the new demand for water is. So, let's see what happens when we enlarge the diameter of Section E of our piping system based upon the new demand requirement.

In Figure 14.2, Section E's diameter has been changed and, subsequently, the flow of water has increased. If you correctly selected your new diameter based on the new demand requirements, you will have "fixed" this problem. But what if there is another surge in demand for water? What would you do? The correct answer would be that you now need to enlarge Section B's diameter, which is again based on the new demand requirement. Section E and now Section B are referred to as *system constraints* (aka bottlenecks). The inevitable conclusion in any business is that system constraints control the flow and throughput within any system. Ask yourself how this might apply to your business.

For any type of business, there is a process that is at least similar to what you see in Figure 14.3. Materials, SKUs, or parts are delivered to your business and enter into your manufacturing system. Step by step, things happen at each step in your process to either change the materials or, if you're a retailer or distributor, maybe you sell your product directly to your customers. Parts or raw materials enter Step 1, are processed for 30 minutes, and

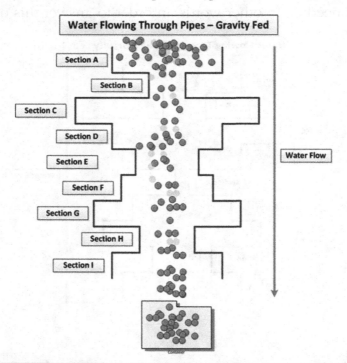

**Figure 14.2**

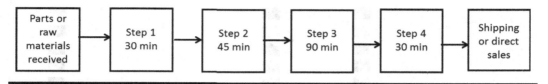

**Figure 14.3**

are then passed on to Step 2. Step 2 processes what it has received from Step 1 for 45 minutes and then passes it on to Step 3. Steps 3 and 4 complete the processing and the finished product is either shipped to the company that ordered it or directly sold to consumers.

Suppose that you wanted to sell more parts to your customer base. Ask yourself what you would need to do to increase the throughput of parts through this simple four-step process. (Hint: remember the piping system). Because Step 3 takes the longest amount of time to complete, it is the system constraint (i.e., just like Section E in the piping diagram). The bottom line is the only way to increase the throughput of this process; you must reduce the time required in Step 3 (i.e., 90 minutes), simply because it is the system constraint. What would determine by how much to reduce Step 3's processing time? Just like the piping system, the required processing time for step 3 would depend on the demand requirements. Would reducing the processing time of any other step in this process result in increased output or sales? The answer is no, so the inevitable conclusion is that the system constraint controls the output of any process.

Many businesses are using manpower efficiency or equipment utilization to measure the performance of their processes and, as a result of these performance metrics, they work to increase these two metrics. Since increasing efficiency is only achieved by running close to the maximum capacity of each process step, what happens when this takes place? That is, Step 1 makes one part every 30 minutes and passes it on to Step 2 which takes 45 minutes to complete, etc.

As demonstrated in Figure 14.4, after the first eight hours, this is what this process looks like. Work-in-process (WIP) inventory begins to accumulate, which causes the total processing time to increase, which then results in on-time delivery deteriorating and, ultimately, angry and frustrated customers, frustrated because of your company's inability to ship product on time, which negatively impacts their own ability to ship their products on time.

In Figure 14.5, we see this same process after three eight-hour days. WIP levels continue to grow, negatively impacting flow and, unless something changes, the system becomes overwhelmed with WIP. This increase in WIP

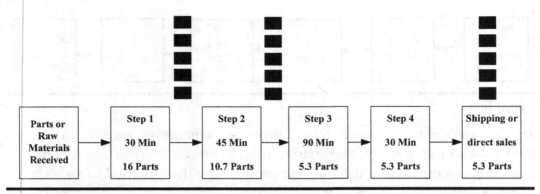

**Figure 14.4**

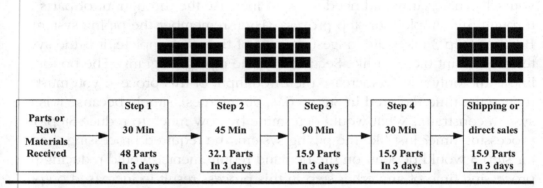

**Figure 14.5**

extends processing times even further which negatively impacts on-time delivery and customers end up threatening to take their business elsewhere. So, what is the answer?

As you have just witnessed, the performance metric efficiency or equipment utilization both have negative consequences, so maybe they're not such good metrics after all, at least not with respect to non-constraints. They are both excellent metrics that are used to drive the output of the constraint, but not in non-constraints. In order to avoid this explosion of WIP, doesn't it make sense that Steps 1 and 2 should be running at the same speed as the constraint (i.e., one part every 90 minutes)? In order to increase the output rate of this process, Step 3's processing time must be reduced because it is the system constraint. What happens if we focus our improvement efforts on Step 3 only? By focusing our improvement efforts on Step 3 only, we get an immediate increase in the throughput of this process, which improves our on-time delivery of product to our customers. This is the essence of the Theory of Constraints…it provides the necessary focus for your improvement efforts. So, let's move on to our distribution and replenishment discussion.

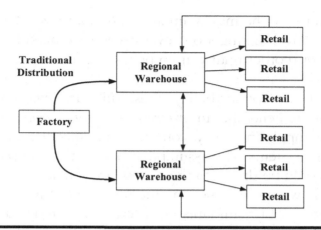

**Figure 14.6** Note: The above figure is from *Reaching the Goal* by John Arthur Ricketts – a book I recommend.

Originally, replenishment was invented to manage the distribution of goods, but it can equally be used by service providers and even direct sales businesses. Replenishment gets its name from the specific way in which goods or services are distributed or supplied. Figure 14.6 is a simplified version of a distribution chain. I say "simplified" because many businesses have many more factories, warehouses, and retail outlets in their distribution chain. In traditional distribution, product generated by the factories is immediately shipped in large batches to regional warehouses. Each regional warehouse, in turn, intermittently ships (pushes) smaller but still sizeable batches to numerous retail locations.

The key point here is that most inventory is *pushed* through the chain to retail locations on the assumption that it will eventually be sold to the end consumer. Regrettably, because variability is highest at retail locations, several undesirable effects will most likely occur. Some of the retail locations might end up having plenty of one particular product, whereas, at the same time, unfortunately, others will not have any of it. And because there's no easy way to ship inventory from one retail location to another, in an attempt to reduce both over-stocks and stock-outs, some locations end up having plenty of one particular SKU, whereas others simply don't have any of the same SKU. When the inevitable stock-outs occur, if the time required to restock a retailer from the warehouse is longer than customers are willing to wait, stock-outs turn into *lost sales* rather than backorders. So, what is the primary cause of all this confusion?

Many companies today are using a replenishment system referred to as the Min/Max System. The traditional rules and measures for these systems are actually quite simple:

■ Rule 1: Determine the maximum and minimum levels for each SKU.
■ Rule 2: When re-ordering, don't ever exceed the maximum level.
■ Rule 3: Never reorder until you go below the minimum level.

The foundational assumptions behind these rules and measures are primarily based on the belief that in *order to save money and minimize your expenditures* for supply inventory, you must minimize the amount of money you spend for these items. The assumption here is that the purchase price per SKU (unit) could be driven to the lowest possible level by buying in bulk and the company would *save* the maximum amount of money on their purchase by buying excessive amounts of materials. But, in reality, what we end up seeing is that there always seems to be circumstances of excess inventory for some items, whereas others are in a stock-out condition. So, why is it that, even though you might have plenty of inventory, you continue to have stock-outs? Let's try to answer that question by pointing out the "rules of engagement" for the Min/Max System.

As specified in the basic rules for the Min/Max System, the system re-order amount must never exceed the pre-established level of the maximum. In addition, most supply systems we see today only allow for one order at a time to be in the ordering system for a specific SKU. In addition, total SKU inventory is held at the lowest possible level of the distribution chain – the point-of-use (POU) storage location.

SKUs are typically inventoried once or twice a month, and orders are placed based on the inventoried levels as required. Remember, orders for SKUs are triggered only after going below the minimum amount value that has been set. The problem is that, many times, the replenishment time to receive the replacement orders creates a temporary stock-out condition, as depicted in Figure 14.7. Unfortunately, sometimes the duration of these stock-outs is extended, which negatively impacts a company's ability to ship orders in a timely manner.

The Min/Max System is based on being in a reactive mode, waiting for the part to reach the pre-defined minimum stock level before re-ordering the SKU (i.e., the re-order point). Stock-outs occur when the lead time to replenish the part (Vendor Replenish Time) exceeds the minimum stock available. In addition, when variability enters the picture, stock-outs can happen in shorter time periods. This pattern of possible stock-outs repeats itself over time, as depicted in Figure 14.8.

Figure 14.8 demonstrates the negative consequences of the typical Min/Max supply system where, at times, you have excessive levels of inventory,

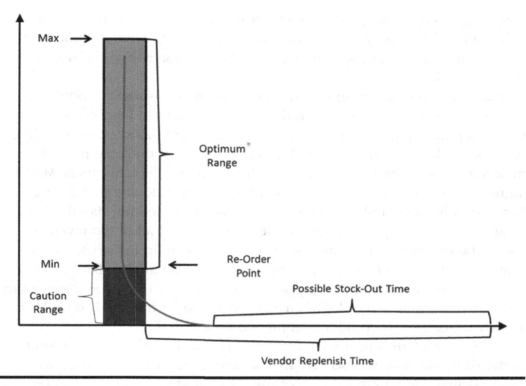

**Figure 14.7**

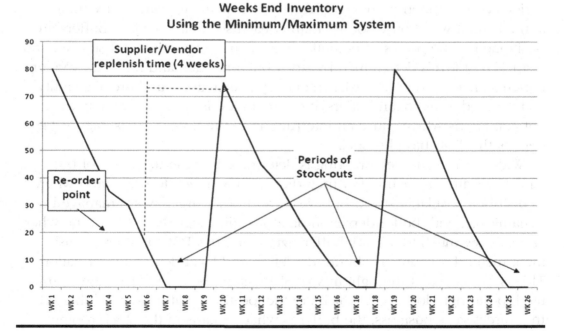

**Figure 14.8**

whereas, at other times, SKUs are out of stock. The reality is that, in most cases, the most prominent measures for the Min/Max System are focused on cost-world thinking (i.e., saving money) rather than satisfying the needs of the system. So, what's the answer?

The Theory of Constraints Distribution and Replenishment Model is a robust SKU replenishment system that allows the user to be proactive in managing the supply-chain system. It's also a system based on usage, either daily or weekly, and, unlike the Min/Max system, not on some pre-deter-mined minimum amount. The TOC Distribution and Replenishment Model argues that the majority of the inventory should be held at a higher level in the supply chain and not at the lowest level, like the Min/Max System promotes. For example, in a direct sales business, not all of the inventory should be on shelves, but rather some should remain in the stock room. The TOC Distribution and Replenishment Model also argues that the use of Min/Max amounts should be stopped, and, instead of using some minimum amount to trigger the reorder of an SKU, it should be triggered by daily or weekly usage and the vendor lead time to replenish it.

In TOC's replenishment model, stock is positioned at the highest level in the distribution system so that all available inventory can be used to satisfy demand at multiple points of use. More frequent ordering can be completed because the central warehouse sums the demand usage at the various consumption points and larger order quantities can be accumulated at the central warehouse sooner than at each separate location. Buffers are positioned at the points of potential high-demand variation and stocked and restocked at levels determined by stock on hand, demand rate, and vendor replenishment lead time. Order frequency is increased, and order quantity is decreased to maintain buffers at optimum levels so as to avoid stock-out conditions which cause an interruption to the flow of parts. Figure 14.9 depicts the TOC-based model.

With the TOC model, ordering is determined by the depletion of buf-fers. The status of each buffer then dictates how much to order, and where to distribute available stock. Buffer size and order urgency are managed dynamically, with buffer depletion data providing signals to determine when and by how much to modify buffer size. Using the TOC-based replenish-ment method accounts for buffer depletion and local demand information. This is done so that the right mix of SKUs is ordered, and SKUs are distrib-uted to the right locations, which are the locations that most need the SKUs. In a direct sales business, the buffer is what remains in the stock room; when the buffer is depleted, it's then time to re-order.

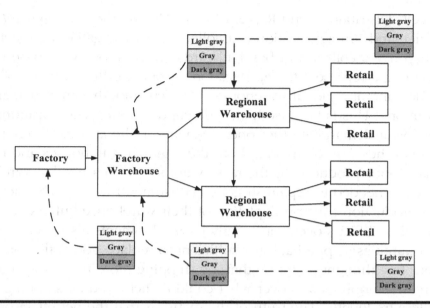

**Figure 14.9** Note: The above figure is from *Reaching the Goal* by John Arthur Ricketts – a book I recommend.

The criteria for the TOC Distribution and Replenishment Model is as follows:

- The system reorder amount needs to be based on daily or weekly usage and SKU lead time to replenish.
- The system needs to allow for multiple replenish orders, if required.
- Orders are triggered based on buffer requirements, with possible daily actions, as required.
- All SKUs/inventory must be available when needed.
- SKU inventory is held at a higher level, preferably at central supply locations or comes directly from the supplier/vendor.
- SKU buffer is determined by usage rate and supplier lead time to replenish. Baseline buffer should be equal to 1.5 times the time required. If lead time is one week, then buffer is set at 1.5 weeks. Adjust as required, based on your historical data.

As demonstrated in Figure 14.9, buffers are placed at strategic leverage points in the supply chain, with most inventory being held in the factory warehouse. Likewise, the regional warehouses and retail locations also have buffers for each SKU. Also, as depicted in Figure 14.9, physical buffers are divided into light gray, gray, and dark gray zones based upon the level remaining in stock.

The TOC Distribution and Replenishment Model relies on *aggregation* to smooth demand. An aggregation is a collection, or the gathering together of things. If you're a collector of baseball cards, for example, your baseball card collection might represent the aggregation of lots of different types of cards. That is, demand at regional warehouses is much smoother than demand at retail locations. This is because higher demand at some retail locations is offset by lower demand at other ones. Demand at the factory warehouse is even smoother than demand at both the regional warehouses and retail locations. Goods produced by the factory are stored in a nearby warehouse until they are needed to replenish goods consumed by sales. The factory bases its production runs on depletion of their warehouse buffers.

Since sales of SKUs occur on a daily basis, shipments also occur daily, and the quantities shipped are just sufficient to replace goods that have been sold. Your first thought might be that, by shipping more frequently, this will increase shipping costs over what could be achieved by shipping large batches less frequently. The truth of the matter is that the net effect on total shipping costs is actually a significant decrease in shipping costs! Why is this the case? Simply because you will have significantly reduced the shipment of things like obsolete goods and re-shipment of misallocated goods. By shipping goods more frequently, it more than compensates for increased costs created by smaller shipments of saleable goods. Think about it: the ability to capture sales that would otherwise be lost, due to insufficient inventory, makes the TOC replenishment solution a much, much better alternative.

Remember, in the TOC replenishment solution, replenishment is driven by actual consumption and not a sales forecast. For those of you who don't know, forecasts are always wrong! As sales are made, the buffer levels at retail locations drop, which triggers orders from regional warehouses, which triggers replenishment from the factory warehouse, which ultimately triggers a manufacturing order to resupply the appropriate buffer before it runs out.

So, how large or small should you make these buffers? Buffer-sizing is based on two basic factors: *variability* and the *time* it takes the vendor to replenish the SKU. For example, the more variable the consumption is, the larger the buffer must be to cover the variability. Similarly, the longer it takes to re-supply the SKU, the larger the buffer needs to be to be able to cover the demand during the re-supply waiting times.

The benefits of TOC's replenishment solution can be very striking. For example, a company currently using the Min/Max System, that is 75% to 85% reliable, should reasonably expect to increase its reliability to 99% or more, while cutting inventory by at least 50%! In addition, the average time to re-supply retail locations typically drops from weeks or months to a day or two. Remarkably, you can reasonably expect to reduce your on-hand inventory by 50% while virtually eliminating stock-out! But one of the central benefits of TOC's replenishment solution is that it transforms your distribution system from a *push* system to a *pull* system. That is, nothing gets distributed unless there are sales. Market pull is the external constraint and optimizes the distribution while minimizing inventory.

To summarize the basic key differences between the Min/Max System and TOC's Distribution and Replenishment Model:

- The Min/Max System "pushes" products into the manufacturing and distribution system, whereas the TOC Model "pulls" products through the manufacturing and distribution system based upon usage.
- The Min/Max System holds inventory at the lowest possible distribution level, the point of use. The TOC Model argues that the majority of the inventory should be held at a higher level in the distribution system.
- The Min/Max System establishes a minimum re-order point (the Min) that must be achieved before re-ordering. And when you do re-order, you order a predetermined amount of product (the Max). The TOC Model believes that you should re-order based on usage, supplier variability, and replenishment time.
- The TOC Model uses buffers that are based upon variability, the amount of product remaining, and the time it takes the vendor to replenish the SKU.

The bottom line is that, instead of having prolonged periods of excess inventory and frequent stock-outs, as is observed with the Min/Max System, you have much lower inventory levels with the virtual elimination of stock-outs. Perhaps the best way to describe the difference between these two distinctly different methods is by way of the following graphics (Figures 14.10 and 14.11). Instead of having this with the Min/Max System in Figure 14.10, you have something better with the TOC Model in Figure 14.11.

In closing this chapter, let's look at a very common replenishment method that is based upon the TOC Distribution and Replenishment Model. Consider a simple soda vending machine. When the supplier (the soda vendor) opens the door of a vending machine, it is very easy for the supplier to see what products have been sold. The soda person knows immediately which inventory must be replaced and at what level to replace it. The soda person is holding the inventory at the next highest level, which is on

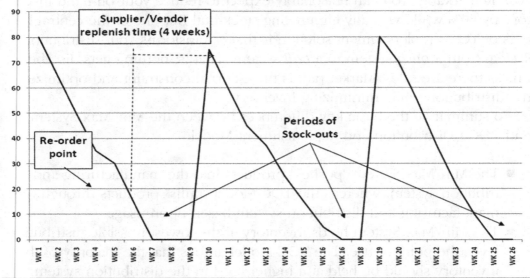

**Figure 14.10**

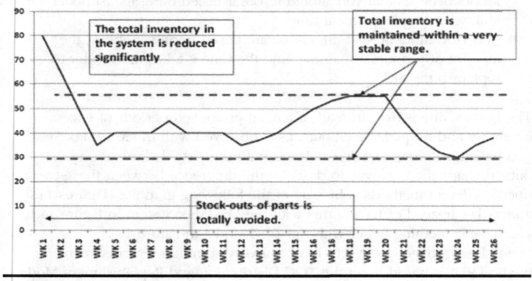

**Figure 14.11**

the soda truck, so it's easy to make the required distribution when needed. The soda person doesn't leave six cases of soda when only twenty cans are needed. If the soda person were to do the former, when they got to the next vending machine, they might have run out of the necessary soda because distribution was made too early at the last stop.

After completing the daily refill of the vending machines, the soda person returns to the warehouse, or distribution point, to replenish the supply on the soda truck and get ready for the next day's distribution. When the warehouse makes distribution to the soda truck, they move up one level in the chain and replenish what's been used from their supplier. Replenishing in this way significantly reduces the on-hand inventory while significantly reducing stock-outs. If a specific type of soda always seems to run out, then more should be added to the vending machine (i.e., another row of this high-demand soda).

Let's look at the potential benefits of using the TOC Model:

- The first benefit is the reduction of total inventory required to manage and maintain the total supply-chain system. This reduction is typically of the order of 40–60%. From a profitability perspective, this inventory reduction should lead to significant dollar savings.
- The second benefit is the virtual elimination of SKU stock-outs. Not having parts available when needed is an expensive situation because production stops. Production lines sitting idle results in frustration, with a corresponding loss of revenue.
- Another benefit is that the distribution of SKUs is made at the right time, to the right location, and the frustration caused by stock-out situations virtually disappears, not only because you can complete the work, but also because the time spent looking for and waiting for SKUs to become available is eliminated.
- Because waiting due to stock-outs virtually disappears, parts flow and synchronization improves dramatically which improves the throughput of parts through the entire supply chain.
- And because throughput improves, on-time delivery improves, and profitability increases proportionately to the level of sales.

Stock-outs and high inventory levels are common problems for many companies and most supply-chain systems. If the current supply-chain system is continued (i.e., the Min/Max system), then the results will remain unchanged. The TOC Distribution and Replenishment Solution offers a way to positively impact your company's on-time delivery and ultimately its profitability.

In the next chapter, I will discuss the different types of plant configurations that can exist within a manufacturing facility. The reason is that the type of plant configuration that exists can have a pronounced effect on the actions you might need to take as you move forward in your improvement effort.

## Chapter 15

---

# Plant Types, Control Point Theory, and Volts Concepts

---

## Types of Plant Configurations

When you are considering implementing improvement efforts, such as things like Drum-Buffer-Rope, into your system, it is important to know what type of plant configuration you might be dealing with. In this section, we will discuss the various plant layouts that exist in today's manufacturing companies. This section was taken from my book with Bruce Nelson, [1] *Epiphanized – A Novel on Unifying Theory of Constraints, Lean, and Six Sigma.*

Principally, there are four different types of plant configurations that can exist. Because the shape of each type of configuration resembles a letter in the alphabet, they are commonly referred to as "A," "V," "T," and "I." Each configuration offers its own type of challenges and, when your plant includes a combination of these four configurations, it can pose an even greater challenge. Knowing what type of plant configuration and the characteristics and consequences will benefit you in the long run as you work to improve the flow of product through your plant. Let's look at each type of configuration in more detail. As you might have guessed, the configurations refer to the basic shape they exhibit.

# The "A" Plant

An "A" plant configuration is exhibited when there are numerous parts and/or sub-assemblies that come together to produce a single end product. The end product of an "A" plant is completed at the top of the "A." A common example of an "A" plant might be the assembly of the many individual components required to make a computer. It could also be illustrated as the sub-assemblies of a computer, such as the manufacture of circuit boards or other assemblies.

Like all configurations, "A" plants have certain defined and predictable characteristics and potential consequences. Figure 15.1 provides the basic structure of an "A" plant, which starts with many raw materials until you finally end up with a single finished product.

The typical characteristics of an "A" plant include things like numerous raw materials unique to the end item(s), few end item(s) relative to raw materials, many different routings, and generic equipment. Potential "A" plant consequences can include things like misallocation of capacity (starting work too early), frequent part shortages, large batch sizes, long lead times, and high levels of work-in-process (WIP) inventory.

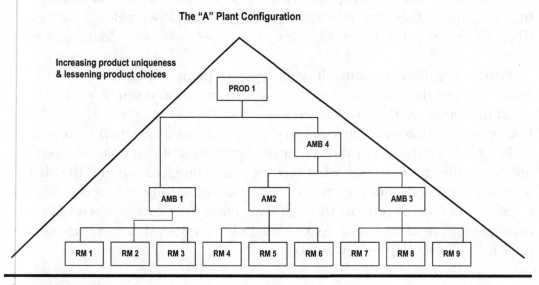

**Figure 15.1**

# The "V" Plant

With a "V" plant configuration, you start with a single raw material, and then produce several different products. The base of the "V" configuration starts with a single raw material and then branches out to multiple products. Figure 15.2 displays an example of a "V" plant configuration, starting with a single raw material of steel and progressing up the lines to the many varied products that can be produced.

Another example of a "V" plant might be a sawmill, where your starting raw material is a log that is cut into 2×4s, 2×6s, 2×8s, or whatever size is needed. Once you commit to making 2×4s, you can't go back and change to making 2×8s. The raw material is already committed to making a certain product and cannot be changed.

The "V" plant also has characteristic and consequences. The characteristics might include things like the number of end items being large (relative to the number of raw materials), all end items are produced essentially the same way, the equipment needed to produce the end items can be

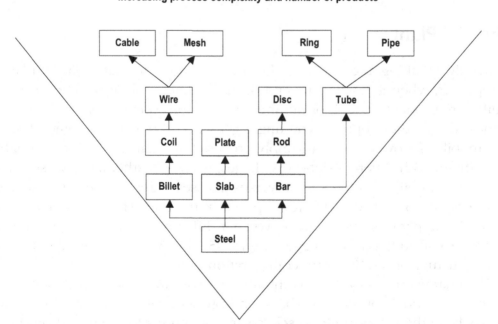

**The "V" Plant Configuration**
Increasing process complexity and number of products

**Figure 15.2**

capital-intensive, and many different machines are needed to produce many different products.

The predicted consequences can include things like misallocation of material, meaning you might commit raw materials too soon in the process; poor customer service, where you can't seem to get orders out on time; constantly changing priorities or multitasking; and continual customer complaints that manufacturing is being unresponsive to their needs.

## The "I" Plant

The "I" plant is strictly a sequence of processes all in a straight line. The characteristics of an "I" plant include, typically, what you start with in the "I" line is similar to what you end up with. "I" plant production lines offer the simplest analysis possible, in that you need only discover the slowest operation in the line to isolate the constraint; with an "I" plant configuration, this is usually a relatively easy task to accomplish. The consequences of an "I" plant are few and far between. Usually, the only consequence of this type of plant is using the performance metric efficiency which only serves to grow WIP and extend cycle times.

## The "T" Plant

Generally speaking, the flow of a "T" plant is similar to that of an "I" plant, except that, when it reaches the end of the "I" line, it branches and becomes a different product, model, or number. A common example of a "T" plant is the different options you might get when producing automobiles. Automobiles follow a single assembly process but, near the end, they might be outfitted with different option packages, such as leather seats versus cloth seats, or a premium stereo system versus a lesser stereo system. In essence, it's the same car, but with different options at the end. The "T" plant concept could also apply to software when you get different versions of the same computer with different languages. Figure 15.3 below is an example of the basic structure of the "T" plant configuration.

The characteristics of a "T" plant are the possibility of creating multiple versions or models of the same basic end product. Like an automobile, customers have the opportunity to select various options for their end product.

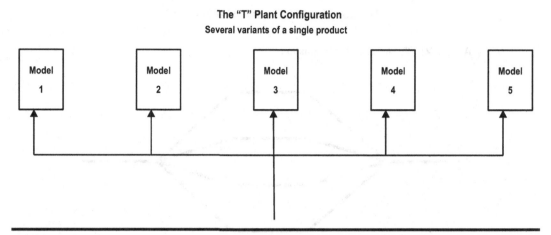

**The "T" Plant Configuration**
Several variants of a single product

**Figure 15.3**

The consequences of a "T" plant are similar to an "A" plant, especially in terms of part shortages, which will have a major impact on process synchronization. "T" plants also suffer from the misallocation of parts, a feature that is also common to the "V" plant. Some parts can be robbed along the way to make other products.

## Combination of Plant Configurations

While it may not be obvious to you, many manufacturing systems will actually contain a combination of different plant configurations. For example, it's possible that your system might start with an "I" line, then move into a "V" line, and then back to one or more "I" lines and then recombine into an "A" line and finish with an "I" Line. Figure 15.4 provides an example of the combined configurations. As you can imagine, many of the consequences already discussed for each individual configuration could be manifested in the combined plant configuration.

## Control Point Theory

The basic definition of "Control Point" is a point or stage of manufacturing where it is essential to control, reduce, or eliminate a risk to avoid downtime. Control point theory had its origin when it was understood that, during a Drum-Buffer-Rope implementation, the cycle between Step 1 (Identify

**The Combined Plant Configurations**

An "I", "V", "I", "A," and "I" combination

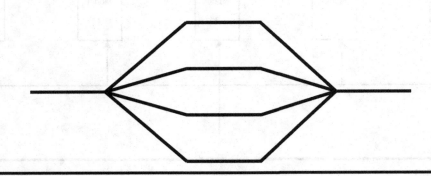

**Figure 15.4**

the system constraint) and Step 2 (Decide how to exploit the system constraint) could happen in very rapid succession. Control point theory argues that you can select any location you want in the system to be your control point. Having said this, there are some recommended guidelines for selecting your control point location.

First, your control point should be a process that currently has excess capacity. This permits the control point to keep up with system improvements as your capacity demands increase. In other words, it's a location within your system that won't be hampered by system capacity demands anytime soon, as improvements are completed at other locations in the system. Second, it should be a process located at or near the end of the system in question. The reason for this is that you want to actively track work that is about to exit the system, and not work that has been measured early on, but then gets caught in a rework cycle or worse yet, gets scrapped. With this single-point concept, the single process can be used to control the system, monitor the system, and create performance metrics for the entire system. This concept becomes especially important when the system is undergoing the implementation of improvements, especially during a Drum-Buffer-Rope implementation.

As the single-point measurement location, the *control point* can be used to track both productivity and financial measures. The bottom line is that it's a single pulse point to measure the health and wellness of your system. There is no need to wait until the end of the month or the quarter to determine how good or bad your system might be performing. With a control point, you should have key information supplied daily to show how your system is performing, according to your plan.

## Productivity and Financial Measures

Productivity can be measured in terms of throughput based on the number of units that pass through your control point. As long as work passes through the control point, your productivity measure will remain accurate, provided that it is not recycled back through the system as rework. When the product becomes throughput, then the financial measures can also be calculated. There is a simple and robust tool that can be used to measure the financial performance of your system. This simple concept is known as on-the-line charting. Figure 15.5 provides an example of an on-the-line chart, showing a random twenty-day period.

This chart is constructed using calculations based on the Throughput Accounting (TA) formula for Operating Expenses (OE) and Throughput (T) dollars. In Figure 15.5, you are looking at a twenty-day period of time, with each day having an Operating Expense (OE) of $1,000. The OE becomes cumulative through time to express the OE for each day in a month. The Throughput (T) is derived from the calculation of Selling Price (SP) – Total Variable Costs (TVC), or:

$$T = SP - TVC$$

The Net Profit (NP) is derived from the calculation of Throughput minus Total Operating Expenses, or NP = T – OE. If the financial performance of the plant is based on these calculations, then when Throughput is above the

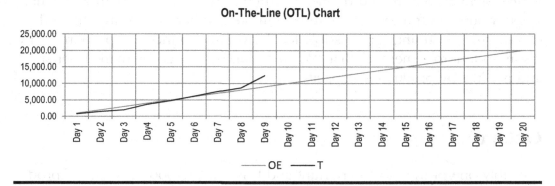

**Figure 15.5**

line, the company is making money; in other words, when NP = T − OE is seen as being positive and your company is making money. On the other hand, if the Throughput is below the OE line, then the company is not making money. In fact, you are not even making enough to cover your OE costs. As long as the Throughput line is above the OE line, then you are making money and the higher the Throughput is above the OE line, the more money you are making.

This chart could be used on a daily basis by a company owner, operations manager, or production manager to determine if there are gaps between T and OE that need attention. One key benefit of this method is that it is no longer required to wait until the end of the month or end of the quarter to get a report from Cost Accounting, to determine whether you are making money. You will have the necessary information to make good decisions daily about adjustments that might be required.

## The Concept of VOLT

With all of this discussion about Drum-Buffer-Rope, and setting up a system to operate at an optimized level, it's important to have a discussion about VOLTS. No, VOLTS in this case is not referring to something electrical. VOLT, in this case, is an acronym for Volume, Octane, and Lead Time. Let's define each of the individual components of VOLT in more detail.

## Volume

Volume refers to the amount of product and product mix moving through your system as determined by the constraint. The constraint output is equal to the volume output of the entire system. Remember, if you find, fix and elevate the constraint, it is possible for the volume to increase proportionally. It's important to remember that "Volume" can be limited by market demand and not just by production capacity.

## Octane

Probably one of the most important and least understood concepts of product pricing is the product *octane*. Different products will have different product octane ratings. The product octane is calculated based on the overall selling price (SP) minus total variable costs (TVC). The difference between these numbers is the product throughput or, in this case, product octane. Throughput is determined to be the dollar value after the total variable costs have been subtracted from the selling price of each unit (T = SP − TVC). In this case, the Octane is equal to the Throughput. As an example, suppose you have a product "A" that sells for $10.00 and it has a TVC of $6.00, then the Octane is equal to $4.00 or 40%. If you have a second product "B" and it sells for $11.50, and has a TVC of $6.00 (same as product "A"), then the Octane rating is equal to $5.50 or 47.8%. If the constraint time is equal for both products, then product "B" will make the most money in the same time period.

However, if there is a constraint utilization time difference, and product "B" takes longer than product "A" to produce, then product "A" will become the product of choice to push with regard to sales. Cost Accounting (CA) thinking will point you in the opposite direction because it would say that product "B" is the better product to produce, simply because it has a higher margin. However, CA does not consider constraint production time and its effect on making money, whereas Throughput Accounting does!

Octane becomes an extremely important number to understand simply because Net Profit (NP) is determined when the total Operating Expense (OE) is subtracted from the total Throughput (T) value (NP = T − OE). If operating expense is fairly constant through time (and it usually is), then the amount of NP will increase if the Throughput number increases. The greater the Throughput numbers, when Operating Expenses are subtracted, then the greater the profit margin.

Many organizations believe and follow the principle and business model that "any work is good work!" They assume this because CA implies you should make money on all of the work you do. The bottom line is that, if capacity is finite, which products should you spend your time making? When you evaluate products in terms of their Octane rating, it becomes painfully obvious which product mix is the most likely contributor toward higher Throughput dollars and correspondingly higher NP.

It is very possible that some of your products may be consuming large amounts of constraint time, but yield only minimal Throughput in terms of dollars. And there may be other products that zoom through the constraint quickly, but don't seem to offer nearly the margins of other products. If you were looking strictly on the surface, and using the CA mentality, then these lower-margin products might be the products you would consider avoiding.

However, it is highly recommended that you look again and determine constraint time and product Octane values.

## Lead Time

In conjunction with Volume and Octane, consider the Lead Time through your system. How fast does it move from start to finish? If Drum-Buffer-Rope is in place and the rule of subordination is followed, then product should move quickly through your manufacturing system. Fast-moving products with higher Volumes and an exceptional Octane rating can be a gold mine. Don't make these decisions based on the traditional Cost Accounting rules because it will most likely point you in the wrong direction. Be bold and consider the VOLT concept. Let's now look in the next chapter at key performance metrics that companies must consider as they progress through their improvement efforts.

How you measure your company's performance is critical to your success in terms of profitability. In the next chapter, I will discuss performance metrics in detail and lay out which metrics are key to your success.

## Reference

1. *Epiphanized – A Novel on Unifying Theory of Constraints, Lean, and Six Sigma*, CRC Press, 2015.

# Chapter 16

# Drum-Buffer-Rope (DBR)

In their book *The Goal* Dr Eliyahu Goldratt and Jeff Cox effectively use a story, written in a business novel format, to walk the reader through the steps necessary to move a manufacturing organization from the traditional manufacturing concepts to a facility managed using the concepts of Drum-Buffer-Rope (DBR). This non-traditional approach, through logical thinking, is the masterpiece of a character named Jonah. Jonah is able to help Alex Rogo, a general manager of a manufacturing company, understand the incorrect thinking and assumptions being used to manage his plant and the negative consequences associated with that type of thinking. By helping Alex focus his thinking on how the plant is being managed, Jonah helps Alex logically discover a new and better way to schedule and run his organization. Drum-Buffer-Rope (DBR) is the centerpiece of this process.

The thinking behind Drum-Buffer-Rope (DBR) is not only simple, but it is also very logical. And while thinking logically isn't anything new, it is *not* the way that most people think. The fundamental view of DBR is to focus on the entire system, rather than on only a single piece of the system, at least until you have clearly identified your system constraint. This idea of looking at the *global system* is really a major shift in the way systems have previously been understood and managed. Prior to global systems thinking, the predominant point of view was that any system's improvement, at any location, would improve the overall system. The basic idea of this thinking was that the sum total of the isolated improvements would somehow equal a corresponding improvement to the entire system. But, I assure you, such

DOI: 10.4324/9781003462385-16

is not the case. The effects of employing the "shotgun approach" to systems management typically results in a series of disturbing systemic effects.

The definition of a system, as explained in Chapter 11, is a sequence of steps or processes that are somehow linked together to produce *something* as an end result. The System Test told us that systems must have a well-defined purpose, elements, and a clear understanding of how these elements are interconnected. With that definition in mind, it's easy to understand how virtually everything can be linked to some kind of system. Engineering organizations have systems, banks have systems, hospitals have systems, and even grocery stores have systems. Almost anything you can think of is the product of some kind of system, provided it passes the System Test.

By design, a system can be as small and unique as two processes linked together, where the output of one process becomes the input for the next process.On the other hand, systems can be very complex, with many steps or processes linked together to generate a product or deliver a service. Having said this, it's important to understand that, just because a system is complex, does not mean that it can't be improved: it just means it's complicated. Even in a system as simple as two linked processes, most of the time, one of those two processes will constrain the other. It's just the nature of how things work.

Think about what the concept of a system constraint actually means. If the system's constraints did not exist, then theoretically the system should be able to produce at an infinite capacity. But infinite capacity is not the level that is ever achieved from a system, simply because all systems contain constraints. *All* systems are limited at some point in time, by some type of output limitation or system constraint. No matter how good the system is, there is still only so much it can do. And sooner or later, whatever kind of system you're looking at or studying, it will reach its maximum system capacity and be unable to produce more. If a higher system output is required, then it should be clear that the system in question must be changed.

## Managing Variation with Drum-Buffer-Rope

When viewing a system through the eyes of Drum-Buffer-Rope (DBR), it quickly becomes evident that improving every step in the process is not required. Nor will the sum total of all of the system improvements necessarily equal an improved system overall. When conducting a full systems analysis, with your intent to implement DBR, one very important consideration to understand is the actual location of the *system constraint*. As Goldratt explained in his famous Five Focusing Steps, this is Step 1: identify the current constraint. Once you know where the slowest operation is located, you now have the information necessary to know where to focus your improvement efforts within the system. Why is it important to understand where the slowest operation is? Because this is the location that controls and determines the output for your entire system. In essence, the entire system will produce no faster than the slowest operation can produce.

With the constraining operation now identified, you will have identified the *drumbeat* for your entire system. Knowing the drum beat is of strategic importance when implementing any improvements to your system. The drum, or system constraint, also provides you with the necessary information in terms of knowing where the focal point for your improvement efforts should be. Many organizations conduct countless improvement projects in the mistaken belief that their organization should attempt to improve every process, the thought being that each process step should be improved at some level of frequency in order to make the whole system better. It's important to understand that the sum of many efforts does not equal improvements to your system output.

The problem with this type of reasoning, in which each step or process is optimized, is that it is a totally unfocused *shotgun approach* to improvement. In effect, it presents an improvement policy that believes that, if you select a wide enough range of improvements, then you should eventually hit the target, or at least come close to it. When you take the shotgun approach, you might hit everything a little bit but still miss the full impact required to make the substantial changes resulting in overall improvement. If your shotgun approach includes trying to improve non-constraints, as many do, then the system as a whole gains nothing or, at most, very little! At least, any improvement will not be equal to the level of resource involvement you might have expected.

Attempts to make improvements to non-constraints in isolation, without an all-inclusive systems analysis, is just another way of dealing with symptoms of a problem and not the real issue, which is ultimately the system constraint. Without the necessary information needed to focus on the real issue, the disorder goes merrily along without the improvements you had hoped you would get. Improvement of non-constraints is certainly a noble gesture, but one that yields little, if any, real improvements to the overall system. Not every process within a system needs to be improved at the same time, meaning that some system processes are more important than others.

Without knowing where your system constraint is located, your efforts to improve everything will be unfocused, and, many times, not worth the effort. This kind of effort only serves to consume large amounts of time, money, and resources without the payback that you wanted or at least hoped for.

Once the systems constraint has been identified, you must realize that, essentially, nothing else in your system is more important than the constraint! As soon as you have this important bit of information at your disposal, your next job is to develop a plan on how to best exploit and manage the system constraint. Think about it. If the output of your entire system is completely dependent on the output of the constraint, then doesn't it make sense that you should only focus your efforts there? Having said this, if you had a quality or downtime problem in other steps, you certainly can't ignore them. The bottom line is that what's in front of you is to decide just how best to *exploit* the system constraint. Exploitation simply means that you must evaluate the process to get the most out of the weakest link, your system constraint.

It's important for you to understand that typically the constraint is not being utilized at or near its full potential. The exploitation effort typically involves looking for those things that the constraints can either stop doing or reduce the time it takes to complete them. Every time the constraint can stop doing something that takes away valuable production time, it is an opportunity to increase the constraint's output proportionally. This could be an excellent opportunity to employ the Interference Diagram (ID) that we discussed in Chapter 13, in order to define those key interferences that prevent you from getting more from your constraint. For example, you may want to implement Lean concepts to reduce waste and/or Six Sigma to reduce and better control variation and improve quality.

Like our examples in the previous chapters, it might mean taking actions like keeping the machine or process busy during breaks and lunchtime, using overtime, or off-loading work to the non-constraints. It's also very important for you to understand that exploiting the current constraint *does not* mean going out and buying a new machine or even adding more resources, at least not yet. It simply means that you need to find new ways to get more out of the constraint operation than you are currently getting, without spending lots of money to do so.

There's a very good chance that during the exploitation phase of Goldratt's Five Focusing Steps, the constraint capacity will have improved beyond the capacity of the next constraint in the system. If this happens, you simply go back to Step 1 and identify the new constraint. In a typical improvement effort, it's not unusual for this cycle between Steps 1 and 2 to be repeated many times before the system has fully stabilized. When the system does stabilize, it's time to go to Step 3 of the Five Focusing Steps: *subordination.*

*Subordination* simply means that all non-constraint process steps that feed the constraint should produce at the same rate as the system constraint and never out-pace it. Achieving system subordination will stabilize and synchronize the flow of product through the entire process and, ultimately, the system. One of the key benefits of subordinating the non-constraints to the constraint is that you will avoid generating mountains of work-in-process (WIP) inventory, which needlessly ties up cash and ultimately extends the overall cycle time. What you must do is to have the non-constraints work as required to produce just enough quantities to keep the constraint busy all of the time and never let it sit idle

As I just explained, it is vital to make sure the constraint is busy *all the time* simply because, as the constraint stops or slows down, the entire system will stop or slow down proportionally. The best way to accomplish this objective is to make sure there is always work to perform in front of the constraint. One of the most effective ways to do this is to create a *buffer* of work in front of the constraint. This buffer can be in the form of either time or physical inventory or a combination of both. The bottom line is to think in terms of the right amount of work, in the right location, at the right time. The system constraint not only determines and controls the amount of throughput through your system, but it also determines the correct amount of WIP inventory that should be maintained within your system. The correct inventory level will be reached almost by default when system subordination is activated.

The *rope* portion of Drum-Buffer-Rope is the alert mechanism that controls two distinctly different functions. First, it determines how much and when to release inventory into the system. The most common practice is to tie an artificial "rope" from the constraint operation back to the front of the line to know when to release raw materials into the first step in the process. When the constraint produces and completes one unit of work, and passes it to the next operation, the rope is then pulled to signal the front end of the line to release one more unit of work into the system. The rope signal is quite simply equal to the output of the constraint operation. This release mechanism is tied to the drumbeat of the constraint and will allow for a synchronized flow of work and a smooth transition of work through the entire system.

The second function of the rope is to initiate, control, and maintain subordination for *all* other steps contained within the process. By default, following the pace of the rope release signal will automatically result in subordination of the non-constraint processes. The non-constraint processes can only work on what has been released to work, so, by releasing work only to the drumbeat of the constraint, all other operations are held in check to the rule of subordination. Even if the non-constraints can do more work, they are restricted by subordination and only permitted to work on parts or products that are required by the constraint.

The system's inventory not only includes the work located in the *buffer* but also the total of all inventory at other process steps. I always recommend that you should establish an additional buffer at the shipping location. The shipping buffer is needed to help control any system variation that might occur beyond the system constraint. For example, if the process step receiving output from the constraint develops a quality problem or downtime, there is a high probability that shipments will be late.

The constraint buffer provides the necessary protection in front of the constraint, whereas the shipping buffer provides protection after the constraint. The shipping buffer is simply a mechanism that will absorb and manage the inevitable variation that will most likely occur. Buffer sizing at these two locations is a variable, but consider it as a starting point for the buffer in front of the constraint, to be about one and a half (1.5×) of whatever units of time you are measuring. Let's look at an example.

For example, if your constraint can produce ten units of product in one day, then your buffer should be set at fifteen units (i.e., $10 \times 1.5 = 15$). In time, you may decide that the buffer is too large or even too small, so you will be able to adjust the buffer size either up or down depending on your need and how well the system is flowing. The shipping buffer should be three or four days or perhaps even a bit less, depending on the speed of product through your system and the reliability of process steps after the constraint. It doesn't need to be large in quantity or long in time, but rather it simply needs to be sufficient to protect against the inevitable variation that could occur after the constraint.

It's also important to consider your shipping buffer time in your scheduling calculation to determine the correct release date into the system for on-time delivery. If you watch your buffer locations carefully, you will be able to make good decisions on whether to either increase or decrease them based on historical data, such as on-time shipments and deliveries to your customer base. The rules are very simple. If your buffer is constantly on the high end with the build-up of excess inventory, then reduce it. By contrast, if your buffer is constantly running out of product, then increase it. Common sense rules and data should be followed to determine the correct buffer size.

When you know and understand the constraint location, and you buffer the work activity correctly and send the correct release signal to the front of the line to release more work, then you have, in essence, implemented a system of *synchronized flow*. Figure 16.1 defines Drum-Buffer-Rope's basic steps and integration.

With a synchronized flow and actively implementing system subordination, there is a very high probability that the performance metric *efficiency* will deteriorate, at least for some period of time. If you are using Cost Accounting to make your financial decisions, this will result in an unacceptable level of your efficiency performance metric. The resulting message from leadership will probably be to, "Stop this synchronization nonsense in order to improve the efficiency." In reality, you must be very careful when you consider this to be nonsense. In this case, the real nonsense is using efficiency to measure non-constraint productivity. When the synchronized flow is implemented, excess capacity at non-constraints will be the result, at least for some period of time. Based on the efficiency metric, it will appear that everything is falling apart and that you are headed in the wrong direction. But trust me, through time, the new system reality and thinking will expose

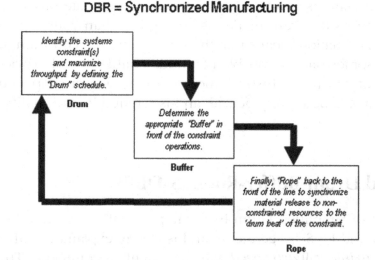

Figure 16.1

new evidence about what is actually happening in your system. In fact, your new reality will be throughput rates increasing, lead times through your system decreasing, WIP inventory decreasing, on-time delivery rates improving, and ultimately profit levels increasing to new levels.

If you consider these results to be nonsense, then think of the possible consequences if you return to the "high efficiency" metric. Throughput rates will decrease, lead times through the system will become extended, WIP inventory will increase, on-time delivery will deteriorate, and profit levels will return to the old levels. So, be careful when answering the question about which one of these methods is really the nonsensical approach.

## Types of Constraints

Constraints exist as basically one of two types. The first type of constraint is an *internal constraint*, which simply means that the market demand for your product is higher than the capacity of your system to satisfy the demand. Customers want more of what you have to offer, but unfortunately you're unable to produce enough to satisfy this high level of demand. If you can't come up with a way to satisfy your market demand, then your competitors will frequently figure out a way to do it and you will end up losing potential sales. This is an ideal situation for implementing the traditional Drum-Buffer-Rope (DBR) to meet the demand and, ultimately, capture more market share.

The second type of constraint is an *external constraint*, which means that the market demand is less than your capacity to generate product. In simple terms, this means that your market is buying less than your capacity to produce. This situation means that there is no internal constraint to contend with, so it's somewhat improbable that traditional DBR will provide relief to this kind of constraint. Instead, there is a modified or simplified form of DBR which might be more practical, and is referred to as Simplified DBR or S-DBR.

## Simplified Drum-Buffer-Rope (S-DBR)

The concept of Simplified Drum-Buffer-Rope (S-DBR) was developed by Bill Dettmer and Eli Schragenheim, and is clearly explained in their book [1] *Manufacturing at Warp Speed*, which I highly recommend! The basic concept behind S-DBR is that the constraint is external to your system and therefore resides in the market segment. S-DBR also assumes that significant variation exists in the market demand, which causes the system constraint to fluctuate back and forth between internal to external locations. This fluctuation between internal and external constraints can cause chaos in deciding which market segments should be pursued and which ones might be better left alone.

In the situation of an external constraint, the *drum* is determined and activated only when the system has firm orders in place. The *rope* is determined by the orders that actually exist, which are released based on customer due dates. If the orders exceed the capacity of the system, then the constraint has moved back to being internal and different actions need to be taken. This also assumes that the internal constraint will exist for only short periods of time and can be overcome with actions like implementing short-term overtime. Dettmer and Schagenheim have argued, quite successfully, that the market is the true constraint of any system.

## Multiple Drum-Buffer-Rope (M-DBR)

There is another unique situation that can require the implementation of a third type of DBR, which Bruce Nelson and I refer to as Multiple Drum-Buffer-Rope (M-DBR). The situation for M-DBR is created when a single buffer location is required to supply products (or services) to more than one assembly or service line, and each assembly or service has its own drum that is reacting to orders at a different pace. Figure 16.2 is an example of what an M-DBR configuration might look like. This figure depicts an actual maintenance operation on multiple aircraft that Bruce Nelson and I were charged with improving.

In the case of M-DBR, the drum is the length of time required to repair each aircraft, whereas the buffer is equal to the number of aircraft waiting to enter the repair system. Each hangar repairs the same type of aircraft, with the difference being the duration of the repair cycle time. Some will be faster and some will be slower, depending on the type of repair required. It's the total repair time duration that determines the drumbeat in each "I" line. Aircraft waiting in the buffer would be required to have the repair problem isolated to some reasonable level and be fully ready to enter with the necessary repair parts in place, as well as the ability to move aircraft in and out of the hangar and a crew waiting and ready to perform the repair.

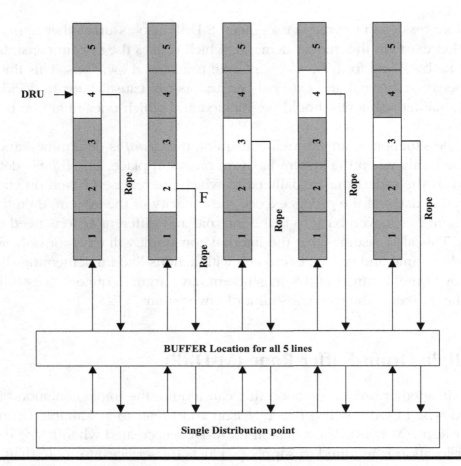

**Figure 16.2**

Figure 16.3 is another example of an M-DBR configuration, with this example being from a hospital Emergency Department. Patients enter the Emergency Department into a triage area and are either treated and released, or they are admitted into the hospital for additional treatment. In this case, the hospital has a buffer of patients waiting to be admitted. The time buffer is based on the estimated time to complete treatment of the current patient. The drum, in this case, is represented by the hospital beds, whereas the rope is the signal that another bed is available.

Another example might be a Surface Mount Technology (SMT) machine that is required to make different types of circuit cards for different assemblies, and each circuit card assembly flows down different assembly lines. It's similar to moving from the apex of an "A" plant into the base of a "V" plant, with different parts now required for a number of different "I" lines. The drumbeat for each "I" line will vary, but each line requires input from

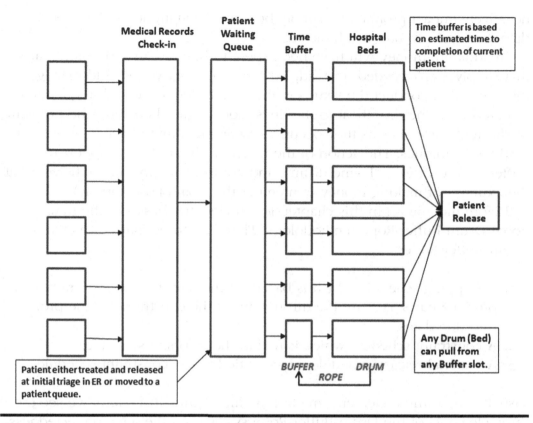

**Figure 16.3**

a single SMT machine or a series of SMT machines. For those of you not familiar with the different plant types, I recommend reviewing Chapter 15.

When multiple drums exist, as in M-DBR, there are also multiple ropes, with each have distinctly different requirements. In fact, there are two signal points for the multiple ropes. The first rope signals back to the buffer to release more work for that particular line, while the second rope goes directly back to the SMT machine to support the needs of the buffer, which then releases work at the front of the SMT line. The advantage of this concept is to reduce the tendency for economic batch size quantity at the SMT.

Many organizations incorrectly believe that, when they set up a machine to make parts, they should make as many parts as possible, especially if the machine is expensive or the setup times are extremely long. The thought that this economic batch size quantity somehow saves money simply defies logic. The reality is that the economic batch size will serve only to reduce the throughput through the system and needlessly tie up cash. The economic reality is that no money has been saved at all! The fact is that it will negatively impact profitability simply because throughput will have been damaged and revenue will be lost.

In addition, money will have been spent to buy raw materials and parts that simply aren't needed. Instead, I recommend that you should manage the constraint, conduct the setups in the correct sequence and frequency required from the drumbeat in the lines. You should then solve the problem of shorter setup times as they occur, using Single Minute Exchange of Dies (SMED) techniques. The action of the machine should be to support the buffer for the various "I" line drums, and not to maintain "high efficiency" at the expense of making money (remember the Goal of a company).

Before moving on in this chapter, let's review the basics of the traditional Drum-Buffer-Rope methodology. There are three main elements of Drum-Buffer-Rope:

1. A shipping schedule which is based on the rate that the constraint can produce parts; i.e., use the throughput of the constraint for the promised due dates.
2. A constraint schedule which is tied to the shipping schedule.
3. A material release schedule which is tied to the constraint schedule.

Visually, these three elements might look like Figure 16.4. Here, we see the three elements of the Drum-Buffer-Rope system and the interconnectedness of each one. The drum sets the pace of the production line and its capacity is, hopefully, greater than the number of orders in the system. In order to satisfy the shipping schedule, we must first fulfill the constraint schedule. In order to meet the constraint schedule, we must satisfy the material release schedule. Failure to release materials according to the schedule will jeopardize the constraint schedule, which will, in turn, jeopardize your shipping schedule. Because of this linkage of schedules, managing the buffers becomes critical!

## The Total View

Even with all the improvements that can be realized with a synchronized flow, using traditional DBR, S-DBR or even M-DBR, there can also be some problems related to these achievements, especially with traditional DBR. When you follow Goldratt's Five Focusing Steps, it is possible that, during Step 2 (i.e., decide how to exploit the system constraint), a constraint can be

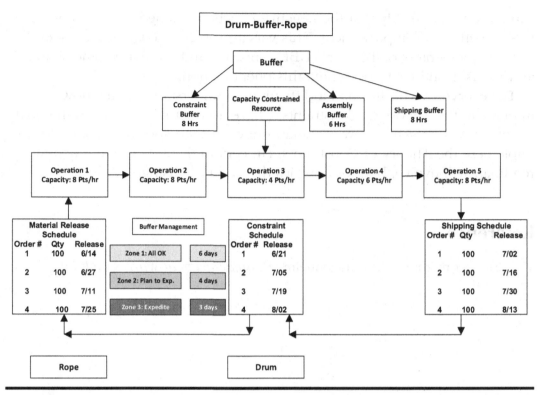

**Figure 16.4**

improved to the point that it is no longer the constraint, and, at times, this can happen very quickly. When it does happen, you have essentially *rolled* the constraint to a new location, which means you only just finished Step 2 before it is now time to go back to Step 1 again.

The original system process that was considered to be the constraint today is no longer the constraint tomorrow. These types of rapid system improvements can obviously cause some problems. When a new constraint is identified within the system, then the system effectively has a new drumbeat. When that happens, you have to move the buffer location to reside in front of the new constraint. In addition, you will need to move the rope signal to this new location, back to the release point at the front of the line. In some systems, it's possible that you will need to roll the constraint several times, to several different locations, before an acceptable level of system stability is achieved.

This fast action of fixing and rolling the constraint can and does cause a certain amount of chaos in a system. Workers will quickly become confused and ask the question, "Where is the constraint today?" Improvements can happen so quickly that the negative effects of change will outweigh the positive effects of improvement. This was a problem recognized early on by some implementers of TOC and DBR concepts, and there are some simple and robust solutions to overcome this phenomenon.

For everyone who has had a difficult time understanding just how to implement the Theory of Constraints, I have a new tool for you. In the next chapter I will present a new roadmap I have created specifically for how to implement the Theory of Constraints. I'm certain that, over time, my new roadmap will evolve, but, for now, it's the one I am using.

# Reference

1. Bill Dettmer and Eli Schragenheim, *Manufacturing at Warp Speed*, CRC Press, 2000.

# Chapter 17

# The Theory of Constraints Roadmap

Much has been written over the years about the Theory of Constraints and how to implement it. Even for myself, when I first learned about the basics of the Theory of Constraints, I had wished that there would have been a step-by-step procedure on how to implement it, a sort of "roadmap," if you will. Well, for all of you who have had the same wish, this chapter is for you. Figure 17.1 is my version of the Theory of Constraints roadmap, which, hopefully, will make life easier for all of you who wanted to see something like this when you first heard about the Theory of Constraints.

In this version of my roadmap, there are seven major sections and eighteen individual steps. The seven major steps are as follows:

1. Define the span of control, sphere of influence, and goal.
2. Identify the system constraint.
3. Decide how to exploit the system constraint.
4. Subordinate everything to the constraint.
5. If necessary, elevate the constraint.
6. When your current constraint is broken, return to Step 3 to identify your new system constraint.
7. Seek more business to satisfy your new capacity.

Let's now walk through the eighteen individual steps of this roadmap to define the necessary actions you must take to successfully implement the

DOI: 10.4324/9781003462385-17

## Theory of Constraints Implementation Roadmap

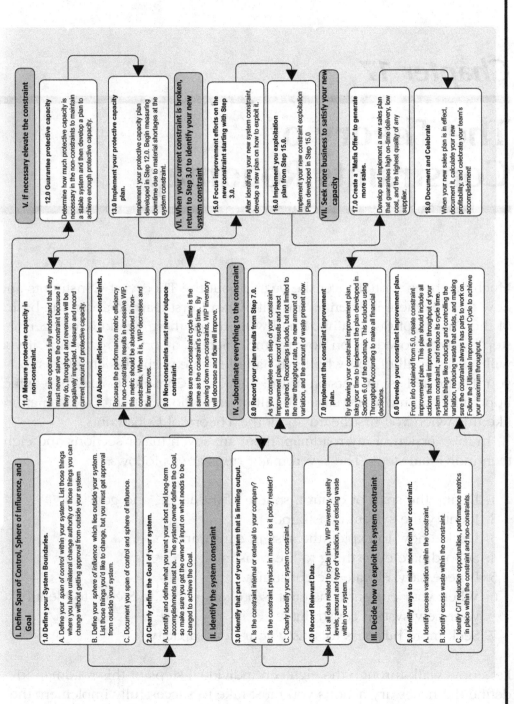

**I. Define Span of Control, Sphere of Influence, and Goal**

**1.0 Define your System Boundaries.**

A. Define your *span of control* within your system. List those things where you have unilateral change authority or those things you can change without getting approval from outside your system

B. Define your *sphere of influence* which lies outside your system. List those things you'd like to change, but you must get approval from outside your system.

C. Document you span of control and sphere of influence.

**2.0 Clearly define the Goal of your system.**

A. Identify and define what you want your short and long-term accomplishments must be. The system owner defines the Goal, so make sure you get the owner's input on what needs to be changed to achieve the Goal.

**II. Identify the system constraint**

**3.0 Identify that part of your system that is limiting output.**

A. Is the constraint internal or external to your company?

B. Is the constraint physical in nature or is it policy related?

C. Clearly identify your system constraint.

**4.0 Record Relevant Data.**

A. List all data related to cycle time, WIP inventory, quality levels, amount and type of variation, and existing waste within your system.

**III. Decide how to exploit the system constraint**

**5.0 Identify ways to make more from your constraint.**

A. Identify excess variation within the constraint.

B. Identify excess waste within the constraint.

C. Identify C/T reduction opportunities, performance metrics in place within the constraint and non-constraints.

**11.0 Measure protective capacity in non-constraint.**

Make sure operators fully understand that they must never starve the constraint because if they do, throughput and revenues will be negatively impacted. Measure and record current amount of protective capacity.

**10.0 Abandon efficiency in non-constraints.**

Because the performance metric efficiency in non-constraints results in excessive WIP, this metric should be abandoned in non-constraints. When it is, WIP decreases and flow improves.

**9.0 Non-constraints must never outpace constraint.**

Make sure non-constraint cycle time is the same as the constraint's cycle time. By slowing down non-constraints, WIP inventory will decrease and flow will improve.

**IV. Subordinate everything to the constraint**

**8.0 Record your plan results from Step 7.0.**

As you complete each step of your constraint Improvement plan, record results and react as required. Recordings include, but not limited to the new throughput rate, the new amount of variation, and the amount of waste present now.

**7.0 Implement the constraint improvement plan.**

By following your constraint improvement plan, take your time to implement the plan developed in Section 6.0 of the roadmap. This includes using Throughput Accounting to make all financial decisions.

**6.0 Develop your constraint improvement plan.**

From info obtained from 5.0, create constraint improvement plan. This plan should include all actions that will improve the throughput of your system constraint, and reduce its cycle time. Include things like reducing and controlling the variation, reducing waste that exists, and making sure the constraint always has parts to work on. Follow the Ultimate Improvement Cycle to achieve your maximum throughput.

**V. If necessary elevate the constraint**

**12.0 Guarantee protective capacity**

Determine how much protective capacity is necessary in the non-constraints to maintain a stable system and then develop a plan to achieve enough protective capacity.

**13.0 Implement your protective capacity plan.**

Implement your protective capacity plan developed in Step 12.0. Begin measuring downtime due to material shortages at the system constraint.

**VI. When your current constraint is broken, return to Step 3.0 to identify your new system constraint**

**15.0 Focus improvement efforts on the new constraint starting with Step 3.0.**

After identifying your new system constraint, develop a new plan on how to exploit it.

**16.0 Implement you exploitation plan from Step 15.0.**

Implement your new constraint exploitation Plan developed in Step 15.0

**VII. Seek more business to satisfy your new capacity**

**17.0 Create a "Mafia Offer" to generate more sales.**

Develop and implement a new sales plan that guarantees high on-time delivery, low cost, and the highest quality of any supplier.

**18.0 Document and Celebrate**

When your new sales plan is in effect, document it, calculate your new profitability, and celebrate your team's accomplishment!

## Figure 17.1

Theory of Constraints. I might add that like my other roadmaps, I'm sure, over time, that it will evolve.

## Step 1: Define your System Boundaries

In this step, there are three actions that you must complete as you work to implement the Theory of Constraints within your organization. The three steps include:

A. Define your *span of control* within your system. In other words, list those things where you have unilateral change authority or those things you can change without getting approval from outside your system.
B. Define your *sphere of influence* which lies outside your system. List those things you'd like to change, but you must get approval from outside your system before you can implement them.
C. Document your span of control and sphere of influence for future reference.

It's very important to clearly define your span of control and sphere of influence simply because those issues that fall within your span of control are relatively easy to resolve, but those within your sphere of influence will most likely be somewhat more difficult to address and resolve. As you will also learn, you may have no impact on those issues outside your sphere of influence. My advice is to take your time when addressing these issues.

## Step 2: Clearly Define the Goal of Your System

In this step, I recommend identifying and clearly defining what you want your short- and long-term accomplishments to be. Keep in mind that it's the responsibility of the system owner to define the Goal, so make sure you get the owner's input on the Goal so that you can clearly define what needs to be changed to achieve the Goal of your system.

[1] Bill Dettmer, in his classic book, *The Logical Thinking Process – A Systems Approach to Complex Problem Solving*, tells us that

> Determining what needs changing requires that we first know
> what we're trying to achieve – where we want to be when all is

said and done. Or as Steven Covey suggests, 'Begin with the end in mind.'

Dettmer further explains that there is a simple reason for doing this.

> The desire to change something stems from dissatisfaction with the current situation. Dissatisfaction, in turn, grows from the perception of a gap between what *is* and what *should be*. Before we can legitimately criticize what is, it's essential for us to have a clear impression of what *should be* – in other words, our system's goal.

I couldn't agree more with Bill Dettmer! Bill also explains,

> By definition, a goal is an end to which a system's collective efforts are directed. To that extent, it might be considered a destination of sorts. A destination naturally implies a journey across the aforementioned gap between where we are and where we want to be. In order to determine the size of the gap, and the direction of the correction needed, agreement on the system's goal is essential.

We now move to Section 2 of the roadmap, which tells us to identify the system constraint. This is perhaps the most important step in our roadmap, simply because it sets the stage for improvements needed to reach the Goal of the system. This is especially true if the Goal of the system is tied to your company's profit levels.

## Step 3: Identify the System Constraint

In this step, there are three actions/questions that must be completed/ answered which are:

A: Is the constraint *internal* or *external* to your company?

  Knowing whether your constraint lies within the boundaries of your company, or outside your company, is critical in determining the actions you will be taking as you move through this roadmap. The basic question that you must answer is: which is larger, *capacity* or *demand*? In other words, is your system capable of totally and immediately satisfying the demand being placed on it? If your system can't satisfy the demand placed on it, then your constraint is internal. If the system constraint is located within your company, then it implies that your current configuration is not supplying enough parts to fulfill your current orders. If this is the case, then you must work on increasing the capacity of your constraint.

On the other hand, if the constraint is external to your company, this typically means that you have more capacity than you have customer orders. If this is the case, you must work to differentiate your company from your competitors, in order to attract more customer orders. This would involve creating what Eli Goldratt referred to as a "Mafia Offer." Eli Goldratt defined a Mafia Offer as "an offer so good that your customers can't refuse it." It has also been referred to as an *unrefusable offer.* We'll discuss this concept in more detail later in this chapter.

B: Is the constraint *physical* in nature or is it *policy* related?

It's important to understand that most of the constraints we run into in our systems have policies as their origin and are not physical in nature. Actually, physical constraints are much easier to identify and break than those associated with policies. But, even though policy constraints are much more difficult to break, when they are broken, there's usually a much larger degree of system improvement obtained than with a physical constraint.

Knowing whether your constraint is internal or external will identify where you must focus your improvement efforts, but will also give you an idea of what you need to do. If your constraint is external, there's a high probability that it is related to an existing policy. On the other hand, if it's internal, it could be either physical or policy related.

C: Clearly identify your *system constraint.*

I have added this comment in the roadmap because you must clearly define your system constraint if you are to be successful in breaking it. Because of the level of importance of both B. and C, it is imperative that you take your time and clearly identify what your system constraint is. If it's a physical constraint, be very specific as to what part of your system it resides in. If it's a physical process, clearly state which process step it is, along with the corresponding cycle time. I also recommend that you identify and record the amount of work-in-process (WIP) inventory that currently exists.

If your system constraint is policy related, then clearly define and state which policy it is. For example, one of the common policy constraints that companies face is the mandate to measure efficiencies at each step of the process. Typically, companies that use efficiency as one of their performance metrics will attempt to drive it higher and higher and all this does is bog down the flow of product through the process and create mountains of work-in-process inventory.

## Step 4: Record Relevant Data

In this step, I explain that you should list all constraint data related to things like cycle time, work-in-process inventory, quality levels, defects, and rework, plus the amount and type of variation, and existing waste that is currently in your system constraint. I have added this step to prepare you for Step 5, where you will identify ways to make more from your current constraint. In collecting this information, you should be able to get a good idea of where and by how much you could increase the capacity of your system constraint.

## Step 5: Identify Ways to Make More from Your Constraint

One of the keys in this step is to discover what keeps your system from doing more. Think about it: if there was no constraint, then doesn't it make sense that your system could produce unlimited amounts of product? If you were to ask others why your system can't produce more, you would probably get a plethora of different reasons. My advice to you is to stay away from opinions and instead, go through your system and collect data.

In Step 5, one of the first things you should be doing is looking for and identifying excess variation that exists within your system constraint. Excessive variation can take the form of both rework and scrap, so, if these things exist, this is an opportunity for your process, and specifically your system constraint, to be producing at a higher rate. By the same token, look for excessive waste that is present within your constraint. Look for and record things like excessive wait times, excessive transportation, excess inventory, unnecessary motion, overprocessing, and overproduction. All of these and more sources of waste work to steal time away from your system constraint. In Step 5, I indicate that you should identify opportunities to reduce cycle time, but I also instruct you to record all constraint and non-constraint performance metrics that are in place. Incorrect performance metrics can have a negative impact on the output of your system.

## Step 6: Develop Your Constraint Improvement Plan

In this step, you now take all of the information collected in Step 5 and transform it into a plan to improve the output of your system constraint. This plan should include all actions that will reduce its cycle time, so as to improve the throughput of your system. Include things like reducing and controlling the variation, reducing any waste that exists, and making sure the constraint always has parts to work on.

In Step 6, I advise you to follow the Ultimate Improvement Cycle to develop your constraint improvement plan. In doing so, you will achieve your maximum throughput. This plan will include the integration of Lean Manufacturing, Six Sigma, and the Theory of Constraints. The impact of this integration will be a streamlined process or system with the ultimate outcome being maximized throughput. This integration will result in net profits beyond what you've ever seen in the past. In the next chapter, I go into detail on how to implement my Ultimate Improvement Cycle (UIC). In Chapter 16, you will see another new roadmap on my UIC, which will help you with this effort.

## Step 7: Implement the Constraint Improvement Plan

In Step 7, you should begin implementing the constraint improvement plan that you just developed in Step 6. My advice here is very simple and that is, take your time! Don't rush off in reckless abandon, trying to achieve quick results. One of the key actions you will undertake in this step is to abandon your current Cost Accounting system in terms of making real-time financial decisions. Because GAAP rules require that you report results based on the rules of Cost Accounting, you cannot abandon it completely, but you must use Throughput Accounting when you are forced to make real-time financial decisions. In several chapters of this book, I go into great detail on the benefits of using Throughput Accounting to make financial decisions, so review and learn the material before making this significant change.

## Step 8: Record Your Plan Results from Step 7

In this step, it is important to understand how well what you implemented in your constraint improvement plan is working. It's also very important that you make certain that you've successfully implemented Throughput Accounting and that your financial decisions are all being made on the basis of this new accounting methodology. Your recordings will include, but are not limited to, your new throughput rate, your new rate of variation, and the amount of waste that might still exist in your system. If you are to successfully continue to improve your throughput, you must take your time and do things correctly.

## Step 9: Non-constraints Must Never Outpace Your Constraint

In order to avoid excessive amounts of work-in-process (WIP) inventory, your non-constraints, that feed product into your constraint, must never outpace your constraint. This is the concept of *subordination*, which is Goldratt's third step of his five focusing steps. Excessive WIP inventory will only serve to "bog down" the flow of product through your processes which, in turn, extends the cycle time of your processes and system. And when processing times are extended, there are numerous negative side effects that will occur. If you have mountains of WIP inventory within your system, you will be tying up cash needlessly and running the risk of producing parts that could become obsolete in the future. Also, with excessive amounts of WIP inventory on hand, your on-time delivery will suffer as well. In Step 10, I will demonstrate the simplest and most effective way to "slow down" your process.

## Step 10: Abandon Efficiency in Non-constraints

Eli Goldratt coined the phrase, "Show me how you measure me, and I'll show you how I'll behave." Goldratt got it exactly right when he said this, especially as it applies to the performance metric "operator efficiency." If you are measuring operators on their ability to produce more and more product, the bottom line is that they will over-produce! And, while this may sound like good behavior, in reality, it is a negative behavior.

The goal of for-profit companies is to make money now and in the future, and measuring operator efficiency is counterproductive when this is a company's goal. Why, you may be wondering? When attempting to drive this metric higher in non-constraints, the output when using the performance metric efficiency results in over-production, causing excessive WIP inventory. And when this occurs, lead times become extended, unnecessary cash is tied up, throughput declines, and revenue decreases, all of which negatively impact profitability.

On the other hand, what happens when efficiency is measured only in the system constraint? Driving efficiency upward in the system constraint has several positive impacts. It significantly improves throughput and revenue, reduces operating expenses due to less WIP inventory, and, ultimately, profit margins are significantly improved! So, with these benefits in mind, doesn't it make sense to stop measuring efficiency and trying to drive it higher and higher in non-constraints?

## Step 11: Measure Protective Capacity in Non-constraints

Protective capacity represents the extra capacity at non-constraint resources, which is intended to absorb random disruptions in the planned level of performance so that the constraint is more effectively utilized. The placement of protective capacity has very little influence on your system's flow time, but it will guard against the bottleneck shifting to a new location. When there is high utilization/efficiency, it is necessary to place protective capacity both before and after the system constraint.

## Step 12: Guarantee Protective Capacity with Drum-Buffer-Rope and the TOC Replenishment Solution

In this step, you must determine how much protective capacity is necessary in the non- constraints, in order to to maintain a stable system, and then develop a plan to achieve enough protective capacity. One of the most effective ways to do this is through the use of TOC's scheduling system known as Drum-Buffer-Rope (DBR) in combination with TOC's replenishment solution. Drum-Buffer-Rope, which I presented in the previous chapter, is the Theory of Constraints scheduling process which is focused on increasing flow by identifying and leveraging the system constraint. DBR was developed by Dr. Eli Goldratt, who is widely recognized as the father of the Theory of Constraints. Even though I dedicated a previous chapter to DBR, let's now discuss the basics of DBR in this context.

If you've never read Goldratt and Cox's book, [3] *The Goal*, I strongly recommend that you get a copy. The book centers around a story of a plant manager who ends up applying the Drum-Buffer-Rope methodology. Figure 17.2 is a simple graphical image of the basic layout of a Drum-Buffer-Rope system that we discussed in Chapter 16. The layout of this process is a simple four-step process with the cycle times listed for each step. Raw material enters into Step 1, is processed for one day and then passes it on to Step 2. Step 2 processes the material for five days and then passes it on to Step 3. Step 3 takes eight days to process the semi-finished material before it passes it along to Step 4, which takes four days to complete.

Because Step 3 has the longest cycle time, it is the step that is limiting your output. Step 3 is recognized as the system constraint, or as it is also known, the *drum*. The constraint is referred to as the drum because it sets the pace for the entire operation. Remember, a constraint (drum) is any resource that has demand that is greater than its available capacity, and any time lost on the constraint is output lost by the entire system. So, if you increase the output of the constraint, the output for your entire system increases by the same amount.

Listed in Figure 17.2, you will see three different buffers, namely a *raw material buffer*, a *constraint buffer*, and a *shipping buffer*. The buffer is defined as a *period of time* to protect the drum resource from problems that might occur, either upstream or downstream, from the drum operation. Its effect is to synchronize the work as it flows through the process. In effect, the buffer acts to compensate for process variation that exists in all processes, and results in DBR schedules being very stable and somewhat immune to most problems. DBR has one additional effect, which is the elimination of the need for 100% accurate data for scheduling.

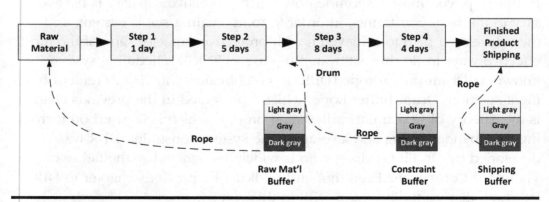

**Figure 17.2**

Since the buffer acts to aggregate variation, it results in much lower levels of work-in-process (WIP) inventory, which dramatically reduces the overall production lead times. In addition, because the WIP inventory is much lower, cash that was tied up as excess inventory is significantly reduced. Once the drum has been scheduled, raw material release and shipping are connected directly to it, using the buffer offset, as depicted in Figure 15.2. Material is released at the same rate as the drum can consume it, and orders are shipped at the rate that the drum produces.

The process of scheduling your facility first focuses on your primary objective, which is to ship based upon the delivery date to which you have committed. So, with this in mind, you must first determine the due date of the order, and then add a shipping buffer, which creates the needed confidence that you will ship on time. Once you know the planned finish date, you then backward schedule to recognize an "ideal" time to work on the drum resource. The drum is then forward scheduled to avoid potentially late jobs that must be identified. After the drum is scheduled, the operations after the drum are forward scheduled in time, from the drum completion date. The final step is that the jobs feeding the drum are backward scheduled from the start of the resource buffer.

So, how do you determine the size of these buffers? As depicted in Figure 17.2, these three buffers are divided into three different zones, namely light gray, gray, and dark gray. If the buffer zone is light gray, then no action needs to be taken. If the buffer falls into the gray zone, then you must prepare to take action, if necessary. If it falls into the dark gray zone, then appropriate action needs to happen. My recommendation is that the constraint buffer should be sized so that it turns dark gray no more than 5–10% of the time. My rule of thumb is that, if your buffer falls within the dark gray zone more than 10% of the time, then you should add more protective capacity at one or more of the non-constraints. On the other hand, if you never move into the dark gray zone, then you can reduce the size of your buffer, simply because you have more protective capacity than you really need.

The next buffer is the shipping buffer, which, as its name implies, is intended to protect the due date. The underlying purpose for this buffer is because your cycle times are just estimates, and, in many cases, they are incorrect. The bottom line is that there will be variability in every step in the process, but this buffer is based upon the variability of the drum or the constraint.

According to the Constraints Management Group, in their white paper entitled, [4] *About Drum-Buffer-Rope (DBR),*

Readers of *The Goal*, often have no problem acknowledging that the concepts in the book make a lot of sense. So why are these common-sense concepts so hard to implement in our operations? In our experience, the answer is often centered around people's inability to transfer the concepts from *The Goal* to their unique environment and effectively deal with an organization's resistance to change. There are three critical components in implementing DBR that overcome these problems:

1. The transfer of Drum-Buffer-Rope know-how.
2. The construction of a unique tailored Drum-Buffer-Rope system.
3. The transfer of thought process tools for effective problem-solving now and in the future.

So, let's dive into these three problems in more depth. And, again, this part is taken directly from the Constraints Management Group, in their white paper entitled, *About Drum-Buffer-Rope (DBR)*.

### 1. The Transfer of Drum-Buffer-Rope Know-How

Before a management team, as well as an organization, can be expected to put a Drum-Buffer-Rope (DBR) system in place, they must be effectively educated about what DBR really is and how to make decent operational decisions within its framework. Additionally, this is crucial for people that must later sell these concepts to others. How many times have you been forced to explain something that you did not fully understand? What were the results?

People have to realize that education is not enough. Too often, organizations stop here and expect results from their people or choose to purchase software with the expectation that they are now in a position to get results from it. How can a manufacturing team deliver results when there is no effective and comfortable blueprint for how the concepts specifically translate to their environment?

### 2. The Construction of a Unique, Tailored Drum-Buffer-Rope System

Once the education is provided, it must be used to unleash the intuition of an implementation team. In other words, the best people in the world to apply Drum-Buffer-Rope in your facility are sitting in your facility. First, the team must be educated and then their intuition must be organized to fully construct a robust blueprint for the system to make sense for and to them. This means the critical points that define their system must be fully defined, and measures and policies put in place to support their ability to make the right decisions at the operational level, whether it is around up-front scheduling or decisions around dealing with a crisis.

Without this critical step, they will struggle to implement anything lasting. Additionally, practical issues, including scheduling software options, must be addressed. At this point, the organization is able to make an informed choice about supporting software packages.

Think about where the implementation team will be at this point: knowledgeable about the concepts of DBR and, most importantly, about how those concepts specifically apply to the environment where they must make it work. Now, the team is in a much better position to clearly explain to its subordinates, as well as other functions within the organization, what the system is trying to do and what is expected from them and why. This is a recipe for breaking down people's resistance to change, the single biggest killer of any major improvement initiative. But ensuring initial implementation is not enough. To ensure long-term success, people must be left with the ability to innovate on top of and to improve the existing system.

### 3. The Transfer of Thought Process Tools for Effective Problem-Solving, Now and in the Future

An implementation team must have the ability to effectively deal with people's reservations around change. Often, the knowledge around the common-sense approaches and how they apply to the environment are enough, but what happens when someone raises a legitimate reservation that was not yet fully considered? We know that the people who run the environment every day have strong intuition and often their concerns are very legitimate. Do we scrap the plan? Of course not.

What we really need is for our implementation team to have the ability to understand these reservations, solicit or come up with comfortable solutions, and re-incorporate them back into the solution. Furthermore, we know the one thing in our environments that is a constant is change. Given that, we need to make sure that people have tools to evolve the system in the face of change. These tools will provide the common language, the DBR education, and the tailored solution to provide the framework in which to communicate. When those two things are present, an organization has the ability for rapid and robust solutions to changing conditions.

In addition to DBR, TOC offers a solution that will almost guarantee no stock-outs of raw materials, while at the same time reducing your raw material inventory by about 50%. Since this solution was already presented in Chapter 14, I won't go into it in detail, but it's important for you to understand that, when used in conjunction with Drum-Buffer-Rope, your throughput will rise to levels you've probably not experienced before.

The basic context of the TOC replenishment solution is that, rather than restocking raw materials based upon a forecast, the restocking happens based upon usage, i.e., you will re-order raw materials more frequently than you would with the traditional Min/Max system. And while it might seem that your shipping would increase significantly due to more orders, because you never have to worry about stock-outs that cause delays in production, the net financial gain is significant. My advice to you is to re-read Chapter 13 to get the details on how to implement this solution.

## Step 13: Implement Your Protective Capacity Plan

You are now ready to implement your protective capacity plan which takes the form of Drum-Buffer-Rope (DBR) coupled with TOC's replenishment solution. Just like any improvement plan, my advice is to not rush through the implementation of this key effort. The implementation of DBR and TOC's replenishment solution will clearly change the way that your organization operates and will lead you to levels of profitability that you haven't experienced before.

Your Buffer-Rope system is managed through its buffers and the buffers will tell you about the health of the system, as well as any individual operation, the status of a work order, and where to focus improvement. The buffer is sized according to variables including average process batch size, the rate and volume at which a batch can be transferred to the area to be buffered, the reliability of the processes in front of the buffered area, and the potential for other types of problems, such as stock-outs of raw materials. A company shouldn't debate for weeks and months calculating this number. Define what is good enough and go with it because it will change on you as you manage and adapt it.

To manage the buffer, you should divide it into three zones, as described in the previous step of the roadmap and, as in Figure 17.3, light gray, gray,

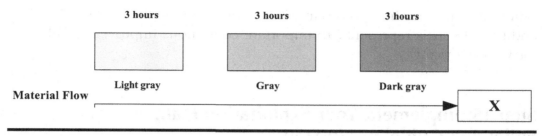

**Figure 17.3**

and dark gray. The zones are not always of equal size but, for demonstration purposes, they will be depicted as equal.

For our example we have defined a nine-hour buffer (i.e., three hours each for light gray, gray, and dark gray zones). Material flows to the constraint "X" from left to right. Light gray defines a time frame where we can expect a work order to begin queuing in front of the constraint (six to nine hours before it is being run). Light gray means things are going fine, you don't need to micromanage this order. When things don't show up in the buffer according to plan, we have what we call a "hole." If we don't see it with six hours left, we will penetrate into our gray zone, which is "watch and plan." Walk up the line, find the order, and see what the problem is. Begin to make your plans around ensuring that the constraint does not go down.

When you penetrate into the dark gray zone, act on your plans. If you are always living in the light gray zone, what do you know about your buffer? It is too large. Remember that smaller buffers reduce the amount of WIP and, with less WIP, lead time can be reduced. If you are living in the dark gray zone too often, what do you know about your buffer size? It is too small. Raise the level of inventory in the short term, identify the problematic upstream issue, and address it. This will allow you to reduce your buffer once the issue has been addressed. Thus, Buffer Management can provide the focus for things like SPC, Kaizen, and Lean tools.

## Step 14: Focus Improvement Efforts on the New Constraint Starting with Step 6 of the Roadmap

At this point in time, you will probably have "broken" your constraint and a new one will appear immediately. When this happens, return to Step 6 and develop your new constraint improvement plan. Because you have already completed this step at least once, the actions you take will be different from your first go-around. You then continue on to Steps 7, 8, 9, and then 15. This represents an important continuous improvement effort for your company.

## Step 15: Implement Your Exploitation Plan, Following Guidelines in Step 7

Just like you did earlier in Step 7, you now need to implement your "exploitation plan" for your new constraint. You will now see record levels of capacity, revenue, on-time delivery, and ultimately profit levels that you never dreamed possible. It is now time to go back to the marketplace and seek out new customers. You will be able to do this by creating something we referred to earlier in this chapter as a *Mafia Offer*. Think about what you've accomplished thus far. By following the steps outlined in this roadmap, you probably have metrics that are the best in the business and results that will surely attract many new orders.

## Step 16: Create a "Mafia Offer" to Generate More Sales

If you are like most business owners, you're probably looking for ways to make more money now and in the future by doing what you do best. You've just taken your company to new levels of customer satisfaction through much higher levels of on-time delivery, the highest levels of quality in your business arena, and ultimately significant improvement in your profitability. And, although you're very happy with your results, you simply want more sales. The bottom line is, generating more sales is not a matter of beating your competition's prices or service. In this step, I will show you how to generate more sales and, ultimately, even more profits. We do this by creating something referred to as a *Mafia Offer*.

A Mafia Offer is an offer that you can create which will allow you to close new orders on the order of maybe more than 80% of prospective buyers. Think about what would happen to your profit levels if you were successful in closing on 80% of the customers who view your products or services. I know this sounds too good to be true, but, by creating a Mafia Offer, it is not only true, it's only the beginning for your company. A Mafia Offer is essentially an offer that is so good that the purchaser would have to be absolutely illogical if they were to buy goods or services from anyone but you.

So how do you create a Mafia Offer? In order to create your own Mafia Offer, you need to recognize that it's a methodology based upon what we've discussed throughout this book, in other words, the Theory of Constraints. The Theory of Constraints states that, in any business, there is always an internal or external constraint that limits your system's performance relative to its goal. There is always a constraint in any business structure that will limit how much profit can be generated for a given amount of overhead. The Mafia Offer is principally building a business proposal for clients that aims at removing constraints on their perception of the value of your product or service. In other words, it is seen as an offer that is too good to refuse.

To get a better idea of what a Mafia Offer is, and how to create one, we will dive into Chapter 22 in [5] *The Theory of Constraints Handbook, Mafia Offers: Dealing With a Market Constraint.* This chapter, which you can purchase as a separate entity, was written by a world-renowned TOC expert, Dr Lisa Lang. I highly recommend this chapter! Dr Eli Goldratt first introduced the concept of a Mafia Offer in his book, *It's Not Luck* (Goldratt, 1994). He later defined a Mafia Offer as *An unrefusable offer.* According to Dr Lang, a Mafia Offer is "simply the offer you make to your market – your prospects and customers – to make them desire your products or services and something that your competition cannot quickly match." The reason you would want to create a Mafia Offer is because, after completing several iterations of this roadmap, your constraint is probably now outside your system and is, therefore, external to your company. In other words, you now have more internal capacity than you have orders.

Dr Lang explains that,

> A Mafia Offer typically requires that you do something entirely different than what you have been doing as far as sales go. A Mafia Offer is a sustainable market offer that prospective customers would truly desire. The question you must answer is, 'Do you have a market constraint?'

Dr Lang asks a question that will help you answer this question. She asks,

> If I could increase your sales tomorrow by twenty percent, could you handle the increase while:
>
> ■ being 100 percent on time, to your very first commitment;
> ■ without going into firefighting mode; and
> ■ still maintain a competitive lead time?

Dr Lang tells us that the bottom line is this:

> If the only way that you could handle the increase is to increase
> your lead times; work overtime; or miss due dates, then you have
> an internal operational constraint. On the other hand, if you can
> answer yes, and you could take a 20 percent increase in sales, and
> not have any negative effects, then you do have a market or sales
> process constraint.

So, with this in mind, how do you go about developing a Mafia Offer?

According to Dr Lisa Lang, in order to develop a Mafia Offer, there are
three things that we need to consider:

*1. Your capabilities, both what they are and what they could be, compared
with your competition.* Your capabilities are how you deliver your product
or service. What are things like your lead time, your due date performance,
your quality, and other key metrics? The answers to these questions are, in
reality, your capabilities.

*2. Your industry – how you and your competitors sell whatever you sell.*
The second thing you must consider as you develop your Mafia Offer is how
your industry sells whatever it is you sell. There are many questions that will
fit your industry, but here are two important ones:

- Is the industry practice to use a price/quantity curve?
- How do you and your competition typically charge? By the hour? By the
  day? By the project? Time and materials? Flat rate? Who pays for shipping? Paid at the start? Paid at the end? Progress payments?

The key is to understand how your industry interacts in the selling
and delivering your products/services, with your typical prospects and
customers.

*3. Your specific customers, how they are impacted by typical capabilities,
and how your industry sells.* Since your customers are the only judge of
your Mafia Offer, you also need to understand how your current capabilities,
and those of your competitors, affect the companies in your target market,
as well as how they are affected by the way you sell to them. It is in these
interactions and interfaces that you may be having negative effects on your
customers and prospects. Understanding these negative effects leads you to
uncover your customer's core problem, relative to doing business with your
industry.

When you develop a Mafia Offer, you start by asking to whom will the offer be made? You then select a target market, or the type of customer, you want to make the offer to. According to Dr Lang, you then ask the following types of questions to further refine your offer. Some of the questions might be:

- What market do we want to grow?
- What market has the best margins?
- Do we have too much business with one customer or in one market?
- Which customers or types of customers do we want to avoid?
- What market has tons of room for us to grow?

One of the best examples of what a good Mafia Offer can do for your company comes from a man named [6] Jim Schleckser, from Inc.com. Schleckser wrote an article or blog post entitled, *Make Your Customers An Offer They Can't Refuse*. He wrote, "For years, Blockbuster dominated the market for videotape and, later, DVD rentals. The Blockbuster sign became just about ubiquitous in neighborhoods around the country where people flocked to rent movies for the weekend."

But then Netflix came along. Not only did they have a more expansive inventory to choose from, they also made it more convenient where you didn't have to go into the store anymore to get your movie. You could do it all from your computer and the movie would show up in the mail (that's obviously now evolved into online streaming as well). And, oh yeah, they made it a lot cheaper to rent movies as well. In other words, Netflix made movie watchers a Mafia Offer where they were twice as good and half the price. Not surprisingly, Blockbuster went out of business just a few years later. They just couldn't compete.

And finally, here's an example from Dr Lisa Lang's Chapter 22 about a manufacturer or service company creating a decisive competitive advantage to make a Mafia Offer to another manufacturer, or project-based company, or service company.

> *Mister Customer, most equipment suppliers put all the risk of purchase on you. At best, you might be offered a lease or rental agreement. We can reduce your risk to 5 percent of the purchase price, and you pay only as you use the equipment. Since you pay per use, our incentive is to maximize your uptime and quality. Then you can focus on your business instead of worrying about when and if to buy.*

The bottom line is that a Mafia Offer can significantly help you to increase your sales by answering the question, "Why should I buy from you?" And if it's developed and delivered correctly, you will absolutely have much better control of your sales. The Mafia Offer will help you close deals to the tune of as high as 80%. This happens because the customer will be unable to refuse it, and your competition can't or won't match it. A Mafia Offer is only one part of how the Theory of Constraints can help you improve your marketing, but it is an essential part if your capacity to produce is greater than the amount of sales that you have.

## Step 17: Document and Celebrate

After your new sales plan has gone into effect, based upon your Mafia Offer, make sure you document everything. This includes your new level of profitability and, if you measure customer "happiness" in some way, make sure you document your new level of this metric. Why? Because if you have to repeat this effort in the future, this will serve as your justification for doing it again. Equally important, when you have completed this effort, is that you need to get everyone together to celebrate your new level of success! By doing this, in the future when you need to repeat this roadmap, and you will, your employees will remember what happened the last time and will absolutely support your new effort.

This completes your first iteration of the Theory of Constraints Implementation Roadmap, and, based upon my own experience, your company will have been transformed to a new, much higher level of success. Your on-time delivery rates will surpass anything you've ever done in the past, and profit levels will be higher than you ever dreamed possible. In addition, your customer satisfaction rates will be the best they've ever been. The bottom line is that your customer base will be strongly supportive of your company! Congratulations on a job well done!

Now that you have a better idea of how to implement the Theory of Constraints, let's look in the next chapter at how best to combine Lean and Six Sigma with TOC to take profit levels higher and higher. In the next chapter, I present the details of how to do this with another new roadmap.

# References

1. H. William Dettmer, *The Logical Thinking Process – A Systems Approach to Complex Problem Solving*, American Society for Quality, Quality Press, 2007.
2. Stephen R. Covey, *The Seven Habits of Highly Effective People: Powerful Lessons in Personal Change*, Simon and Schuster, 1989.
3. James F. Cox III and John G. Schleier, Jr., McGraw-Hill, 2010.
4. Constraints Management Group, *About Drum-Buffer-Rope (DBR)*.
5. Dr Lisa Lang, *Theory of Constraints Handbook – Chapter 22, Mafia Offers: Dealing With a Market Constraint*, McGraw-Hill, 2010.
6. Jim Schleckser, *Make Your Customers An Offer They Can't Refuse*, Inc.com, 2017.

# Chapter 18

# The Ultimate Improvement Cycle Roadmap

One question I always asked, when I was consulting for a new company, was, "How's your improvement effort working for you?" The majority of companies that I worked with had invested lots of money in training, but they weren't seeing enough profit hitting the bottom line to justify the money they had spent. Like any other investment, they expected a rapid and suitable Return on Investment (ROI), but it just wasn't happening the way they imagined or at least hoped that it would. Some had invested in Six Sigma and had trained many of their employees to become Green Belts and/or Black Belts. Some may have even gone out and hired a Master Black Belt.

Some of the companies I consulted for had invested a large sum of money in training people on Lean Manufacturing. Still others had tried going the Lean Six Sigma route. So, if you were one of the companies, the question you may have asked yourself was probably something like, "Why aren't we seeing a better return on our investment?" You knew improvements were happening, because you were seeing all of the improvement reports, but you just weren't seeing these same improvements positively impacting your bottom line at a high enough rate, again to justify all of the money you had spent on training.

In one of my own positions, I too experienced this same dilemma, so I decided to analyze the results of both failed and successful improvement initiatives in which I had been involved. And what I found changed my approach to improvement forever. What I discovered was that it was all about having the correct *focus* and *leverage*. Knowing where to focus my

DOI: 10.4324/9781003462385-18

improvement efforts absolutely transformed me because I now knew where to focus my improvements to leverage it. The key to my epiphany was that I discovered something called the *Theory of Constraints* (TOC).

The Theory of Constraints explains that, within any company, there are key leverage points that truly control the rate of money generated by a company. Sometimes, these leverage points are physical bottlenecks, but many times they are just policies that prevent us from realizing our true profit potential. In my analysis, the successful efforts all had one thing in common, and that was the *focal point* of their improvement effort. In this chapter, I'm going to demonstrate to you how to use the power of the Theory of Constraints to truly jump start your improvement efforts. But better yet, I'm going to help you turn all of those training $s (or whatever currency you use) into immediate profits, and then illustrate how to sustain your efforts over the long haul.

If you're like many companies, there always seems to be a rush to run out and start improvement projects, without really considering the bottom-line impact of the projects selected. Many companies even develop a performance metric that measures the number of ongoing projects, and then attempt to drive this metric higher and higher. Instead of developing a strategically focused and manageable plan, many companies try to, in effect, "solve world hunger!" Many Lean initiatives attempt to drive waste out of the entire value chain, while Six Sigma initiatives attempt to do the same thing with variation. There's nothing wrong with either of these strategies, but they must be focused on the right area within your company to achieve the maximum benefits. The real problem with failed Lean and Six Sigma initiatives is really two-fold. There are typically too many projects and most of the projects are focused primarily on cost reduction. Many companies simply have too many ongoing projects that drain valuable resources needed for the day-to-day issues facing them. The true economic reality that supersedes and overrides everything else is that companies have always wanted the most improvement for the least amount of investment. Attacking all processes and problems simultaneously, as part of an enterprise-wide Lean Six Sigma initiative, quite simply overloads the organization and does not deliver an acceptable ROI. In fact, according to some studies, the failure rates of many Lean Six Sigma initiatives are hovering around 50%. With failure rates this high, is it any wonder why companies abandon their improvement initiatives and simply back-slide to their old ways? Earlier, I said that focusing projects on cost reduction was one of the primary reasons that many Lean Six Sigma initiatives are failing. Across-the-board cost-cutting initiatives are pretty much standard for many businesses. My belief is that focusing solely on cost reduction is a colossal mistake. So, if this misguided focus isn't right, then what is the right approach? What is it that companies should be doing to maximize their profits? Based upon my experiences in a variety of organizations and industries, the disappointing results coming from Lean and Six Sigma are directly linked to failing to adequately answer three questions:

1. What to change?
2. What to change to?
3. How to cause the change to happen?

Take a look at your own company. Are your improvement projects focused on cost reduction? Do you have an army of Green Belts and Black Belts? Do you have so many projects that they are actually bogging down your company? Are your Six Sigma projects typically taking 3–6 months to complete? Are they providing you with real bottom-line impact or are they simply a mirage?

Earlier, I said I wanted to demonstrate where to focus your improvement efforts. But before I do this, I want to explain TOC, or at least some basic concepts of TOC, to those of you that don't have much experience in or exposure to TOC. One of the best ways to demonstrate these concepts is through the use of simple graphics.

Figure 18.1 is a simple gravity-fed piping system that is used to transport water. As you can see, the pipes all have entirely different diameters. Suppose you were asked to increase the rate of water flowing into the receptacle at the base of this piping system. How would you answer this question? If you wanted to increase the flow of water through this process, what would you do and where would you focus your efforts? If you said you would increase the diameter of Section E, you would be absolutely correct. You would focus your efforts on Section E to improve the throughput of water through this piping system. Why? Because Section E, with the smallest diameter, is constraining the flow of water through the entire system. In simple terms, your improvement action would be to focus your efforts on Section E in order to increase the flow of water. OK, so let's assume most of you got this correct. Would focusing on any other section increase the flow of water? The correct answer is, no, it wouldn't, it would be wasted effort, simply because Section E controls the total output of water through this piping system.

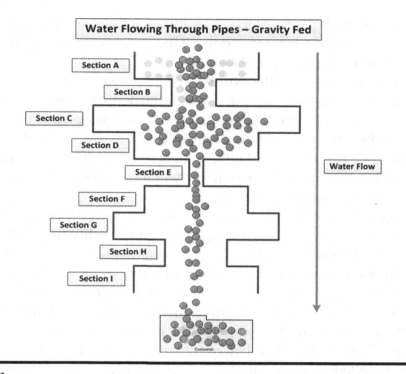

**Figure 18.1**

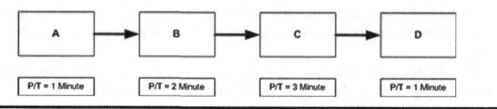

**Figure 18.2**

Now, let's look at Figure 18.2. This is a simple four-step manufacturing process, with each of the step's processing times listed. Using the piping analogy that we just discussed, which step prevents more parts from being produced? Or, another way of saying this is, which step is preventing us from achieving more throughput of product? If you answered Step C, you were correct. Why? Because Step C requires three minutes to process the product, so the total system cannot produce product any faster than twenty parts per hour (i.e., 60 minutes in an hour divided by 3 minutes per part). If you reduced the processing time of Step B from two minutes to one minute, have you increased the throughput of this process?

The answer is no, because you're still limited by Step C at three minutes per part. So, just like the piping system example, you would have to focus your improvement efforts on Step C to improve the throughput of this process. That is, you would have to reduce Step C's processing time. So why am I so worried about improving throughput?

Earlier, I said that going after cost reductions is not the best way to make more money for your company. So, if cost reduction isn't the best way to make more money, then what is? In order to demonstrate this to you, I need to introduce you to a different brand of accounting called Throughput Accounting (TA). Yes, we described Throughput Accounting in a previous chapter, but, because it's so important for you to understand and grasp its impact, let's go through the basics again.

Throughput Accounting (TA) was developed by Dr Eli Goldratt, the architect of the Theory of Constraints, in order to simplify financial decisions. I know this will seem like a lot of new terms but, as you will see, they actually are very simple, or at least much simpler than a traditional Cost Accounting (CA) report. If you can learn these simple terms now, and apply them in your company, you will be well on your way to making more money for your company than you ever dreamed possible. However, I want to make one thing crystal clear before moving on. Throughput Accounting was never intended to replace traditional CA, simply because companies are required by law to follow Generally Accepted Accounting Principles (GAAP) reporting rules and requirements. Throughput Accounting was developed to help make much better *real-time* financial decisions and not to replace GAAP.

In order to judge whether an organization is moving toward its goal of making more money, three basic questions need to be answered:

1. How much money is generated by your company?
2. How much money is invested by your company?
3. How much money do you have to spend to operate your company?

Traditional CA as many of you have experienced, is not only difficult to use and understand, but it's all about what you did last month or even last quarter. Cost Accounting also teaches us that the pathway to profitability is through how much money can be saved, and this is simply a flawed approach! The correct pathway to improving profitability is through making money. And no, these are not the same. Goldratt recognized the need to have real-time financial data, so he created his own version of accounting, or, as it's also known, Throughput Decision-Making. He developed the following three financial measures:

**Throughput (T):** The rate at which the system generates "new" money, primarily through sales of its products or delivery of its services. Throughput represents all of the money coming into a company minus what it pays to suppliers and vendors. The actual equation for Throughput is this simple equation:

$T = P - TVC$

where P is the price/unit of the product and TVC is the Totally Variable Costs associated with the sale of the product. TVC is typically the cost of raw materials, but could also include things like sales commissions, etc., things that will vary for each unit of product sold.

**Investment or Inventory (I):** The money the system invests in items it plans to sell. This typically includes both work-in-process and finished goods inventory. This is money associated with inventory, machinery, buildings, and other assets and liabilities. TOC recommends inventory be valued strictly on totally variable costs associated with creating the inventory, not with additional cost allocations from overheads.

**Operating Expense (OE):** The money spent on turning investment (inventory) into Throughput, including labor costs, supplies, overheads, etc., basically any expense that is not in the TVC category. OE is the money the system spends in generating "goal units." For physical products, OE is all the expenses, except the cost of the raw materials.

The important point here is that Throughput is not considered Throughput until *new money enters the company by producing and shipping product or delivering services to its customers and then receiving payment for the goods and/or services*. Anything produced that is not shipped is simply inventory, which costs the company money and ties up needed cash. Cost Accounting actually views finished product inventory as an asset, but is it really, if it's just sitting in a storage rack gathering dust? Accordingly, Goldratt defined Net Profit (NP) and Return on Investment (ROI) as follows:

- Net Profit equals Throughput minus Operating Expense, or $NP = T - OE$
- Return on Investment equals Throughput minus Operating Expense divided by Investment (I), or $ROI = (T - OE) \div I$

So, with these three simple measures, T, I, and OE, Goldratt reasoned that organizations are able to determine the impact of their actions and decisions on the company's bottom line, Net Profit and Return on Investment, in real time.

OK, let me explain why I say that focusing on Throughput is so important. If you consider inventory reduction, it is a one-time improvement that frees up cash, but, after the initial reduction, there's really nothing left to harvest. Operating Expense has a functional or practical lower limit, and, once it is reached, nothing more can be harvested without having a negative impact on the organization. That is, companies that typically focus on Operating Expense often engage in layoffs which, if cut too deeply, will negatively impact the performance of the company. What about Throughput? Theoretically, Throughput has no upper limit! As long as you have the sales and you can reduce the *cycle time* of the *constraint*, Throughput continues to rise. Yes, Throughput has a practical upper limit, but the potential is there to continue growing profits.

Figure 18.3 represents a graphic of what I just explained. Look at the potential of all three profit components. OE, the target of most improvement projects, is actually the smallest component, followed by Investment (I), which is slightly larger, but is limited at zero. Throughput, on the other hand, is much larger than either I or OE. The point here is, if you want

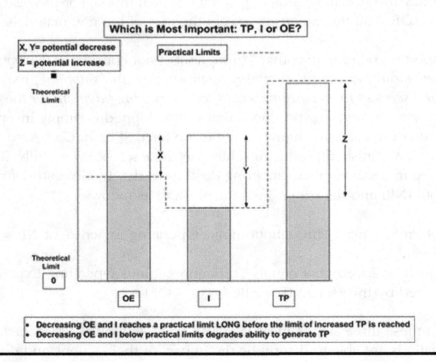

**Figure 18.3**

to drive profitability higher and higher, you must focus your improvement efforts on the process that is limiting your ability to do so, the constraint, to drive Throughput higher and higher. As we have seen, Throughput Accounting is much simpler to use and understand, allows for faster decisions (using real-time data), and decisions that are linked directly to your company's bottom line.

As mentioned earlier, Throughput Accounting is used to make real-time decisions, so is it obvious to you that the best decisions are those that result in increasing T while decreasing OE and I? Keep in mind that I'm not suggesting that traditional Cost Accounting should be discarded, simply because we have to respect GAAP requirements. But if you're trying to determine where to focus your improvement efforts, use Throughput Accounting.

So, the question now becomes, how do I know where to focus my improvement efforts? Goldratt also developed his own version of a process of ongoing improvement, and he gave us five simple steps to follow. These five steps will form the framework for significant and sustainable improvement for your company.

1. Identify the system constraint.
2. Decide how to exploit the constraint.
3. Subordinate everything else to the above decision.
4. If necessary, elevate the constraint.
5. Return to Step 1, but don't let inertia become the constraint.

Let's look at each of these in a bit more detail so that they make sense to you from an improvement perspective.

1. **Identify the system constraint**. Since the goal of a typical "for-profit" company is to make more money now and in the future and, since we learned earlier that focusing on Throughput (T) is the most effective and fastest way to make more money, we need to identify the resource or policy in our system that is preventing our company from producing and shipping more goods or delivering more services. It is important to understand that the constraint is not always physical. In fact, in my opinion, the majority of the time the constraint is a policy or procedure that limits our ability to improve our throughput. It's also important to understand that the constraint is not always internal to your company. By that, I mean, what if you have the capacity to produce much more of your products or deliver more of your service, but you don't have the sales? In this

case, the market is the constraint and, when this is the case, the actions you take are much different than if the constraint was internal due to a lack of capacity. In Chapter 17, I discussed something called a Mafia Offer, so if you have a market constraint, re-read Chapter 17.

2. **Decide how to exploit the system constraint**. The key here is to make sure that the constraint's time is never wasted doing things that it shouldn't be doing and is *never starved for work*. Remember, every minute lost at the constraint is a missed opportunity to increase Throughput. Focus everything you do on reducing the cycle time of the constraint and improving/synchronizing the flow of product (or service) through the constraint. If the constraint is market-related, then you must enhance your competitive edge factors, including things like on-time delivery, quality levels, overall cycle time from order to delivery, etc. What you want in this case is to become best in class, so that customers come to you.

3. **Subordinate everything else to the above decision**. This step is typically the most difficult of all for most companies to understand and accomplish. By definition, if a process step is not a constraint, and the constraint is internal to your company, then any process step that is faster than the constraint and therefore has more capacity to produce than the constraint does, is a non-constraint. Think about it. Why would you ever want a non-constraint to produce at a faster rate than a constraint? If you did, you would only serve to increase inventory within the system, which needlessly ties up cash and impedes the flow of the process. Subordinating, in its simplest form means to produce at the same rate as the constraint...nothing more and nothing less.

4. **If necessary, elevate the system constraint**. One of the terms everyone is familiar with is take time, which is really the throughput rate required to meet customer requirements. But what if, after all the improvements you've made in Steps 1–3, you still aren't supplying enough to meet market requirements? If this is the case, then you may have to spend some money to either purchase a new piece of equipment or even hire additional labor. You need to do whatever it takes to meet the market demand. This is what elevating the constraint means. And, as a side note, you need to use Throughput Accounting to help you make that decision.

5. **Return to Step 1, but don't let inertia become the constraint**. After completing Steps 1–4, you should see significant reductions in the cycle time of the constraint, so you must prepare for a new one to take

its place. That is, after you essentially "break" your current constraint, another one will immediately appear at a new location, so you must move your improvement efforts to the new location. So, what does it mean when we say, "Don't let inertia become the constraint"? It simply means that you should not become complacent when you break the current constraint. Immediately move your improvement resources to this new constraint or, following these five steps, return to Step 1 to identify the new constraint.

OK, so that's our Process of On-Going Improvement (POOGI), introduced by Goldratt back in the '80s. Think back to my drawings of the piping system and the four-step process, and try to imagine your POOGI and how it might apply to your company. Are you following a logical pathway for improvement or are you instinctively moving to the next improvement project? This is what I call the Ultimate Improvement Cycle (UIC) and, in the next section, I'll give you the details of how this improvement methodology should be implemented in your company.

## How to Implement the Ultimate Improvement Cycle

In the previous section, an improvement methodology referred to as the Ultimate Improvement Cycle (UIC) was introduced. The case was made for combining the two most popular improvement methodologies, Lean and Six Sigma, with the Theory of Constraints. In this section, details on how to implement the Ultimate Improvement Cycle will be presented, along with results that could be reasonably expected.

One of the most important points presented in the previous section was the need to combine the two most popular improvement methodologies, Lean and Six Sigma, with the Theory of Constraints (TOC). And, whereas Lean and Six Sigma are integral parts of this integrated method, both are missing a key ingredient, a focusing mechanism. TOC clarifies where you must focus your Lean and Six Sigma initiative, in order to realize an acceptable return-on-investment (ROI). That focal point is the system constraint. The system constraint represents the leverage point for your improvement efforts and delivers the Return on Investment needed to justify your training investment.

As explained in the previous section, most of the improvement efforts being pursued today mistakenly focus their horde of projects on cost reduction. It was pointed out that across-the-board cost-cutting is standard practice for many businesses as part of their continuous improvement initiatives. This practice, along with the failure to identify the improvement leverage point, are the primary reasons that many of the improvement initiatives are failing to deliver an acceptable return-on-investment, resulting in many companies either abandoning their improvement efforts or significantly scaling them back.

There was one other very important message brought forward in the previous section, and that was the reason for not pursuing cost-cutting to drive a company's ROI. In order to demonstrate why cost-cutting is not the right pathway to improve ROI, a different accounting method, referred to as Throughput Accounting (TA), was introduced. It was also stated that TA was never intended to replace traditional Cost Accounting (CA) because companies are required by law to follow GAAP reporting rules and requirements. TA was developed to help make easier and more logical real-time financial decisions.

In order to judge if an organization is moving toward its goal of making more money, we stated that three basic questions need to be answered:

1. How much money is generated by your company?
2. How much money is invested by your company?
3. How much money do you have to spend to operate your company?

It was explained that Traditional Cost Accounting is not only difficult to understand, but it's all about what you did last month or last quarter. The key point brought forward in the previous section was that CA teaches us that the pathway to profitability is through cost-cutting (i.e., saving money), and this belief is simply wrong. The correct pathway to improving profitability is through *making money*, which is completely different from *saving money*. I explained that, in order to have real-time financial decisions, TOC pursues profitability by using three simple financial measures:

1. *Throughput* (T): The rate at which the system generates new money, primarily through sales of its products.
2. *Inventory or Investment* (I): The money the system invests in items it plans to sell.
3. *Operating Expense* (OE): The money spent on turning I into T.

From these three basic financial measures, you are then able to calculate Net Profit (NP) and Return-On-Investment (ROI) as follows:

1. Net Profit = Throughput (T) − Operating Expense (OE) or NP = T − OE
2. Return-On-Investment = (Throughput − Operating Expense) ÷ Investment or (T − OE) / I

So, with these prominent points in mind, let's now begin our discussion on how to implement the Ultimate Improvement Cycle in your company. The basis for this section was taken from a book I wrote, published in 2009, under the title of *The Ultimate Improvement Cycle – Maximizing Profits Through the Integration of Lean, Six Sigma, and the Theory of Constraints* [1].

## Implementing the UIC

As the title of this chapter suggests, it will be demonstrated just how to implement a blend of the Theory of Constraints, Lean, and Six Sigma. In order to do this, it's important to first understand the basics of each of these methodologies independently. With this in mind, let's begin with a basic understanding of the Theory of Constraints (TOC).

TOC was first introduced to the world by Dr Eliyahu M. Goldratt and Jeff Cox in their classic business novel, *The Goal* [2]. Goldratt and Cox explained to us that systems are composed of interdependent processes and functions which they equated to a chain. Every chain has a weakest link and, in order to strengthen the total chain, you must identify, focus on, and strengthen its weakest link. Any attempts to strengthen the other links will not result in a stronger chain because it will still break at the weakest link.

Goldratt and Cox analogized the concept of a chain to organizations and explained that failing to identify and strengthen the organization's weakest link, or system constraint, will not strengthen the global system. Similarly, attempts to improve non-constraint operations will not necessarily translate into significant organizational improvement. It's kind of like a professional baseball team signing free-agent sluggers when the real constraint is relief or starting pitching. They can score lots of runs, but, in the end, if they can't hold the other team to fewer runs than they score, they'll never win a pennant.

Theoretically, the implications of the Theory of Constraints to improvement initiatives can be very profound. From a throughput accounting perspective, reduction in inventory (one of the benefits of Lean) has a functional lower limit of zero and, once you've reached zero inventory, there is none left to harvest. Lowering inventory can lead to substantial dollars, but it's a one-time occurrence. Operating expense reduction, the favorite of many Lean and Six Sigma aficionados, also has a functional lower limit but, when this lower limit is surpassed, further attempts to reduce it can actually debilitate an organization.

Throughput improvement, on the other hand, has no upper limit! Even if the productive capacity of the organization exceeds the number of customer orders, then the market becomes the constraint and creative sales techniques, like lead time and on-time delivery, can be used to generate more sales. It's important to remember that, if you have excess capacity, then, as long as your new product cost covers your cost of raw materials and you haven't added excess labor to achieve this excess capacity, the net profit flows directly to the bottom line! Of course, all three of these actions (i.e., throughput increases, inventory reductions, and operating expense reduction) have a positive impact on net profit and return on investment. Think about this: if there were no constraints in a company, wouldn't their profits be infinite?

As explained previously, the Theory of Constraints' process of on-going improvement is a direct result of always focusing your efforts toward achieving the system's goal. In order to achieve this focus, Goldratt and Cox developed a five-step process toward that end:

1. *Identify* the system's constraint(s).
2. Decide how to *exploit* the system's constraint(s).
3. *Subordinate* everything else to the above decision.
4. *Elevate* the system's constraint(s).
5. If, in the previous steps, a constraint has been broken, *return* to step 1, but do not allow inertia to cause a system constraint.

In the Lean Improvement Cycle, you are primarily interested in removing unnecessary waste from your process in an effort to improve the flow of products through your processes. You do this by using the following five steps:

1. *Define* and *identify* what *value* is.
2. *Identify* the entire value stream.
3. Make value *flow* without interruptions.
4. Let customers *pull* value from the producer.
5. Relentlessly pursue *perfection*, making our processes less and less wasteful.

A true Lean implementation will definitely produce a better process, as long as it is done correctly, but this is sometimes a big "if".

In the Six Sigma Improvement Process, you are primarily interested in identifying variation, then reducing it, and finally controlling it. The steps for Six Sigma are as defined by the acronym DMAIC as follows:

1. *Define* problems and requirements, and set goals.
2. *Measure* the key steps and validate and refine the problems identified in Step 1.
3. *Analyze* the pertinent data to develop or validate our causal hypotheses.
4. *Improve* the process by testing solutions and removing root causes.
5. *Control* our processes by establishing standard measures.

Like Lean, if done correctly, Six Sigma creates a much better process, with much less variation, but again, this is sometimes a big "if".

So, by now, you must be wondering why we are going to such great lengths to explain these three, very separate and, to this point, mostly stand-alone initiatives. What does the Theory of Constraints have to do with either Lean or Six Sigma, or vice versa? The answer to this question is quite simply, *everything*! The key to successful Lean, Six Sigma, and TOC implementations, in terms of maximizing throughput and return on investment, is to ensure that your company's efforts are focused on the right area of the business and the Theory of Constraints provides this focus. The right area of focus is always the system constraint! Whereas TOC provides the needed focus, Six Sigma and Lean provide the tools needed to reduce waste and variation. In effect, Lean, Six Sigma, and TOC form the *Ultimate Improvement Cycle*!

The major difference between the Lean, Six Sigma, and TOC improvement initiatives is simply a matter of *focus* and *leverage*. Whereas Lean and Six Sigma implement improvements and then measure reductions in inventory and operating expenses, as well as increases in throughput, TOC focuses up-front on throughput and looks for ways to achieve higher and higher levels. The only way to increase throughput is to focus on the operation that is *limiting it*! The net effect of this *Ultimate Improvement Cycle* is greater throughput coupled with reductions in operating expenses and inventory costs. All three financial profit components are moving in the right direction at a faster rate than if you had attempted stand-alone initiatives.

It's quite likely that there could be some disparaging and reproachful comments from both the Lean and Six Sigma camps, and there will no doubt be attempts to discredit this approach. Zealots of any kind seem to always assume a defensive posture when their beliefs are being challenged. But the fact is we're not challenging the validity of Lean or Six Sigma or the Theory of Constraints. We're simply presenting a better approach for all three initiatives. All three initiatives are vital pieces of the improvement pie and this combination of the three is a better approach to improvement than each being pursued in isolation as stand-alone initiatives. With the failure rates of all three initiatives being as high as they are, it seems that combining forces would intuitively be a better approach.

So, just what would happen if you were to combine the best of all three improvement initiatives into a single improvement process? Just what might this amalgamation look like? Logic would say that you would have an improvement process that reduces waste and variation, but primarily focusing on the operation that is constraining throughput. That is exactly what we have! Figure 18.4 is a depiction of combining these three separate but dependent improvement methodologies.

The above graphic (Figure 18.4) is what I refer to as the Ultimate Improvement Cycle (UIC) [1], which combines the power of Lean, Six Sigma, and Theory of Constraints improvement cycles to form a more powerful and profitable improvement strategy. This improvement cycle weaves together the DNA of Lean and Six Sigma with the focusing power of the Theory of Constraints to deliver a powerful and compelling improvement methodology. All of the strategies, principles, tools, techniques, and methods contained within all three improvement initiatives are synergistically blended and then time-released to yield improvements that far exceed those obtained from doing these three initiatives in isolation from each other. So, let's look at the actions we should take and what we're trying to accomplish with each one.

## UIC Actions

By combining Lean, Six Sigma, and the Theory of Constraints, we are attempting to:

*1. Identify, Define, Measure and Analyze the Process.* The actions in Steps 1a, 1b, and 1c serve to characterize the process value stream by identifying which step is limiting the full potential of the process (the constraint operation), defining value, pinpointing the potential sources of waste, and locating and measuring potential sources of defects, scrap, and variation. There will be a compelling urge to make changes during this phase but resist this

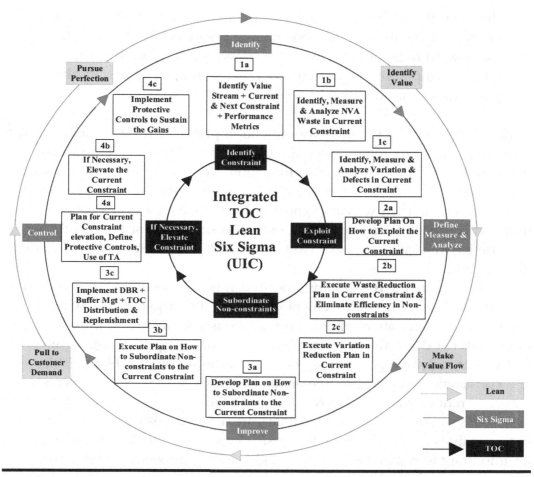

**Figure 18.4**

temptation. In this phase of the improvement cycle, you are simply trying to define, analyze, and understand what is currently happening in your process. Taiichi Ohno used a technique known as "standing in the circle" [3] which emphasized going to the process to observe and understand. It was not uncommon for a person to have been left standing for eight solid hours or more before Ohno was satisfied that they had seen the waste in the process and the reasons why it exists. During this "standing in the circle exercise," it is best to simply acknowledge that the waste exists without trying to eliminate it just yet.

By the same token, we are also looking for sources of variation within the process. What are the things you see that are preventing your process from being consistent and stable? Keep in mind that the next phase deals with stabilizing the process by reducing both waste and variation in the constraining operation, so it's important, for now, to remember that you are simply trying to understand what is happening in your current process and, more specifically, your constraint operation.

Although you will be focusing your attention primarily on the operation that is limiting your throughput, since the upstream and downstream process steps could be contributing to this limitation, they must be observed as well. For example, if an upstream process consistently stops the flow of product to the constraint, then we can't ignore it. Conversely, if a downstream operation is consistently losing constraint output to scrap and/or rework, then it can't be ignored either. In both cases, the result would be less than optimal throughput.

*2. Create Stability.* Before any process can be improved, a focused plan must be developed or improvement efforts will be disjointed. In Steps 2a, 2b, and 2c, you are attempting to simultaneously stabilize and improve your process. What does stabilize actually mean? Quite simply, stabilizing means that you are attempting to make your process more predictable, reliable, and consistent. In this sense, the actions in Steps 2a, 2b, and 2c serve primarily to reduce waste and variation within the constraint operation so that new levels of consistency and reliability are achieved. What you observed in the analysis phase will form the basis for your plan to achieve stability. It's important to remember that true and lasting improvement will never occur unless and until the process is consistent and stable over time. You will use a variety of tools and techniques during this phase of the Ultimate Improvement Cycle to accomplish this end. In order to achieve improved process flow, you must be patient and deliberate when reducing waste and variation.

*3. Create Flow and Pull.* Specifically, the actions in Steps 3a, 3b, and 3c are intended to optimize flow. Flow in this phase includes the flow of materials, information, and products through the system. Although you are seeking to create flow, creating it will also surface any problem that hinders it! So, in order to sustain flow, you must stop and solve these problems. Because of your past experiences, you might be tempted to fix these problems on the fly, but don't do it! You must begin to view problems as opportunities for long-term improvement and not as a failure, so, by stopping and fixing problems, is actually a sign of strength in an organization.

*4. Control Process to Sustain Gains.* The actions in Steps 4a, 4b, and 4c serve to both increase constraint capacity, if you need to, and to assure that all of the changes made, and improvements realized won't be squandered. What a shame it would be to make big improvements that you can't sustain. Sustaining the gains is a hallmark of great organizations!

So, again, the four phases of the UIC are *analyze, stabilize, flow,* and *control.* Each phase is critical to the optimization of revenue and profits. Don't jump from one to the other, simply follow them in sequential order.

The Ultimate Improvement Cycle accomplishes five primary objectives and serves as a springboard to maximizing revenue and profits:

1. It guarantees that you are *focusing* on the correct area of the process or system (i.e., the constraint operation) to maximize throughput and minimize inventory and operating expense.
2. It provides a superior *roadmap for improvement* that ensures a systematic, structured, and orderly approach that will assure the maximization and utilization of resources to realize optimal revenue, which translates into maximum profitability.
3. It *integrates* the best of Lean, Six Sigma, and the Theory of Constraints strategies, tools, techniques, and strategies, that serve to maximize your organization's full improvement potential.
4. It assures that the necessary, *up-front planning* is completed in advance of changes to the process or organization, so as to avoid the "Fire, Ready, Aim!" mindset.
5. It provides the synergy and involvement of the *total organization* needed to maximize your return on investment.

If you are seriously committed to following the steps of the UIC, in the sequence illustrated in the figure above, then you will see bottom-line improvements that far exceed what you've experienced using stand-alone initiatives. Just like any new initiative, it requires the entire organization's focus, discipline, determination, and a little bit of patience. This is new territory for you, so follow the path of least resistance that has been provided for you…it truly does work!

So, just how do you go about achieving each of the steps in the UIC, you may be wondering? You do so by using all of the tools and actions that we would use if we were implementing Lean and Six Sigma as stand-alone improvement initiatives, but this time you focus most, if not all, of your efforts primarily on the constraint operation. In the figure below, the tools and actions you will use and perform at each step of the UIC can be observed. As you can see, there are no new or exotic tools that are being introduced here. In creating the UIC, one of the objectives was to keep things simple and the tools depicted in the figure below are all of the basic and time-tested tools that have been around for years.

The Ultimate Improvement Cycle (UIC) is not simply a collection of tools and techniques but rather a viable and practical manufacturing strategy that focuses resources on the area that will generate the highest return on investment. The UIC is all about focusing on and leveraging the operation or policy that is constraining the organization and keeping it from realizing its full potential. So, let's look at a new roadmap (Figure 18.5) I have created that lays out the step-by-step procedure on how to implement the UIC.

In keeping with the overriding theme of this book, I have created a roadmap on how to implement the Ultimate Improvement Cycle. Figure 18.5 is this roadmap that contains seven major sections and seventeen individual steps that must be completed in order to successfully implement this improvement methodology. Let's now walk through this roadmap.

In Section I of this roadmap, you are instructed, by using Lean, Six Sigma, and TOC, to identify, measure, and analyze. In Step 1A, your primary objectives are to clearly identify the value stream you are attempting to improve, identify the current and next constraint, and the performance metrics that are currently in place used to monitor the process being improved. In Step 1A, you are instructed to identify the current value stream, the current and next constraint, and the current performance metrics being used to monitor the process. You are then instructed, in Step 1B. to identify, measure, and analyze non-value-added waste in the current constraint based upon the principles and tools of Lean. In Step 1C, you are instructed to identify, measure, and analyze variation and defects that exist in the current constraint based upon the principles and tools of Six Sigma.

In Step 2.0 of the roadmap, you are instructed to develop a plan on how to exploit the current constraint. In Step 2A, you are instructed, by using the information from Step 1.0, to create an exploitation plan for the current constraint. The plan should include waste and variation reduction and defect elimination, but, for now, only focus the plan on the current constraint. Once these three steps are completed, you then move on to Step 3.0 of the roadmap where you are instructed to execute the exploitation plan you developed.

**Ultimate Improvement Cycle Roadmap**

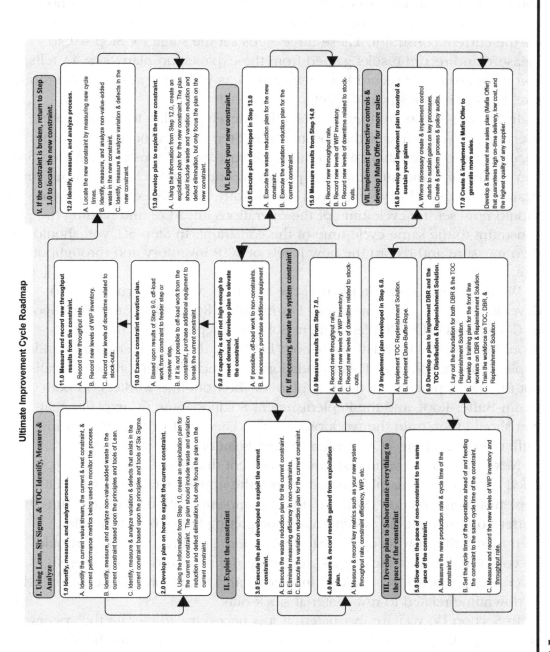

**I. Using Lean, Six Sigma, & TOC Identify, Measure & Analyze**

**1.0 Identify, measure, and analyze process.**

A. Identify the current value stream, the current & next constraint, & current performance metrics being used to monitor the process.

B. Identify, measure, and analyze non-value-added waste in the current constraint based upon the principles and tools of Lean.

C. Identify, measure & analyze variation & defects that exists in the current constraint based upon the principles and tools of Six Sigma.

**2.0 Develop a plan on how to exploit the current constraint.**

A. Using the information from Step 1.0, create an exploitation plan for the current constraint. The plan should include waste and variation reduction and defect elimination, but only focus the plan on the current constraint.

**II. Exploit the constraint**

**3.0 Execute the plan developed to exploit the current constraint.**

A. Execute the waste reduction plan for the current constraint.
B. Eliminate measuring efficiency in non-constraints.
C. Execute the variation reduction plan for the current constraint.

**4.0 Measure & record results gained from exploitation plan.**

A. Measure & record key metrics such as your new system throughput rate, constraint efficiency, WIP, etc.

**III. Develop plan to Subordinate everything to the pace of the constraint**

**5.0 Slow down the pace of non-constraint to the same pace of the constraint.**

A. Measure the new production rate & cycle time of the constraint.

B. Set the cycle time of the operations ahead of and feeding the constraint to the same cycle time of the constraint.

C. Measure and record the new levels of WIP inventory and throughput rate.

**6.0 Develop a plan to implement DBR and the TOC Distribution & Replenishment Solution.**

A. Lay out the foundation for both DBR & the TOC Replenishment Solution.

B. Develop a training plan for the front line workers on DBR & Replenishment Solution.

C. Train the workforce on TOC, DBR, & Replenishment Solution.

**7.0 Implement plan developed in Step 6.0.**

A. Implement TOC Replenishment Solution.
B. Implement Drum-Buffer-Rope.

**8.0 Measure results from Step 7.0...**

A. Record new throughput rate,
B. Record new levels of WIP inventory.
C. Record new levels of downtime related to stock-outs.

**IV. If necessary, elevate the system constraint**

**9.0 If capacity is still not high enough to meet demand, develop plan to elevate the constraint.**

A. If possible, off-load work to non-constraints.
B. If necessary, purchase additional equipment

**10.0 Execute constraint elevation plan.**

A. Based upon results of Step 9.0, off-load work from constraint to feeder step or receiver step.

B. If it is not possible to off-load work from the constraint, purchase additional equipment to break the current constraint.

**11.0 Measure and record new throughput results from the constraint.**

A. Record new throughput rate,
B. Record new levels of WIP inventory.
C. Record new levels of downtime related to stock-outs.

**V. If the constraint is broken, return to Step 1.0 to locate the new constraint.**

**12.0 Identify, measure, and analyze process.**

A. Locate the new constraint by measuring new cycle times.
B. Identify, measure, and analyze non-value-added waste in the new constraint.
C. Identify, measure & analyze variation & defects in the new constraint.

**13.0 Develop plan to exploit the new constraint.**

A. Using the information from Step 12.0, create an exploitation plan for the new constraint. The plan should include waste and variation reduction and defect elimination, but only focus the plan on the new constraint.

**VI. Exploit your new constraint.**

**14.0 Execute plan developed in Step 13.0**

A. Execute the waste reduction plan for the new constraint.
B. Execute the variation reduction plan for the current constraint.

**15.0 Measure results from Step 14.0**

A. Record new throughput rate,
B. Record new levels of WIP inventory.
C. Record new levels of downtime related to stock-outs.

**VII. Implement protective controls & develop Mafia Offer for more sales**

**16.0 Develop and implement plan to control & sustain your gains.**

A. Where necessary create & implement control charts to sustain gains on key processes.
B. Create & perform process & policy audits.

**17.0 Create & implement a Mafia Offer to generate more sales.**

Develop & implement new sales plan (Mafia Offer) that guarantees high on-time delivery, low cost, and the highest quality of any supplier.

Figure 18.5

There will be three steps in this effort, namely Steps 3A, 3B, and 3C. Step 3A instructs you to execute the waste reduction plan for the current constraint; Step 3B instructs you to eliminate measuring efficiency in non-constraints and Step 3C instructs you to execute the variation reduction plan for the current constraint. These three steps set the stage for Step 4.0, to measure and record results gained from the exploitation plan. Step 4A tells you to measure and record key metrics such as your new system throughput rate, constraint efficiency, WIP, etc.

In Section 3, you are then instructed to develop a plan to subordinate everything to the pace of the constraint. In Step 5.0, you need to slow the pace of non-constraints down to the same pace as the constraint. In Step 5A, you should now measure the new production rate and cycle time of the constraint, as both will have improved significantly. Step 5B explains that you should now set the cycle time of the operations ahead of and feeding the constraint to the same cycle time of the constraint. In Step 5C, you should then measure and record the new levels of WIP inventory and throughput rate.

We then move on to Step 6.0 of the roadmap, which instructs you to develop a plan to implement both Drum-Buffer-Rope (DBR) and the Theory of Constraints (TOC) Replenishment Solution. Step 6A states that you should lay out the foundation for both DBR and the TOC Distribution and Replenishment Solution. This foundation must include Step 6B, which calls out the development of a training plan for the front-line workers on both Drum-Buffer-Rope and the Replenishment Solution. Step 6C explains that you should then train the workforce on the Theory of Constraints, Drum-Buffer-Rope, and the TOC Replenishment Solution.

Next, in Step 7.0, you must now implement the plan that you developed in Step 6.0. This plan includes both the implementation of the TOC Replenishment Solution (Step 7A) and the implementation of your Drum-Buffer-Rope scheduling system. After completing Step 7.0, you should then follow the instructions for Step 8.0. There are three steps that should be completed, which include 8A, recording the new throughput rate; 8B, recording the new levels of WIP inventory; and 8C, recording the new levels of downtime related to raw material stock-outs.

In Section IV, you are instructed, if it is necessary, to elevate the system constraint. Many times, the actions you've already taken should have delivered capacities that will satisfy your needs as far as completing orders in a timely manner. If this is not the case, then you must proceed to Step 9.0, which states that, if capacity is still not high enough to meet demand, then you should develop a plan to elevate the constraint. When developing this plan, consider Steps 9A and 9B, which tell you, if possible, to off-load work from the constraint to your non-constraints. If this hasn't provided enough capacity to satisfy demand, then Step 9B should be used. Step 9B tells you that, if it is necessary, to purchase additional equipment or hire additional labor. Most of the time, you will not need to follow this step.

Step 10.0 instructs you to execute your constraint elevation plan by following Steps 10A and 10B. Step 10A explains that, based on results of Step 9.0, you should off-load work from your constraint to your constraint feeder step or your constraint receiver step. Step 10B tells you that, if it is not possible to off-load work from the constraint, then it may be necessary to purchase additional equipment or hire additional labor or work overtime in order to break the current constraint. As mentioned earlier, typically, this step will not be necessary.

Step 11.0 instructs you to measure and record new throughput results from the constraint. These recordings will include Step 11A, recording your new throughput rate; Step 11B, recording your new levels of WIP inventory; and Step 11C, recording new levels of downtime related to raw material stock-outs. If you have successfully completed all of the previous steps in the roadmap, you should see significantly higher throughput rates, amazing reductions in WIP inventory, and raw material stock-outs close to zero!

Section V tells you, if the constraint is broken, to return to Step 1.0 to locate the new constraint, which will have appeared immediately after you broke your current constraint. Step 12.0 instructs you to identify, measure, and analyze your process now that you have broken your current constraint. Step 12A instructs you to locate the new constraint by measuring new cycle times. Step 12B tells you to identify, measure, and analyze non-value-added waste in the new constraint you have just located. Step 12C instructs you to identify, measure, and analyze variation and defects in your new constraint.

Step 13.0 then instructs you to develop a plan to exploit your new constraint. You do so by using the information from Step 12.0 to create a new exploitation plan for the new constraint. The plan should include waste and variation reduction and defect elimination, but only focus the plan on the new constraint.

In Section VI, you should now exploit your new constraint. In Step 14.0, you are now instructed to execute the plan developed in Step 13.0. In Step 14A, you should execute the waste reduction plan for the new constraint, while, in Step 14B, you should execute the variation reduction plan for the new constraint. In Step 15.0, you should measure the results that now exist which include 15A, recording your new throughput rate; 15B, recording your new levels of WIP inventory; and Step 15C, recording your new levels of downtime related to raw material stock-outs. All three of these results should be the best your company has ever achieved. In fact, it would not be surprising that your new capacity will be much more than the number of orders you now have.

In Section VII, you are instructed to implement protective controls and develop a Mafia Offer in order to generate more sales. I discussed the Mafia Offer in detail in Chapter 17, so, if you aren't sure about how it works, go back and review it. But, for now, proceed on to Step 16.0, to develop and implement a plan to control and sustain your gains. Step 16A instructs you to, where necessary, create and implement control charts to sustain gains on key processes. In Step 16B, you should create and perform process and policy audits to assure that everything is functioning well.

In Step 17.0, you should now create and implement a Mafia Offer to generate more sales. In this step, you should develop and implement a new sales plan (Mafia Offer) that guarantees high on-time delivery, low cost, and the highest quality of any supplier. Remember, from Chapter 17, that a Mafia Offer is an offer that you can create, which will allow you to close new orders of more than eighty percent of prospective buyers. Think about what would happen to your profit levels if you were successful in closing on eighty percent of the customers who review your products or services. I know this sounds too good to be true, but, by creating a Mafia Offer, it is not only true, it's only the beginning for your company. A Mafia Offer is essentially an offer that is so good that the purchaser would have to be absolutely illogical if they were to buy goods or services from anyone but you.

## Expected Results

Early on in this chapter, we talked about Goldratt and Cox's Throughput Accounting measures (i.e., Throughput (T), Inventory (I), and Operating Expense (OE)). During the first cycle of improvement, you should have lowered inventory by not over-producing product at the non-constraint operations, and you should have also "burned off" any excess inventory that had collected within your system prior to the first cycle of the UIC. If you did these two things, then this reduction should have had an immediate, one-time positive impact on cash flow for your company. In addition, your operating expenses should have decreased as well, because you now have fewer defects, fewer repairs, less scrap, and less waste within your process. Although both the savings in inventory and operating expense should be respectable, in terms of bottom-line improvement, the real impact on the company will have come from increased Throughput! Assuming you haven't added large amounts of labor to break the constraint, which you should not have had to do, all of your new Throughput (revenue minus truly variable costs) should flow directly to the bottom line!

So, now let's try one more time to answer the question of why so many Lean, Six Sigma, and TOC initiatives might have failed. Some authors have stated incorrectly, or at least implied, that the Lean and Six Sigma philosophies are at odds with or are contradictory to the Theory of Constraints. Still others have suggested, also incorrectly, that Lean and Six Sigma are just complementary to TOC. The fact is, Lean and Six Sigma are, in fact, essential ingredients for the success of the Theory of Constraints.

By the same token, success in Lean and Six Sigma initiatives is driven by adopting TOC as the basis for improvement, simply because TOC supplies both the focus and leverage points needed for true improvement. All three initiatives, when implemented in concert with each other, as presented in the Ultimate Improvement Cycle, represent the best possible strategy for maximizing revenues and profits! These three initiatives form a *symbiosis* where not only do they co-exist, but they benefit from each other's presence. In fact, they form the *Ultimate Improvement Cycle* and act as a guide for maximizing profits!

Some of you, or maybe many of you, are saying to yourselves, "Is he crazy, I can't do even one initiative right, let alone all three at the same time!" Although this may be a concern, the reality is that by integrating Lean, Six Sigma, and the Theory of Constraints, life simply becomes much easier on the shop floor. Because you are typically limiting your focus on only one operation at a time (i.e., the constraint) and not attempting an enterprise-wide improvement initiative, you will:

- Have fewer resource allocation problems.
- Have fewer problems to solve at any one time.
- Have lower amounts of waste to remove at any one time.
- Have less organizational chaos and disorder.
- Have products that flow through your operation much faster and more efficiently.
- Have your rate of revenue generation improve dramatically.

■ Have employees who are more motivated.
■ Have faster return on investment.
■ Have much more impressive bottom-line results!

## Conclusion

In any industry, we must learn to recognize each of these methodologies as different steps of the same dance. Perhaps it is time to establish an industry-wide consortium that integrates these as a common technology. Although we shouldn't necessarily agree that Lean, Six Sigma, and TOC are different *entry points*, we should all believe that the Ultimate Improvement Cycle captures the essence of a common technology. Going forward, using the Ultimate Improvement Cycle, your organization will realize its full potential much faster and more effectively than you could have ever dreamed possible. Think about it: less waste, less defective product, less inventory, higher throughput, better on-time delivery, etc., which all translate into a faster revenue stream and higher and higher profits.

In the next chapter, we will discuss the subject of performance metrics, and, as you will see, selecting the correct performance metrics is absolutely critical to the success of your improvement efforts going forward!

## References

1. Bob Sproull, *The Ultimate Improvement Cycle – Maximizing Profits Through the Integration of Lean, Six Sigma and the Theory of Constraints*, CRC Press, Taylor & Francis Group, 2009.
2. Eliyahu M. Goldratt and Jeff Cox, *The Goal*, North River Press, 1986.
3. Jeffrey K. Liker and David Meier, *The Toyota Way Fieldbook – A Practical Guide for Implementing Toyota's 4P's* McGraw-Hill, 2006.

# Chapter 19

---

# Performance Metrics

---

It's important for any organization to be able to perform effectively, but how organizations measure their performance ties directly into their long-term direction and performance. Every for-profit company must understand that their profitability is absolutely not dependent upon how much money they can save, but rather how much money they can make. And the two approaches are dramatically different. I want to relate a short story, originally written by Bruce Nelson in our book, [1] *Epiphanized – A Novel Integrating Theory of Constraints, Lean, and Six Sigma*.

## The Sock Maker

In the early 1900s, Cost Accounting (CA) was in its early stages and beginning to be widely accepted and used. For a business owner, there were many things to consider in the day-to-day operation of the business. One of the most important functions of the business owner was tending to the daily needs of the business's financial situation. Keeping the books, calculating costs for raw materials, calculating labor costs, and making sales were all important issues to be dealt with on a daily basis.

It was understood by business owners that, in order to stay in business and make money, the cost they paid for the products or services rendered had to be less than the selling price of their products or services. If it wasn't, then they would quickly go out of business. Then as now, the needs of business haven't changed much, but other things have changed.

DOI: 10.4324/9781003462385-19

The ideas and concepts about what was important to measure and how to measure it were starting to form and were being passed from one generation to the next. This was considered important information that you needed to know in order to be successful. Without this understanding, it was assumed that you would fail. Back then, the business structure and methods were different from what they are today. The labor force was not nearly as reliable and most workers did not work forty hours a week. When they did work, they were not paid an hourly wage but instead were paid using the piece-rate pay system.

As an example, suppose you owned a knitting business, and the product you made and sold was socks. The employees in your business would knit socks as their job. With the piece-rate pay system, you paid the employees based on the number of socks they knitted in a day or a week, or whatever unit of measure you used. If an employee knitted ten pairs of socks in a day, and you paid a piece rate of $1.00 for each pair knitted, then you owed that employee $10.00. However, if the employee didn't show up for work and did not knit any socks, then you owed nothing. In this type of work environment, labor was truly a variable cost and deserved to be allocated as a cost to the product. It just made sense in a piece-rate pay system. The more socks the employees knitted, the more money they could make. Also, as the business owner, your labor costs were very precisely controlled. If employees didn't make any socks, then you didn't have to pay them.

In time, metrics for calculating labor costs changed and the labor rates changed as well. Many employees were now paid a daily rate, instead of a piece rate. Labor costs had now shifted from a truly variable cost per unit to a fixed cost per day. In other words, the employees got the same amount of money per day, no matter how many pairs of socks they knitted or didn't knit. As time went by, the employee labor rates shifted again. This time, labor rates shifted from a daily rate to an hourly rate. With the new hourly rate came the more standardized work week of forty hours, or eight hours a day, five days a week. With the hourly rate, the labor costs now became fixed.

With these changes, it became apparent to the sock-knitting business owner that, in order to get the biggest bang for the labor buck, the owner needed to produce as many pairs of socks as he could in a day, in order to offset the rising labor costs. The most obvious way to do that was to keep all of your sock knitters busy all of the time, making socks. In other words, efficiency was a key ingredient and needed to be increased. If the owner could make more pairs of socks in the same amount of time, then his labor cost per pair of socks would go down. This was the solution the business owner was looking for, reducing his costs. If everyone was busy, making more and more socks, and they could make a lot of socks in a day, then his new labor cost per pair of socks could be reduced! This had to be the answer! Look how cheaply he could make socks now! Or so he thought.

With these new-found levels of high efficiency came another problem. The owner quickly noticed that he had to buy more and more raw materials just to keep his employees working at such high levels of efficiency. The raw materials were expensive, but he had to have them. The owner knew that his past success was directly linked to his ability to maintain such high efficiencies and keep his cost low. More and more raw materials were brought in. More and more socks were made. The socks were now being made much faster than he could sell them. What he needed now was more warehouse space to store all of those wonderfully cheap socks! So, at great expense, the owner built another warehouse to store more and more cheap socks. The owner had lots and lots of inventory of very cheap socks. According to his numbers, the socks were now costing next to nothing to make. He was saving lots of money! Wasn't he?

Soon the creditors started to show up wanting their money. The owner was getting behind on his bills to his raw material suppliers. He had warehouses full of very cheap socks, but he wasn't selling his socks at the same rate as he was making them. He was just making more socks. He rationalized that he had to keep the costs down and, in order to do that, he had to have high efficiency. The business owner soon realized that he had to save even more money. He had to cut his costs even more, so he had to lay people off and reduce his workforce to save even more money. How did he ever get into a situation like this? His business was highly efficient. His cost per pair of socks was very low. He saved the maximum amount of money he could, and yet he was going out of business! How come?

Reality had changed and labor costing had changed (labor shifted from a variable cost to a fixed cost), but the Cost Accounting rules had not changed. The owner was still trying to treat his labor cost as a variable cost. Even today, many businesses still try to treat their labor cost as a variable cost and allocate the labor cost to individual products. When the labor costs are allocated to a product, then companies try and take the next step – they work hard to improve efficiency and drive down the labor costs per part or unit. This erroneous thought process is ingrained in their mind, and they believe that this action will somehow reduce labor costs. And if you could reduce labor costs, then you are making more profit. But take just a moment and reflect back on the consequences of the sock maker's experience with cost savings and the high-efficiency model. Are these end results anywhere close to what the business owner really wanted to have happen? Was this the real outcome business owners wanted from high efficiency?

## The Efficiency Model

The efficiency model, when measured and implemented at the wrong system location, will have devastating effects on your perceived results. The end results will actually be the opposite of what you expected or wanted to happen. I wonder why, with all of the technological improvements accomplished throughout the years, it is still acceptable to use Cost Accounting rules from the early 1900s. So, let's look more into the "rules" of Cost Accounting.

## Cost Accounting

The primary focus of Cost Accounting is per part or per unit cost reductions. Because perceived cost reductions are viewed so favorably, is it any wonder that there is so much emphasis on efficiency? And yet cost reductions don't seem to be the answer. There have been many highly efficient companies that have come close to going out of business or have gone out of business. Have you ever heard of a company that has saved itself into prosperity? Think about it, any perceived savings that the sock maker thought he was getting were quickly eroded by buying more raw materials. In fact, it ended up costing the sock maker much more money than he realized and not saving him anything! He was doing all of the recommended practices and yet he was failing. How come?

Many companies will emphatically state that the primary *goal* of their company is to *make money*, and yet they spend the largest portion of their time trying to *save money*. It would appear they've forgotten what their goal really is. The strategy you employ to *make money* is *vastly different* from the strategy you would employ to *save money*. For most companies, the assumption is that saving money is equal to making money. That is, if you somehow save some money, it's the same as making money. This is simply not true!

These two concepts are divergent in their thinking – each takes you in a different direction with different results. If the real *goal* of your company is to save money, then the very best way to accomplish your goal is to *go out of business*. This action will save you the maximum amount of money. Goal accomplished! However, if the goal of your company is to make money, then a different strategy must be employed, which is maximizing throughput through the system. Let's now look at a different form of accounting, known as Throughput Accounting.

## Throughput Accounting

Suppose we consider again the same example using the sock maker. Suppose the sock maker wants to make three times as many socks as he is making now. What does he have to do? Using the piece-rate pay system, he would have to hire three times as many employees to be sock makers and pay them a piece rate of $1.00 per pair. So, in order to make three times as many pairs of socks, the labor rate must go up and he has to hire three times as many people. In the piece-rate world, getting three times as much through the system will cost him three times as much in labor.

But let us suppose our sock maker is paying an hourly wage, rather than a piece rate. Furthermore, suppose he figures out a way to make three more pairs of socks per worker, per day. By being able to make three times as many, how much do his labor costs go up? They *do not* go up at all! His labor rate stays exactly the same! He still pays the workers an hourly rate, whether they make one pair of socks or ten pairs of socks. He only has to pay the employees once, not a rate based on the number of socks made. His only increase in cost comes from buying more raw materials to make the socks. So why does modern-day Cost Accounting still try to allocate a labor cost per unit of work, and then claim that increased efficiency drives down the cost per part? It does no such thing! In today's reality, labor costs are fixed, not variable!

Perhaps it is possible that some of these Cost Accounting rules and methods might be wrong and mislead the user into thinking that some results are better than they really are. Is it possible that there might be another way to look logically at the practice of accounting, that will truly get us closer to the goal? What if there was another way? A way that provides an alternative accounting method that allows us to remove, abandon, or ignore the Cost

Accounting rules that are causing so much trouble? Let's now have a look at Throughput Accounting.

Throughput Accounting is not necessarily a frontal attack on Cost Accounting. However, it is a different way to view the accounting measures, solve issues, and manage the company at a much higher success and profitability level. It's an update of the *accounting rules*, if you will, that is much more in line with current business reality. I realize that I have covered Throughput Accounting in previous chapters, but it's my contention that understanding Throughput Accounting will be your company's lever to success.

Throughput Accounting uses primarily three performance metrics, namely Throughput (T), Investment (I), and Operating Expense (OE). These metrics are a simplified methodology that removes all of the mystery of accounting and rolls it into three simple measures.

1. ***Throughput*** is the rate at which inventory is converted into sales. If you make lots of products and put them in a warehouse, that is not throughput, it's *inventory*. The products or services only count as throughput if they are sold to the customer and fresh money comes back into the business system.
2. ***Investment/Inventory*** is the money an organization invests in items that it intends to sell. This category would include inventory, both raw materials and finished goods. This includes buildings, machines, and other equipment used to make products for sale, knowing that any or all of these investments could, at some point in time, be sold for cash.
3. ***Operating Expense*** is all of the money spent generating the Throughput. This includes rent, electricity, phone, benefits, and wages. It is any money spent that does not fit within one of the first two TA categories.

When you read and understand these definitions, it seems likely that all the money within your company can be categorized to fit within one of these three measures.

In thinking about Throughput Accounting (TA), it is important to consider the following thought: Throughput Accounting (TA) is neither costing nor Cost Accounting (CA). Instead, TA is focused on cash, without the need for allocation to a specific product. This concept includes the variable and fixed expenses for a product. The only slight variation would be the calculation for Total Variable Cost (TVC). In this case, the TVC is a cost that is truly variable for a product or service, such as raw materials, paying a sales commission, or shipping charges. The sum total of these costs becomes the product TVC.

TVC is *only the cost* associated with each product. Some would argue that labor should also be added as a variable cost per product. Not true! Labor is no longer a variable cost – it's a fixed cost. With the hourly labor measures, you pay employees for vacation, public holidays, and sick leave. You pay them when they are making nothing! The employees cost you exactly the same amount of money whether they are at work or not. Using this example, labor is an Operating Expense and not a variable cost associated with products.

The following definitions apply to TA:

1. Throughput (T) = Product Selling Price (SP) – the Total Variable Cost (TVC),

or

$$T = SP - TVC.$$

2. Net Profit (NP) = Throughput (T) minus Operational Expense (OE), or NP = T – OE
3. Return on Investment (ROI) = Net Profit (NP) divided by Inventory (I), or ROI = NP/I
4. Productivity (P) = Throughput (T) divided by Operating Expense (OE), or P = T/OE
5. Inventory Turns (IT) = Throughput (T) divided by Inventory Value (IV), or IT = T/I

Some would argue that Throughput Accounting falls short because it is not able to pigeonhole all of the categories of Cost Accounting into Throughput Accounting categories. Things like interest payments on loans, payment of stockholder dividends, or depreciation of machines or facilities. However, this argument appears to be invalid. Which one of those specific categories can't be placed into one of the Throughput Accounting categories? The baseline TA concept is really very simple. If you have to write a check to somebody else, it's either an Investment (I) or an Operating Expense (OE). It's an Investment if it is something you can sell for money at some point in time;

it's an OE if you can't. Put this debt in the category that makes the most sense. On the other hand, if somebody is writing a check to you, and you get to make a deposit, then it's probably a Throughput (T). Cost Accounting rules have made it much more complicated and difficult than it needs to be. When you make it that complex and difficult, and intently argue about the semantics, the stranglehold that CA has on your thinking becomes even more obvious.

Throughput Accounting is really focused on providing the necessary information that allows decision-makers to make better decisions. If the goal of the company is truly to make money, then any decisions being considered should get the company closer to the goal and not further away. Effective decision-making is well suited to an effective T, I, and OE analysis. This analysis can show the impact of any local decisions on the bottom line of the company. Ideally, good business decisions will cause:

1. Throughput (T) to increase.
2. Investment/Inventory to decrease or stay the same. It is also possible that Investment can go up, as long as the effect on T is exponential. In other words, sometimes a very well- placed investment can cause the T to skyrocket.
3. Operating Expenses decrease or stay the same. It is not always necessary to decrease QE to have a dramatic effect. Consider the situation where the T actually doubles, and you didn't have to hire anyone new to do it, nor did you have to lay anyone off.

The decision-making process becomes much easier when these factors are considered. The movement, either up or down, of these three measures should provide sufficient information for good strategy and better decisions. Any good decision should be based on global impacts on the company and not just a single unit or process in isolation. If your thinking is limited to the lowest level of the organization, and you are focused on the wrong area, then the positive impact will never be seen or felt by the entire organization.

## Comparing Cost Accounting and Throughput Accounting

If we compare these two accounting methods at the highest level, then Cost Accounting is all about the actions you take to try and *save money,* and

Throughput Accounting is all about the actions you take to *make money.* Once you've made the cost reductions and you still need more, what do you do next? Where else can you reduce costs? On the other hand, making money, at least in theory, is infinite. What is the limit on how much money your company can make now? Figure 19.1 compares the top-level priorities of these two accounting approaches. With these differences in priorities, it is easy to see why Cost Accounting is focused on saving money, whereas Throughput Accounting is focused on making money. So, consider the real goal of your company before you decide which path to take.

You can pick up the newspaper or watch TV almost any day of the week and see the effects of these priorities. You can read about or hear about company XYZ that is going to lay off 500 employees in order to reduce costs and become more efficient and align themselves to be more vertical with the customer and … blah, blah, blah! What these companies are really saying is they have forgotten how to make money or never learned. They are so focused on saving money that they have forgotten what the real goal of the company is, which is making money!

So, how did all of this come about? Why are things happening the way they are? If all of this Cost Accounting and saving money is so good, then how come so many companies seem to be in financial trouble or, worse yet, going bankrupt? There are many reasons and some could be debated for weeks, if not months or years. But however many reasons there may be, all of them are not equal. Some reasons are bigger players than others, and, as such, have had a far greater impact. Let's look at the cost model associated with both the Cost Accounting and Throughput Accounting concepts. It provides an interesting history of why things are the way they are. Figure 19.2 defines the cost model concept for both Cost Accounting and Throughput Accounting.

| Priority | Common Practice | Common Sense |
|---|---|---|
| 1. | OE | T |
| 2. | T | I |
| 3. | I | OE |
| | Cost World Thinking | Throughput World Thinking |

**Figure 19.1   AAA**

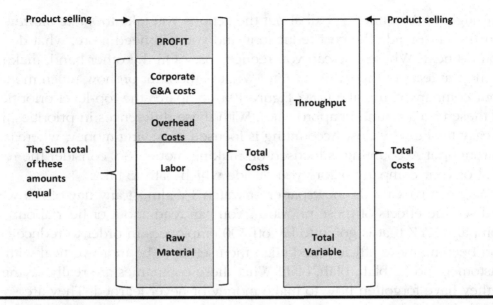

**Figure 19.2  AAA**

The product depicted in Figure 19.2 is exactly the same for both models. It indicates the same selling price, same manufacturing process, same everything. In the Cost Accounting model, you note the layers of allocated cost that are applied to each product as some percentage of the cost or allocated rate. The sum total of all of these costs, whatever it may be, equals what Cost Accounting considers to be the cost to manufacture. Let's look at each layer.

■ *Raw Materials.* This is the total cost of all the raw materials used in the product you produce. An average raw material cost for most companies might be around 40%, but some can, and do, go much higher.
■ *Labor Costs.* This is the allocated labor cost per part. It is usually calculated based on some type of total parts per hour, day, production batch, order, or some other value. Then the total labor cost is divided by the number of parts produced to arrive at the percentage of labor to be allocated to each part.
■ *Overhead Costs.* This is the allocated percentage per part to pay for all of the overhead costs. These include items like the management staff, administrative jobs, training, and so on. Usually, these types of overhead assignments cover many types of parts, but also no part in particular. Human Resources or even Finance are examples of organizations

that fit in the overhead category. You need to have someplace to charge and collect your overhead costs.
■ *Corporate General and Administrative.* This is the allocated cost that pays for all of the corporate staff and everything they provide.
■ *Profit.* This is the location where you add the percentage of profit you want to receive for your product.
■ *Selling Price (SP).* This is the selling price for your product, once you've gone through and added together all of the manufacturing cost categories and the percentage of profit.

There very well could be more layers in your company, but, in the end, the hope is that when you add up all of the costs and sell to the market, consumer, or the next guy in the supply chain, your selling price is always greater than your manufacturing costs. If it is, then you have made a profit.

In reality, the selling price is not determined by the manufacturer, but rather by the consumer. If the price is too high, they simply won't buy your product and will look elsewhere. So, if that happens, what are your choices? Somehow, you have to lower your cost and selling price in order to make your product more attractive to the consumer. So how do you do that? You could cut your profit margins, but most organizations do not like to do that. If you can't do that, then what else do you look for?

How about overhead costs? You can slow down or stop doing some of the things associated with overheads, for example, training. You could cut your raw materials expenses. Perhaps you could find a different vendor, or maybe buy cheaper parts. If you do that, then what about the quality risk? How about cutting labor costs? If you could just get more efficient, then your labor costs would go down. If labor costs go down, then you can make more profit – correct? I think, by now, you understand the cycle of chaos that takes place when you focus on efficiency: disaster usually follows in short order. Such is life in the cost model cycle.

In your company, if you *do not* pay your employees using the piece-rate pay system, then the assumption of using allocated labor costs, or any costs, is invalid! Why is the stigma of allocated costs so strong in Cost Accounting? The assumption that higher efficiency will reduce the cost per part is also invalid. In today's reality of the per hour rate, the cost remains the same.

The Throughput Accounting cost model contains only Total Variable Cost (TVC) and Throughput (T). The calculation is simple: $T = SP-TVC$. Throughput, in essence, equals the dollars remaining from selling the product, after you have subtracted the TVC cost and received payments. Nothing is allocated, nothing is assumed, it's just a simple cash calculation from the sale. Now that you have a good idea of why Throughput Accounting is a superior accounting method for making real-time financial decisions, I want to discuss a closely related subject, local optimum versus global optimum, while also providing more details on why Throughput Accounting is far superior to Cost Accounting for making real-time financial decisions.

## Local Optimum Versus Global Optimum

In this section, I want to discuss a common conflict that exists between *local* and *global* performance measures, especially when operational decisions must be made in real time. Much of what is to follow is based on the writings of [2] L. Srikanth and Michael Umble's book, *Synchronous Management – Profit-Based Manufacturing for the 21st Century, Volume 1*. If you've never read their book, I highly recommend that you do so.

One of the most important functions of performance measures is to motivate the right behaviors, but the standard cost system, based upon the teachings of Cost Accounting, simply encourages what I believe are the wrong behaviors. In addition, I will also recommend what I believe is a superior system to help you make better financial decisions, effectively evaluate and enhance organizational performance, and encourage people to take appropriate actions. The bottom line is that managers need a set of measures that will help them make decisions that enhance the performance of the "global system" rather than local improvements to isolated parts of the system.

If you ask many managers what the goal of their organization is, it's not uncommon to hear things like "to provide high-quality products at competitive prices" or "to provide better customer service" or "to capture market share" or "to reduce costs," etc. In reality, the goal of all for-profit companies should be to "make money, both now and in the future." With this goal in mind, every management decision, from all parts of the organization, must be directed toward helping the organization reach this goal. The problem that I have seen in many companies is that most companies lack the appropriate guidelines to help managers achieve this goal. So, let's focus our attention on the real role of performance measures, as they apply to making decisions that enhance the performance of the organization as a whole and not just parts of it.

In a typical company, during the first part of the month, the actions of the entire work force are heavily influenced by standard Cost Accounting performance measures, which primarily have a "local" focus. Measures like manpower efficiency and/or equipment utilization, as they apply to specific machines, the workers themselves, work centers, and departments are quite common. These measurements stress the standard time to process a part, as well as the cost to produce one unit at each operation. As Srikanth and Umble [2] explain, the supervisors act as if they are wearing blinkers as they strive to meet the established time and cost standards, without regard to how their actions affect the rest of the plant. Individual departments, working in virtual isolation, each striving to meet their own efficiency standards, can have a devastating effect on downstream operations. Perhaps the most glowing example of this is a supervisor running an excessively large batch of a particular part in order to economize on setup time and drive efficiencies higher. Of course, what happens is that we most likely find excess work-in-process (WIP) inventory of some parts and shortages of others.

The excess WIP occurs because the large batches result in more units of the part being produced than are required in the short term to satisfy an order. Shortages occur because a lengthy production run of any one item causes a delay in the timely production of other items that are required at downstream operations. The performance metric looks good, but some operations may develop huge backlogs of work, whereas others may have to shut down while they wait for parts to arrive. In addition, some supervisors may also create bottlenecks by utilizing their most efficient equipment, so as to keep their efficiencies high.

As the end of the reporting period approaches, with shipments now behind schedule, general financial measures (e.g., monthly shipping goals) for the plant as a whole take center stage and the plant manager intervenes. The workers are now told to do whatever it takes to meet the shipping targets for the reporting period. Because the shipping targets are in jeopardy, metrics like efficiency and utilization are temporarily abandoned in favor of the "global measures." As a result, production workers are forced to work overtime, expediters take actions to split/overlap batches, the schedule changes, and a host of other panic-driven actions are taken so that shipping targets (a global measure) can be met. The problem is, when the new reporting period starts, this vicious cycle repeats itself, month after month, year after year.

This example demonstrates just how inefficient and nonsensical this mode of operation really is. This constant shifting back and forth between working on achieving local optimums until the end of the reporting period enters the picture, and then shifting toward meeting global optimums, is ridiculous. The problem is that, for most of the month, individual actions are taken to satisfy local performance measures, when the focus should be on satisfying the company's goal of making money. Clearly, the reason these traditional cost-based procedures are so misguided and cause dysfunctional behaviors is that they reinforce the idea of maximizing the performance of individual subsystems, rather than optimizing the performance of the total system. It should be obvious that, in order to improve the overall system, you must make sure that your performance measurement system supports the overall goal of the organization and not subsections of it.

## Efficiency and Utilization

In the previous section, I talked about what typically happens at the end of the production month, as the typical cost-based performance metrics are abandoned, so that required shipping quantities can be achieved. This phenomenon is referred to as the end-of-the-month syndrome or the hockey stick effect. Throughout the month, individual departments work to maximize their own individual performance measures (e.g., operator efficiency or equipment utilization), until they are forced by leadership to sacrifice their own metrics so that higher-level company objectives can be achieved. So, what drives this curious behavior? The fact is, it is directly related to the metrics used to measure the performance of the organization, namely local efficiency and utilization. So, where do you think these two measures came from?

Efficiency and utilization evolved as part of manufacturing management framework, consistent with the standard cost system. The basic belief within the standard cost system assumes that the higher the level of efficiency and utilization, the higher the profits will be. In effect, this approach assumes that both the plant's and the company's performance metrics are maximized when each of the individual departments within the organization is operating at maximum efficiency and utilization. The problem with this thinking is that, by focusing on local performance optimization, it actually "damages" the performance of the total system. When choosing to maximize efficiency and/or utilization, the system becomes clogged with excess inventory, which, in turn, causes cycle times to lengthen, and ultimately deliveries to be delayed.

Every business that manufactures products is made up of various subsystems within the total system. The product has to be designed, engineered, and the required materials and resources must be purchased. The product then has to be manufactured, marketed, sold, delivered, and payment received from the buyer. It's extremely important for all of these departments to work together, rather than working in isolation. If the company is to be successful, all must act like a winning sports team. So, how can you measure bottom-line success?

The traditional bottom-line financial measurements of making money are net profit (NP) and return on investment (ROI). Net profit is an absolute measure of whether or not a company is truly making money, but net profit by itself is not enough. For example, suppose a firm had a net profit of $1.0 million last year. Is this amount good for a company? We can't answer that question unless we know how much the company had to invest in order to generate $1.0 million. If the investment was $5 million, then $1.0 million represents an ROI of 20% percent, which is a very good return. On the other hand, if the investment was $100 million, then the ROI is 1%, which is not very good. These two bottom-line measurements are adequate to determine whether your company is making money, but they are totally inadequate for evaluating operational and investment decisions. As we saw in our case study example, the use of standard cost-based concepts could very well lead you to make the wrong decisions. So, if these aren't acceptable, then what can we use to improve our decision-making when we're making a purchasing or investment decision?

## A New Decision-Making Perspective

The foundation for this new approach is the development of a set of measures that can be used to correctly assess the impact of specific actions on the productivity and profitability of your entire company. These same measures will also play a key role in the development of ways that will provide you with much better operational decisions in real time. This approach will use three operational and global measures specific to manufacturing companies:

- Throughput (T)
- Inventory (I)
- Operating Expense (OE)

An important point to remember is that, in order to be universally applicable, the performance measures must be common to all manufacturing companies, and they should also accurately describe the key activities that govern a plant's performance. With this in mind, there are three basic activities that a manufacturer undertakes:

- Purchasing of raw materials and/or component parts.
- The conversion of purchased materials into finished goods.
- The sale of the finished goods to customers.

The Theory of Constraints (TOC) offers companies a way to use the three operational metrics, T, I, and OE, to make better operational decisions. Investment/Inventory (I) represents the money invested in materials; Operating Expense (OE) is the money spent by the company for assets and expenses; and Throughput (T) is the money generated and received by the company from the sale of finished goods. Let's look at each of these in a bit more detail.

If you look at a standard dictionary definition of Throughput, it simply states that it represents the total outlook. The TOC definition considers only units sold and not units produced, because the finished goods do not generate revenue until they are sold and money is received from the sale of these finished goods. Traditional Cost Accounting considers inventory as an asset, but TOC tells us that the finished goods are of no value until they are sold, and money is received. [2] The authors tell us that, as support for this argument, just consider the amount of product that is written off, sold at distressed prices, or simply becomes obsolete. So, in order to link manufacturing performance to real profit, you need to measure sales rather than how many units you produced.

One of the major differences between traditional Cost Accounting and Throughput Accounting is how inventory is appraised. The simple change in calculating money generated at the time of sale, and not at the time it is produced is a shift in reality from a seller's market to a buyer's market. Cost Accounting assumes that everything produced would eventually be sold (seller's market). But, in a buyer's market, this is not the case. The bottom line is that you make a profit only when you sell products and receive payment for the products, and not when you produce them. So, the inevitable conclusion is that you need to measure sales rather than production. In this sense, throughput per unit for a given product is calculated as sales revenue per unit minus the cost of the raw materials or component parts added as follows:

t = throughput per unit

t = sales revenue per unit − raw material or component parts cost

So, the total throughput per period of time for a product is the "t" value multiplied by the total quantity sold of that product. For example, if T1 denotes the total product for product 1, then T1 is calculated as follows:

T1 = throughput per unit of product 1 × quantity (q) of product 1 sold

= t1 × q1

From this equation, if T represents the total throughput for a manufacturer for a given time period, total throughput is calculated as follows:

T = the sum of Throughput for each of "n" products sold by the company

= T1 + T2 + T3 + ......+ Tn

Before leaving this discussion of Throughput, it's important to remember that Throughput measures output in dollars and not activity (e.g., work-in-process inventory). Activity that does not contribute to sales or the conversion of materials into products sold is essentially waste. Let's now turn our attention to the subject of inventory.

The authors, [2] Srikanth and Umble, explain that their definition of inventory is different from the traditional definition in two important ways. First, their definition of inventory does not add value to the product as it progresses through the process. Traditional Cost Accounting dictates that, as material progresses through the process, it absorbs both labor and overhead. Because of this, the inventory value of material increases as it is processed through the various steps in the process. If, for example, a part's raw materials are valued at $100, using the traditional costing method, that same part could be valued at $110 after the first step in the process. After it passes through all of the steps in the process, the value of those same raw materials could grow to $175 and more when it's delivered to the finished goods stocking area. Under the authors' definition, the value of the part remains unchanged at $100, as it passes through the various processing steps. Therefore, the authors' definition of inventory is simply the amount of money tied up in materials the company intends to sell.

I = purchased material value of raw materials, purchased parts, work-in-process, and finished goods inventories.

The authors rightfully point out that this assumption of increasing "value" is very misleading. Not only has no value been created, but it is also very possible that value has actually been lost. As materials progress through manufacturing operations, they actually lose flexibility, meaning that they could become limited to single-type products. And if there is no demand for the product, not only was no value (or Throughput) created, but material was consumed and must be replaced when a different product is ordered. In order to avoid these distortions, the authors value inventory at the original value (or cost) of the material. Labor and other expenses incurred in the production process are accounted for in the next category, Operating Expense.

Operating Expense (OE) includes all of the money spent by the system, with the exception of the money spent to purchase inventory (i.e., truly variable expenses), since this latter expense has already been accounted for in the definition of Throughput. Operating Expense is money spent by the company to convert Inventory into Throughput.

$$OE = \text{actual spending to turn I into T}$$

The authors explain that there are two critical differences between their definition and the traditional concept of the cost of operations. First, there is no fundamental difference between direct labor and indirect labor because both assist in the conversion of Inventory into Throughput. Therefore, all personnel-related expenses are included in OE.

The second difference is that, for the most part, Operating Expense includes actual expenses. That is, it counts real money or checks written, as opposed to elements such as variances. Under the traditional Cost Accounting procedure, if an operator is producing parts at a faster rate than the Engineering standard for the operation, then that worker will be generating a positive variance and the cost of operations will be reduced. And this applies even if there is no demand for the product! Under the authors' definitions, the same situation results in no change in Throughput (T), an increase in Inventory (I), and no change in Operating Expense (OE) because the operator's wages don't change. The standard cost system views labor costs as infinitely variable; whereas, in the authors' method (i.e., Synchronous Management measurement system), normal labor costs (excluding overtime) are viewed as fixed in the short term.

# A Simple Example

In order to illustrate the methodology for calculating T, I, and OE, the authors [2] ask us to consider a small wood shop that makes a single product – desks. As discussed in previous chapters, the total Throughput for this shop is the sum of the Throughput contribution of each desk sold. To find the Throughput of a single desk that sells for $400, we need to know the cost of all of the materials used to manufacture a single desk. The [2] authors tell us that the cost of the wood, veneer, hardware, etc., used in the desk totals $100. To calculate the Throughput (T) per unit for this desk, we use the following equation:

■ t = sales revenue per desk – purchased material cost per desk
■ t = $400 − $100 = $300 per desk

Using this formula, we can calculate the throughput for every desk sold. The total Throughput (T) for any specific period is obtained by adding the total Throughput per desk of all desks sold in that period. If the shop sells a total of 50 desks in a given month, then the total Throughput (T) is found by summing up the Throughput per desk for all 50 desks sold as follows:

Total Throughput = throughput per desk $(t)$ × number of desks sold $(q)$

$$T = t \times q$$

$$= \$300 \text{ per desk} \times 50 \text{ desks}$$

$$= \$15,000$$

To determine the value of the inventory in the system, we need to find the purchase value of all of the production materials currently in the shop. This includes all of the wood material in various forms such as chip cores, veneer, and cut and raw lumber; plus, it also includes all of the material that is either in process and in the stockrooms, as well as hardware such as drawer hangers, knobs, and hinges. Remember, using the authors' method, their definition of inventory is valued at the purchase price paid. The value of all of this inventory was $32,000. Also, remember that the inventory does not include production tools, such as saws, drill and router bits, sanders, etc. Nor does this inventory include other supplies such as coffee cups, paper, etc. Operating expense includes all of the costs incurred in running the shop, as follows:

**Table 19.1 Monthly Operating Expense**

| Category | Purchase Value |
|---|---|
| Salaries, insurance, and payroll taxes | $ 10,000 |
| Rent and utilities | $ 750 |
| Supplies (glue, finishing chemicals, etc.) | $ 200 |
| Payment on equipment purchases | $ 1,800 |
| Interest on borrowed funds | $ 400 |
| Other miscellaneous items | $ 300 |
| Total operating expenses | $13,450 |

We then end up with the following values for Throughput (T), Inventory (I), and Operating Expenses (OE) as follows:

$$T = \$15,000 \qquad I = \$32,000 \qquad OE = \$13,450$$

The authors go on to explain that, to make more money, a manufacturing company must generate more sales, spend less money on conversion of raw materials to finished products, and have less money tied up in inventory. The authors summarize this by the following principle:

■ *Operational Measures Principle*: Throughput should be going up, Inventory should be going down, and Operating Expense should be going down, ideally, all at the same time. However, it is possible, and maybe even desirable, to have one of the measures go in the wrong direction (or remain the same) in order to improve another one.

## Effect of Changes in T, I, and OE on Performance

Using our wood shop example presented earlier, we will summarize how the financial performance of this wood shop changes as a result of changes in T, I and OE. In this example, the monthly net profit is equal to Throughput minus Operating Expense, and works out to be $15,000 minus $13,450, or $1,550. At this rate, the annual Net Profit was projected to be $1,550 per month × 12 months, or $18,600. We will now consider three cases, where T, I, and OE are each improved by 10%.

- Throughput increases by 10%, with no change in Inventory and Operating Expense. This can be accomplished in one of three ways: sales price per desk increases, material costs decrease, or additional desks are sold. In this example, the authors elected to have five additional desks sold each month, using the same workforce (because there was excess capacity). T increases by $1,500 per month (i.e., 5 desks × $300 per desk = $1,500) and OE does not change. Remember that the cost of the extra materials to make the extra desks has already been subtracted from the calculation of the total Throughput (T). Therefore, Net Profit (NP) increases by $1,500 per month, from $1,550 to $3,050 or an increase of 97%.
- Investment/Inventory is reduced by 10%, with no change in Throughput or Operating Expense. Since the Inventory value was $32,000, this means there was a reduction of $3,200. Inventory, as the authors have defined it, will eventually affect profitability through a reduction in the inventory carrying cost, which is part of Operating Expense. The authors considered just one aspect of this reduction in carrying cost – a reduction in the interest paid to the bank. Because there is less money tied up in Inventory, less money will be borrowed from the bank. If the interest rate charged by the bank is 10%, then a reduction of $3,200 will result in savings of $320 annually and the NP would go up by this amount. The additional NP of $320 per year represents an increase of 1.72% (based upon an annual NP of $18,600).
- Operating Expense is reduced by 10%, with Throughput and Inventory remaining unchanged. The old Operating Expense was $13,450 per month, so the monthly decrease in expenses is $1,345. This means that the new monthly Operating Expenses would be $12,105. With Throughput remaining the same, the Net Profit would become $2,895 per month ($15,000 − $12,105) for an increase of 87%.

The authors are very clear in stating that, in their Synchronous Management approach, the appropriate question is not "What are the cost savings for a specific action?" Instead, the appropriate question is "What is the impact of the action on the operational measures of T, I, and OE?" It has been shown that changes in T, I, and OE will ultimately have a financial impact on the entire business. They further explain that these same operational measures represent a superior alternative to the standard cost system when evaluating the financial impact of manufacturing actions.

It is also important to understand that these operational measures are not intended to replace those required for GAAP reporting, since they are required by law. But, for real-time decision-making, using T, I, and OE will always result in much better decisions. The bottom line is that the performance measurement and evaluation systems inherent in the standard cost system have contributed significantly to inappropriate actions, poor decisions, and dysfunctional behaviors in many manufacturing companies.

Before closing this chapter, I want to, once again, recommend [2] L. Srikanth and Michael Umble's wonderful book, *Synchronous Management – Profit-Based Manufacturing for the 21st Century, Volume One*. For those of you who utilize Project Management to run your business, in the next chapter I want to demonstrate the Theory of Constraints version of Project Management. Although most of you are probably using some version of the Critical Path Methodology (CPM), I want to explain and demonstrate a superior version of Project Management known as Critical Chain Project Management (CCPM).

# References

1. *Epiphanized – A Novel on Unifying Theory of Constraints, Lean, and Six Sigma*, CRC Press, 2015.
2. L. Srikanth and Michael Umble, *Synchronous Management – Profit-Based Manufacturing for the 21st Century, Volume One*, The Spectrum Publishing Company, 1997.

# Chapter 20

# Critical Chain Project Management

If yours is an organization that relies on project completions as their source of revenue, and you're like many other project-based organizations, then the results of multiple surveys by the Standish Group [1] and others might be of concern to you. In 1994, the Standish Group conducted a landmark study of nearly 10,000 IT projects across America and found that 52% of projects ended up costing greater than 189% of the original budget, 31% were canceled, and only 16% of projects were completed on time and on budget. The costs of these failures and overruns are just the tip of the proverbial iceberg. The lost opportunity costs are probably immeasurable but could easily be in the trillions of dollars. Pretty scary figures, if project execution is your business model.

In 2002, [2] the Public Accounts Committee reported that the UK government had 100 major IT projects underway, with a total value of roughly 10 billion euro. [3] The Spending Review of 2002 allocated approximately 6 billion euro over three years to government electronic service delivery. However, [4] *Computing* magazine calculated that the cost of canceled or over-budget government IT projects between 1997 and 2003 was greater than 1.5 billion euro.

In 2006, the new [5] *Chaos Report* revealed that only 19% of projects begun were considered outright failures, compared to 31% reported in 1994. In addition, 35% of software projects started in 2006 could be categorized as successful, meaning they were completed on time, on budget, and met user requirements. Although this is a marked improvement from their initial

DOI: 10.4324/9781003462385-20

groundbreaking report, it's safe to say that these statistics still aren't acceptable, or at least where they need to be! The point is, project failure rates appear to be a universal problem, spanning virtually all industry types and, although the success rates are improving, they still don't rise to an acceptable level.

So, the question posed to you is, "What if there was a way to demonstrate a method that would push your projects' successful completion rate from where it is now to over 90%? Would you be interested in hearing about it?"

## What's Everyone Using Now?

Approximately 90% of project managers around the world are using a project management methodology known as the *Critical Path Method* (CPM) and have been doing so for many years. If you ask a typical project manager about what factors delayed a completed project, most will tell you that it was something they didn't expect, or even had no control over, or something that cropped up in some of the tasks and delayed them. In other words, uncertainty, or the Murphy bug bit them! Every project from virtually every environment has uncertainty associated with it and how this uncertainty is dealt with determines the ultimate success or failure of the project. So, in order for a project to be successful, there must be a way to protect it from uncertainty. Let's take a look at how traditional project management (i.e., CPM) attempts to protect a project from inevitable uncertainty.

The Critical Path Method attempts to protect a project by using a "fudge factor." When developing the project plan, the duration of each individual task is estimated by the resources responsible for executing them and then a "safety factor" is added to each task by the resource responsible for completing it. For example, suppose the realistic estimate of time for an individual task is one week. Is one week what the resource actually tells his or her project manager? Typically, the resource will add a safety factor of their own to guard against those "things" that might happen that could cause a delay in the completion of the task. As a result, it's not unusual for the original one week to be quoted as two weeks. Resources react this way because they know from experience that as soon as they give the project manager an estimate, it automatically becomes a commitment!

A typical project manager will then add up all of the individual, inflated time estimates and then add his or her own safety factor. Why? Because

Project Managers know that at some point in the project, Murphy will strike and some of the tasks will be delayed. To guard against this delay, the Project Manager adds a safety factor to protect the project from being late. Keep in mind that every resource inflates every task, so it's not uncommon for the estimated duration to be 50% greater than it takes to actually complete the task. So, with all of this built-in safety, the project should be completed on time. Right? You would think so, but the statistics on project completions paint a much different picture. The reasons for this lack of success will be explained in more detail later.

In traditional project management tracking (i.e., CPM), the progress of the project is typically monitored by calculating the percentage of individual tasks completed and then making a comparison of that percentage against the actual due date. Although this may sound like a reasonable method, is this the right way to track progress? The problem with using the percentage of tasks completed is that not all tasks have the same duration estimates. That is, comparing a task that has an estimate of one day with a task that should take one week is really not a valid comparison. Compounding this problem is the mistaken belief that the best way to ensure that a project will finish on time is to try to make every individual task finish on time. This too sounds rational, but, later on, I'll show you why this just isn't so.

## Why are So Many Projects Being Finished Late?

So, the question remains, that if individual project tasks have so much extra time embedded in them, then why are so many projects coming in late? I believe that this is partially explained by two common human behaviors. Resources know that, since they have built this "safety" into their tasks, it's not uncommon for them to delay work on the task until much later than they had originally planned. Think back to your high school days for a minute. When you were given a due date for a paper of Thursday, when did you typically start working on it? How about Wednesday? [6] Eli Goldratt coined the term, the *Student Syndrome*, to explain one of the reasons why the apparent built-in safety gets wasted. When the task start is delayed, and then Murphy strikes, the task will typically be late because the built-in safety was wasted through this procrastination.

The other human behavior that works to lengthen projects is referred to as *Parkinson's Law*. Resources instinctively know that if they finish a task in less time than they estimated, the next time they have the same or a similar task to complete, they will be expected to finish it early. So, to protect against this, even when a task is finished early, the resource doesn't notify the project manager that it has been completed until the original due date is reached. After all, we're talking about someone's personal credibility here, so to protect it, early finishes aren't reported. *Parkinson's Law* states that work expands to fill the available time, so, if the resource has one week to finish a task, the entire week is taken to finish it. The key effect on projects of these two behaviors is that delays are passed on, but early finishes aren't. So, with these two behaviors taking place, is it any wonder why projects are typically late?

Although these two behaviors negatively impact project schedules, there are other reasons why projects are late. Many organizations today have multiple projects going on at the same time and it's not unusual for projects to share resources. In fact, many project managers tend to "fight over" shared resources because they believe their project is the one that has the highest priority. Another significant problem is that, in many project-based companies, leadership initiates projects without considering the capacity of the organization to complete the work. Leadership also mistakenly assumes that the sooner a project is begun, the sooner it will be completed. As a result, perhaps the most devastating problem of all associated with project completion occurs: bad multitasking! But wait a minute, I thought we'd all been taught for years that multitasking is a good thing. The fact of the matter is that good multitasking is good, but bad multitasking is not.

Bad multitasking happens when resources are forced to work on multiple project activities at the same time. Like we've always said, humans aren't very good at rubbing their tummy and patting their heads at the same time. Many people (especially those in leadership positions) believe that multitasking is a good thing, simply because it increases efficiency since everyone is "busy" all of the time. If you've ever read [7] *The Goal* by Eli Goldratt and Jeff Cox (if you haven't, you should), you might remember how focusing on local activities actually damaged the overall system performance. You may also recall how Goldratt used his robot example, wherein running the robots continuously resulted in improved efficiency but at the expense of creating mountains of excess inventory.

The negative impact of bad multitasking in a project management environment is much, much worse. Let's look at an example.

Suppose you have three projects being executed at the same time, as depicted in Figure 20.1. Also, suppose that you are assigned to all three projects, and, in each project, you have estimated that you have two weeks

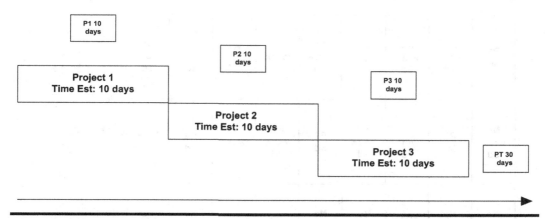

**Figure 20.1**

(ten days) of work on each project for the tasks assigned to you. Assuming Murphy doesn't strike, if you started and finished Project 1 without stopping or working on any other project, it would be done in ten days. Ten days because that's what you told everyone it would take (Parkinson's Law). But having laid it out like this, if all three projects were scheduled to start on the same day, then Project 1 would be on time at ten days, Project 2 would be done in twenty days, but would be ten days late, and Project 3 would be done in thirty days but would be twenty days late. Likewise, for Projects 2 and 3, assuming there were no other interruptions, each would take ten days to complete for a total time to complete the three projects of thirty days. But CPM doesn't usually work like this in a multi-project environment.

Because there are probably three different project managers, each one is most likely telling you (or maybe even screaming at you) that they need you to show progress on their project (remember, projects are typically measured by percentage of tasks complete relative to some due date). You want to satisfy all three managers, so you decide to split your time between the three projects (i.e., you're guilty of bad multitasking). So, as is demonstrated in Figure 20.2, you start with Project 1 and work on it for three days. On the fourth working day, you begin Project 2 and work on only it for three days. You repeat this sequence until all projects are completed.

By using bad multitasking, look what's happened to the time to complete each individual project. Without bad multitasking, each project took only ten days to complete and 30 days to complete all three. With bad multitasking, Project 1 took 28 days, Project 2 took 29 days, and Project 3 took 30 days, again with all of them finished in 30 days. Both methods completed all three projects in 30 days, but which set of results do you think your leadership

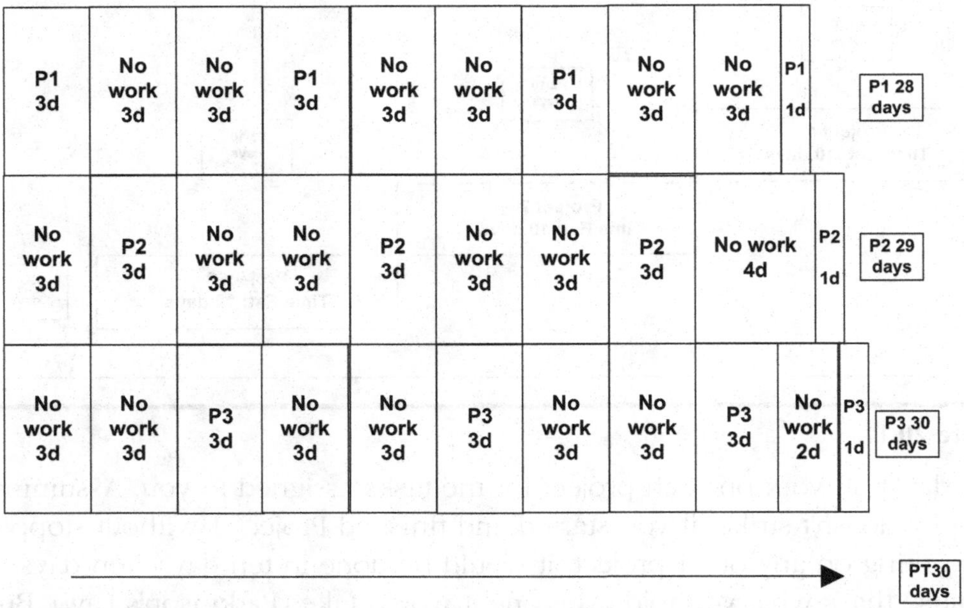

| | | | | | | | | | | |
|---|---|---|---|---|---|---|---|---|---|---|
| P1 3d | No work 3d | No work 3d | P1 3d | No work 3d | No work 3d | P1 3d | No work 3d | No work 3d | P1 1d | P1 28 days |
| No work 3d | P2 3d | No work 3d | No work 3d | P2 3d | No work 3d | No work 3d | P2 3d | No work 4d | P2 1d | P2 29 days |
| No work 3d | No work 3d | P3 3d | No work 3d | No work 3d | P3 3d | No work 3d | No work 3d | P3 3d | No work 2d P3 1d | P3 30 days |

PT30 days

**Figure 20.2**

would prefer? Having two projects done in twenty days and the third one at the thirty-day mark, or the results of bad multitasking? Keep in mind, also, that when you are guilty of bad multitasking, there is also the time required to get re-acquainted with each project so the multitasking times will actually be considerably longer. In fact, some studies have shown that tasks often take 2–3 times their estimated duration when bad multitasking occurs.

So, let's summarize what we've learned before we move on. We've learned that task time estimates for tasks are artificially lengthened as a protective measure against Murphy's Law and all of the negative baggage Murphy brings to the table. We've also learned that, even though excess safety is built in, it is usually wasted because of the Student Syndrome and Parkinson's Law. With the Student Syndrome, we put off work until the last minute, while Parkinson's Law says that, if we're given ten days to complete a task, that's how long it will take, even if it is completed earlier. And finally, we've learned how devastating bad multitasking can be to the completion rate of projects and that if we could eliminate it, we know our on-time completion rate will improve. Although eliminating bad multitasking improves our on-time completion rate, are there other things that can be done to improve these rates even more? Let's take a look.

As we've seen when using the Critical Path Method, task durations are inflated to protect against Murphy. What if we could significantly reduce these embedded safety buffers and still provide the protection that we need? In our example from Figure 20.2, suppose we were able to reduce the estimated duration by 50% and still protect against Murphy. In other words, if we could complete the tasks in five days instead of ten days, wouldn't this be a quantum leap in project completion time reduction?

Figure 20.3 depicts this 50% reduction in duration of each project. We have just reduced the time to complete these three projects from thirty days to 15 days, but can we do this and safely guard against the uncertainty introduced by Murphy? The answer is a resounding "Yes, we can!" But before we explain how to do this, I want to introduce (or re-introduce to some of you) something called the Theory of Constraints (TOC).

TOC came on the scene in the mid-1980s through its creator, Dr Eli Goldratt. Goldratt taught the world that every organization has at least one (and usually only one) constraint that prevents the organization from coming closer to its goal. And, for most companies, the goal is to make money now and in the future. In fact, Goldratt analogized this concept to the strength of a chain being dictated by its weakest link. I believe that the best way to understand TOC is to envision a simple piping system diagram as seen in Figure 20.4.

Figure 20.4 is a diagram of a simple piping system that is used to transport water from Section A through the remaining sections until the water exits through Section G and collects in a receptacle at the base of the

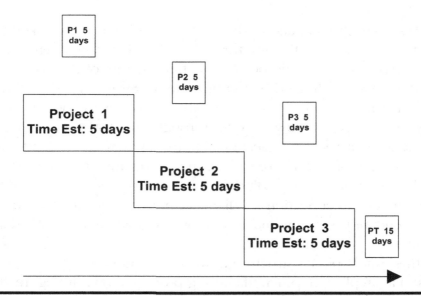

**Figure 20.3**

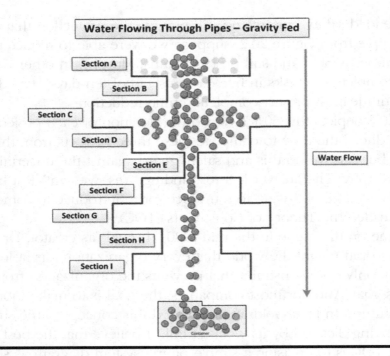

**Figure 20.4**

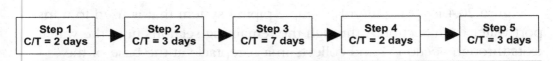

**Figure 20.5**

system. Ask yourself what action should be taken if you were asked to increase the rate of water flowing through this piping system. From a purely physical perspective, it should be obvious that the rate of flow of water through this system is limited by the diameter of Section E because it is the smallest diameter in the system. Equally obvious is the notion that the only way to increase the flow of water through this system is by increasing the diameter of Section E. Section E in this system is referred to as the system bottleneck or system *constraint*. Increasing any other section's diameter would not result in any additional water exiting Section I. The question of by how much larger Section E's diameter must be increased is completely dependent upon how much more water is needed, i.e., the demand requirement.

With this simple piping structure in mind, let's now transfer these thoughts to a simple 4-step manufacturing process shown in Figure 20.5. This process consists of five individual processing steps with the individual processing times for each step listed in each box. Step 1 requires, on average, two days to complete, while Steps 2, 3, 4, and 5 require three, seven, two, and three days on average to complete, respectively. The system constraint in this process is Step 3 simply because the total process throughput is limited by the slowest step in the process...the system constraint. If this process was being initiated for the first time, the total cycle days for this process to deliver its first part would be the sum of the individual process steps, or seventeen days. Once this process is up and running, that is, the process is fully loaded, the shortest time product can flow through this process shrinks to seven days, meaning that we would produce one part every seven days. Like the piping system, the system throughput is dictated by the system constraint.

TOC identifies Step 3 as our constraint and tells us that, if we want to improve throughput, then we must focus our improvement efforts on this step. There are two key points to be made here:

1. Attempts to reduce the cycle times of non-constraint process steps that either feed or receive the output of the constraint do nothing to improve the overall output of the total process or system. Only improvements to the constraint will positively impact the output of the process.
2. The focus must be on protecting the constraint from starvation because any time lost at the constraint is lost to the entire process.

TOC's five-step process of ongoing improvement is as follows:

1. Identify the system constraint.
2. Decide how to exploit the constraint.
3. Subordinate everything else to the constraint.
4. If necessary, elevate the constraint.
5. Return to Step 1, but don't let inertia create a new constraint.

The bottom line is that TOC represents a brilliant opportunity to improve processes. By using TOC to identify your company's leverage point (the system constraint), and then focusing your improvement efforts on it, your company's bottom line will increase significantly. And if your constraint is external (i.e., a lack of sales), the improvements made can become market differentiators to stimulate additional sales. So, with this in mind, let's get back to how TOC and Critical Chain Project Management (CCPM) will positively impact the on-time completion of projects.

Earlier, we demonstrated how, by simply eliminating bad multi-tasking, significant gains could be made in project completion rates, but we still have to address the impact of the Student Syndrome and Parkinson's Law. We know that both of these behaviors work to lengthen the time required to complete projects. Remember how excess safety is embedded into traditional project management plans? Resources estimate task times and add in their own protection against disruptions caused primarily by Murphy. Knowing that this safety exists, resources then delay starting work on their tasks until the due date is close. Even if the resources don't delay the task starts or finish early, these early finishes are not reported or passed on to the next resource. So, how does CCPM deal with these two behaviors?

Whereas CPM relies on individual task durations, as well as scheduled start and completion dates, CCPM does not. The focus is no longer on finishing individual tasks on time, but rather starting and completing these tasks as soon as possible, and this is a major change. So how does this work? Like CPM, CCPM still gathers estimates on individual tasks and identifies its own version of the Critical Path. Unlike CPM, CCPM considers competing resources (i.e., the same resource having to work on different tasks) and makes them a part of the critical path. Let's look at an example of how CPM and CCPM identify the critical path.

CPM defines the critical path as the longest path of dependent tasks within a total project. That is, tasks are dependent when the completion of one task isn't possible until the completion of a preceding task. The critical path is important because any delay on the critical path will delay the project correspondingly. Figure 20.6 is an example of a series of tasks that must be completed in a project, with the critical path highlighted in gray. Traditional project management determines the critical path by looking at the task dependencies within the project. For example, Task A2 can only be initiated after A1 is completed. Task B3 can only be performed after completion of B1 and B2. Task D1 can only be performed after completion of A2,

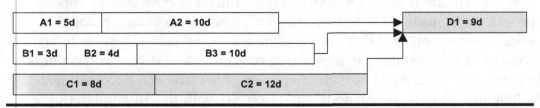

**Figure 20.6**

B3, and C2. Using CPPM, the critical path would have been identified as C1–C2–D1 (i.e., the longest path of dependent tasks) and the project completion estimate would have been twenty-nine days (i.e., 8 days + 12 days + 9 days).

In addition to task dependencies, there are also resource dependencies that CPM fails to recognize. What if, in our example, Tasks A2 and B3 are performed by the same resource? Is the critical path different? In Figure 20.7, we see the new critical path that includes a provision for resource dependencies, and, as you can see, the new critical path is A1–A2–B3–D1 or 5 days + 10 days + 10 days + 9 days, equals thirty-four days. So, the minimum time to complete this project is now thirty-four days. In my opinion, the failure to consider resource dependencies is one of the key reasons why project completion rates are so dreadful.

The simple implication of incorrectly identifying the critical path, which we will now refer to as the *critical chain,* is that the project team will never be able to complete their project on time without heroic efforts, adding additional resources, overtime, or a combination of all three. The practical implication of incorrectly identifying the real critical chain is that the focus will be on the wrong tasks. Is this any different than focusing on non-constraints in our earlier discussion on the piping system? Incidentally, this thing we call the *critical chain* is our system constraint, so, by focusing on the constraint, we can maximize the throughput of projects in your organization.

We said earlier that safety is embedded within each task, as a way to guard against the uncertainties of Murphy. Critical Chain takes a completely different approach by assuming that Murphy's uncertainty will happen in every project. Unlike CPM, CCPM removes these safety buffers within each task and pools them at the end of the project plan to protect the only date that really matters, the project completion date. There are many references that explain the details of how CCPM does this, but here's a simple example to explain it.

CCPM simply removes all of the protection from individual task estimates, which we have estimated to be 50% of the original value. Figure 20.8 demonstrates the removal of this safety. So, the length of the critical chain now

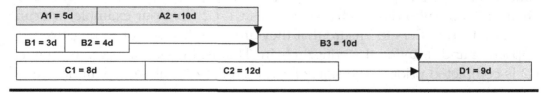

**Figure 20.7**

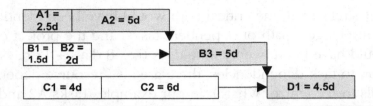

**Figure 20.8**

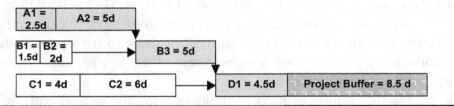

**Figure 20.9**

is no longer thirty-four days, but rather seventeen days (i.e., A1 + A2 + B3 + D1). But, instead of just eliminating the safety buffer, we want to place it where it will do the most good and that is at the end of the project to protect the due date. This isn't exactly how this works, but, for presentation purposes, to demonstrate the theory behind CCPM, it will suffice.

Figure 20.9 is this same process, but this time the safeties that we removed are added to the end of the project to act as a cushion against Murphy's inevitable delays. Actually, we have added only 50% of the safety time removed to create the project buffer. So, the question now becomes, how do we utilize this buffer and how does it improve the on-time completion of the project?

Suppose task A2 takes seven days instead of the five days that are in the plan. In a traditional project management environment, this would be cause for panic. In a CCPM environment, we simply "borrow" two days from the project buffer and we're still on schedule. Suppose now, for task B3, we only take three days instead of the planned five days. We simply deposit the gain of two days back into the project buffer. In traditional CPM, delays accumulate whereas any gains are lost, but not so with CCPM. This is a significant difference! The project buffer protects us from delays. For non-critical chain tasks or subordinate chains, such as C1–C2 from our example, we can also add feed buffers to ensure that they are completed prior to negatively impacting and delaying the critical chain. That is, in our example, as long as C2 is completed prior to the start of D1, then the critical chain will not be delayed.

One of the key differences between CPM and CCPM is what happens at the task level. In traditional project management, we said earlier that each task has a scheduled start and completion date. CCPM eliminates the times and dates from the schedule and instead focuses on passing on tasks as soon as they are completed. This function serves to eliminate the negative effects of both the Student Syndrome and Parkinson's Law from the equation and permits on-time and early finishes for projects. In order for this to work effectively, there must be a way to alert the next resource to get ready in time to begin the next task. This is equivalent to a relay race, where the baton is handed on from one runner to the next. Since the receiving runner begins running before the baton is handed off, very little time is wasted.

Earlier, we explained that, in traditional project management, we track the progress of the project by calculating the percentage of individual tasks completed and then comparing that percentage against the due date. The problem with this method is because we aren't considering the estimated durations that are left to complete, it is nearly impossible to know exactly how much time is remaining to complete the project. Using this method to track progress, it's not uncommon to see 90% of a project completed relatively quickly, only to see the remaining 10% taking just as long. In fact, looking at the number or percentage of tasks completed, instead of how much of the critical path has been completed, only serves to give a false sense of conformance to the schedule.

CCPM measures the progress of a project much differently, and, in so doing, allows the project to make valuable use of early finishes. Critical chain uses something called a *Fever Chart*, which is simply a run chart of the percentage of Critical Chain Completed versus percentage of Project Buffer consumed. Figure 20.10 is an example of such a chart. In this chart, we see that approximately 55% of the critical chain has been completed, whereas only 40% of the project buffer has been consumed, thus indicating that this project is a little bit behind schedule.

The light gray, gray, and dark gray areas of the fever chart are visual indicators of how the project is progressing. If the data point falls within the light gray area of the chart, the project is progressing well and may even finish early. If the data point falls into the gray zone, there is cause for concern and plans should be developed to take action, but not yet implemented. Vertical rises such as that demonstrated in Figure 20.10 above (Day 3) indicate that the buffer is being consumed at too fast a rate, relative to how the project is progressing. If a data point falls into the dark gray zone, then the plan we developed should now be executed. But even if the entire amount

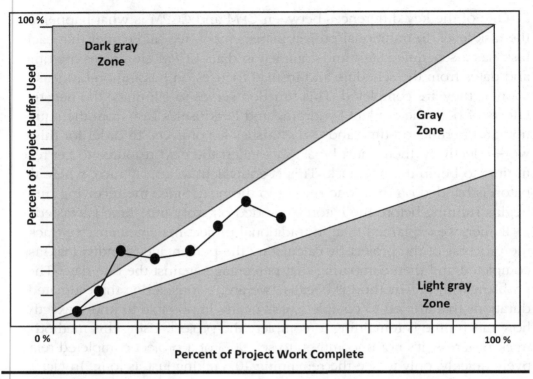

**Figure 20.10**

of project buffer is consumed at the completion of the project, the project is still on time and not late.

In addition to using the fever chart, we also recommend calculating a project index by dividing the percentage of the critical chain completed into the percentage of the project buffer consumed. As long as this ratio is 1.0 or less, then the project will be completed on-time or early. In our example, this ratio would be 40% divided by 55%, or 0.727. This ratio says that this project is progressing nicely with no concern for the project being late.

With most CCPM software, we can also see a portfolio view of the fever chart that tells us the real-time status of all projects in the system. Figure 20.11 is an example of this view and one can see at a glance that four of the projects (Projects 1, 4, 5, and 6) need immediate attention because they are in the dark gray zone, whereas two projects (Projects 3 and 8) are in the gray zone and need a plan developed to reduce the rate of buffer consumption. The remaining two projects (Projects 2 and 7) are progressing nicely and are in the light gray zone. Having this view enables the Project Manager to see at a glance where to focus his or her efforts. It is important to understand that just because a project enters the dark gray zone, it does not mean that

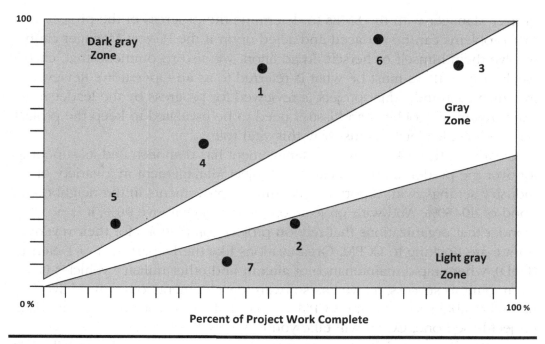

**Figure 20.11**

the project will automatically be late. It only means that, if expeditious action isn't taken to reduce the buffer consumption rate, the project could be late.

The net effect of CCPM will always result in a significant decrease in cycle time with a corresponding increase in the throughput rate of completed projects, using the same level of resources. In fact, it is not unusual for project cycle times to be reduced by as much as 40–50%! These cycle time reductions and corresponding throughput increases translate directly into improved on-time delivery of projects, as well as significant revenue increases.

The key to success using CCPM revolves around utilization of the true subject matter experts (SMEs). That is, by developing a *core team* comprised of 70–80% employees who are actually executing projects, and permitting them to develop the ultimate design solution, the resulting implementation will be owned by the people performing the work. This ownership translates directly into making sure the solution will work. Without this level of involvement and approval authority to develop the applied action plans, CCPM will simply not be as successful as it could or should be.

Another key to successful project management application is a series of regular meetings intended to surface and resolve any problems that surface during the project execution. These include daily "walk-arounds" by the

Project Manager with the SMEs to determine the progress of the project so that problems can be surfaced and acted upon if the Project Manager cannot resolve them himself or herself. In addition, we also recommend that, each week or two, there must be what is referred to as an Operation's Review, in which each individual project is reviewed for progress by the leadership team. Again, if problems and issues need to be escalated to keep the project on schedule, leadership must play this vital role.

Clearly, Critical Chain Project Management has demonstrated its superiority over the predominant Critical Path Project Management in a variety of industry settings, with reported cycle time improvements in the neighborhood of 40–50%. And with project completion rates above 90%, it is no wonder that organizations that rely on project completions for their revenue source are flocking to CCPM. Organizations like the Department of Defense (DoD), where rapid maintenance of aircraft and other military vehicles is paramount to success, as well as software development companies have had incredible success using CCPM versus CPM. So, if your organization is a project-based one, CCPM will take you to a new level of success.

Another problem that I have seen on numerous occasions is the failure of companies to have needed parts available when needed. Many companies in today's world are using what is referred to as the Minimum/Maximum system to satisfy their part's needs. Unfortunately, companies using this system have excessive amounts of inventory, but are seeing numerous stock-out conditions. In the next chapter, I will summarize many of the key learnings I have presented throughout this book.

# References

1. *The Standish Group Report* © The Standish Group 1995. Chaos Report.
2. *Improving Public Services Through e-Government*, Public Accounts Committee, HC845, August 2002.
3. *UK Online Annual Report*, Office of the e-envoy, November 2002.
4. *Government IT problems since 1997*, Computing, 13 March 2003.
5. *The Standish Group Report* © The Standish Group, 2007.
6. *Critical Chain* by Eliyahu M. Goldratt, The North River Press, 1997.
7. *The Goal* by Eliyahu M. Goldratt and Jeff Cox, The North River Press, 1999.

# Chapter 21

---

# Summary of Key Learnings

---

Over the past century, there have been many attempts to improve the quality of both products and services throughout the world, and many different people have contributed to this improvement movement and the body of knowledge associated with it. If you take a moment and look back through the chapters in this book, the list of improvement ideas and acronyms has filled many pages. If it is true that the past helps predict the future, then there will be many more new ideas coming into existence as we move forward. This chapter is intended to review and summarize the key points from the previous chapters.

Currently, three principal improvement methodologies, the Theory of Constraints (TOC), Lean, and Six Sigma, appear to dominate the subject matter of the improvement world, and each brings its own unique perspective to the improvement playing field. Each also has its own following of zealots and believers. Each proclaims that their single method is the way forward, providing the light and the truth, so to speak. It's almost as if each methodology is a religious experience of sorts. But does it really have to be this way? Is there a benefit in keeping these methods separate and apart from each other? Does each methodology have to exist in isolation from the others? Let's look at each methodology in a bit more detail to answer this question.

DOI: 10.4324/9781003462385-21

# Theory of Constraints (TOC)

In the early 1980s, Dr Eliyahu Goldratt introduced the world to a new way of looking at profitability through his now famous Theory of Constraints (TOC), which was presented in his and Jeff Cox's book [1] *The Goal*. In principle, Goldratt and Cox argued that instead of trying to *save money* through cost reductions, companies would be much more profitable if they focused instead on *making money*. But aren't the two ideas synonymous? The answer is, absolutely not! These two ideas represent very different and divergent approaches. Saving money is not the same as making money. And the management strategy you choose to employ to make money is very different from the one you employ to save money.

Goldratt and Cox's emphasis is that the goal of for-profit companies is to *make money now and in the future*. Goldratt and Cox analogized this concept using a chain. They stated that the weakest link in a chain controls the overall strength of the chain and that any attempt to strengthen any link other than the weakest one will do nothing to improve the total strength of the overall chain. Organizationally this means that every action or decision taken by the organization must be judged by its impact on the organization's overall goal of making money. If the decision does not get you closer to that goal, then the decision is probably unproductive.

Goldratt and Cox defined a *system constraint* as anything that limits the system from achieving higher performance relative to its goal. So, if the goal of the organization is to make money, then the system constraint must be identified first. Goldratt and Cox explained that, in order to determine whether an organization is moving toward its goal and not away from it, three simple questions must be asked and answered:

1. How much money does your organization generate?
2. How much money does your organization invest?
3. How much money does your organization spend to make it operate?

From his research, Goldratt developed his own simplified system of accounting that he referred to as Throughput Accounting (TA). The basis for Goldratt's accounting system was three financially based performance metrics:

- *Throughput* (T). This is the rate that the organization generates "new" money, primarily through sales. Goldratt further defined Throughput (T) as the money collected through the sale of a unit of product minus what it pays to its suppliers and others – or Totally Variable Costs (TVC). Therefore, T = Selling price minus Totally Variable Costs, or T = SP – TVC. The bulk of the TVC would be raw materials but could also include any sales commissions and shipping costs associated with products.

■ *Investment* (I). This is the money an organization invests in items that it intends to sell. This category would primarily include inventory, both raw materials and finished goods.

■ *Operating Expense* (OE). This is all the money an organization spends to operate, including labor costs, office supplies, employee benefits, phone bill, electric bill, and so on; in other words, all the money spent to support the organization and turn inventory into finished goods.

What distinguishes Goldratt's definition of Throughput from traditional definitions is that Throughput is not considered to be valuable until money changes hands between the organization and its customers. At any point in time before the *sale*, the product is still considered Inventory, even in a finished goods status. Basically, any product that is produced and not sold to a customer is simply termed Inventory or Investment and it has a cost associated with it. This is a major departure from the traditional definition of Throughput, and its overall implications are far-reaching.

Goldratt and Cox expanded their Throughput Accounting definitions still further by defining Net Profit and Return on Investment as follows:

■ *Net Profit* (NP) = Throughput minus Operating Expense, or NP = T – OE

■ *Return on Investment* (ROI) = (Throughput minus Operating Expense) divided by Investment, or ROI = (T – OE)/I

With these three simple measurements (T, I, and OE), organizations are able to determine the immediate impact of their actions and decisions on the financial performance of their organization. Does it make sense that the superlative actions upon the system are those that increase T, while simultaneously reducing I and OE? You might wonder why a discussion of TOC started first with a financial definition. The relevance should become obvious shortly.

The Theory of Constraints operates under what Goldratt refers to as his Five Focusing Steps:

*Step 1: Identify the System Constraint.* The constraint is commonly considered to be anything within a system that limits the system from achieving higher performance relative to its goal.

*Step 2: Decide how to exploit the System Constraint.* Exploitation implies getting more from what you already have. It requires that you understand *why* you are currently getting what you are getting, and what steps are necessary to maximize the throughput of the constraint. How do you get more from this constraining operation?

*Step 3: Subordinate everything else to the System Constraint.* Subordination implies that *all* other non-constraint processes activate to the same level as the constraint. It seems contrary to popular belief, but sometimes, in order to go faster, you have to go slower.

*Step 4: If necessary, elevate the System Constraint.* Elevation implies more constraint capacity or resources if the market demand on the system still exceeds current capacity. At this point, it may be required to spend some money to increase throughput – but only during Step 4 and not during Step 2.

*Step 5: Return to Step 1.* When the constraint has rolled (moved) to a new location in the system, then go back to Step 1 and follow the sequence again.

So, you may be wondering why these Five Focusing Steps are important to someone who uses Lean, Six Sigma, or the hybrid, Lean Sigma. The facts are simple. Without the understanding of the global system focus provided by TOC, many of the Lean and Six Sigma initiatives will fail to deliver significant bottom-line improvement. The fundamental key to impacting the bottom line is directly proportional to the company's ability to drive Throughput to higher levels while, at the same time, reducing Inventory and Operating Expense. The concept here is driving the system to make money, rather than saving money. Think about it: if your financial model is based upon how much cost you can remove from a process (reducing OE), then your ROI has a mathematical lower limit. Likewise, if your focus is only on reducing Inventory, it too has a functional and mathematical lower limit. Throughput, on the other hand, is devoid of a theoretical upper limit. Consider, just for a moment, the overall impact of simultaneously increasing T while reducing OE and I. The crucial focus of increasing T is what drives NP and ROI!

## Lean

Much has been written about Lean over the past several years, but its basic philosophy is centered on a whole-systems approach that focuses on the existence and removal of non-value-added (NVA) activities within a process or system. These NVA activities are characterized as *waste* in the Lean dialect. As an improvement initiative, Lean teaches you to recognize that waste is present within every process and that we should take extreme actions to either eliminate or significantly reduce it. The entire premise for doing this action is to facilitate a flow of *value* through the entire process. If this is true, then it begs the question, "What is value?" There have been many attempts to define value, but the best definition I have heard is based on the *customer value* and not the producer value.

In its simplest terms, value is whatever the customer feels good about paying for. Customers know what they want, when they want it, and how much it is reasonable to pay for it, so, in the long run, value clarifies itself. Lean has become recognized as one of the most effective business improvement strategies used in the world today, but, if this is so, then why are so many Lean implementations failing at such an alarming rate? In this case, failure implies the inability to not only achieve, but also sustain the needed effort.

## Six Sigma

Like Lean, much has been written about Six Sigma methods and the now-famous acronym, DMAIC. Whereas Lean is attempting to remove non-value-added and wasteful activities, Six Sigma is attempting to remove and control unnecessary and unwanted variation. Six Sigma uses the roadmap *Define, Measure, Analyze, Improve* and *Control (DMAIC)* to seek out sources of variation, and, through various statistically based tools and techniques, and to limit and control variation to the lowest possible level.

The professed power of Six Sigma lies in the disciplined structure and use of tools and techniques. However, this supposed power sometimes ends up being a detriment to some companies, simply because, in many instances, they will experience enormous information overload, coupled with a failure to launch the information into viable solutions. In essence, these companies are suffering from analysis paralysis. Like Lean, many Six Sigma initiatives have failed to deliver true quantifiable bottom-line improvements and, therefore, have been abandoned. Six Sigma can be difficult to employ for one primary reason. It is heavily dependent on mathematics (statistics) and formula derivatives that, quite frankly, most people do not enjoy or involve themselves with. At times, it seems as if you need to call Merlin the magician just to get started.

There is also a popular hybrid of Lean and Six Sigma, known as Lean Sigma which, as the name implies, is a merger of the two initiatives. The primary assumption of Lean Sigma is that eliminating or reducing waste and variation in the system will lead to major cost reductions. It seems to make perfect sense that, if each initiative delivers its own separate improvement, then combining output from both of them should optimize the process and result in a double-dip reduction in cost. However, in the final analysis, the primary functions of Lean and Six Sigma are aimed at cost savings. Saving money is indeed a strategy, but it's just not the most effective strategy for making money.

The overall issue is not with either one of these methodologies, but rather the belief that the way to increase profitability is through cost reduction. The bottom line is that cost reductions have implied mathematical limits, and, once those limits are encountered, the cost-saving improvement effort stops or slows down significantly. Consider this – have you ever heard of a company that has actually saved itself into prosperity? If cost reduction is not the answer, then what is the best route to profitability?

## Focus and Leverage

From what has been stated so far, you might think that I have a negative view of Lean and Six Sigma, but such is absolutely not the case. In fact, TOC by itself cannot and will not deliver sustainable bottom-line improvement. But it does provide the needed global system focus, and that focus is paramount to facilitating organizational growth. In fact, the primary reason why Lean and Six Sigma have failed to deliver an acceptable Return on Investment (ROI) is that they try to improve everything all at once, rather than focusing on the most important leverage point. They encourage improvement because they can, and not because they must. It's like trying to solve world hunger – it's a tough job when you try to do it all at once. So, let us discuss leverage points and what they mean.

## Leverage

The foundational concepts of TOC can be presented in a simple but understandable way as a reference environment. If you understand the reference, you understand the concept. If we use a diagram showing a simple piping system with the primary goal of delivering water, then the reference is defined. By presenting the concept in this format, the basic principles will be much easier to comprehend for people who have not yet had any experience with the Theory of Constraints.

Figure 21.1 describes the piping system with different diameter pipes connected together, supporting the water flowing through this system. The water flows from top to bottom from Section A through the entire length of the system until it exits at Section I and collects in the receptacle at the bottom of the piping system. If you were given this water system and asked what you would do to increase the flow (or throughput) of water through this system, how would you answer the question? Most people would respond by stating that you would need to increase the pipe diameter of Section E, since it is the choke point, bottleneck, or constraint within this system. If you increased the diameter of any other pipe section, it would have absolutely no effect on the throughput of water through this system.

If you were asked how much you should increase the diameter of Section E, how would you answer that question? Most respondents would answer by saying that the increased diameter of the Section E pipe would be determined by how much more water the system needed to deliver (i.e., the demand requirement on the system). So, in order to satisfy the need

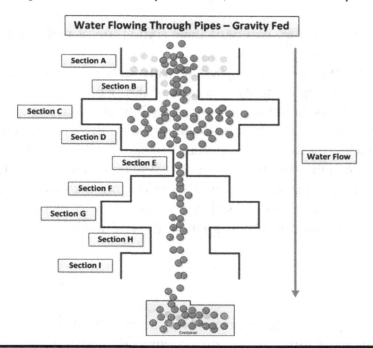

**Figure 21.1**

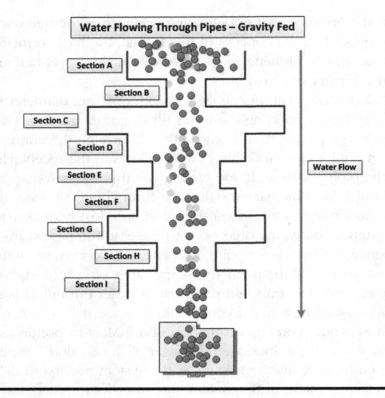

**Figure 21.2**

(demand) for more water, you must have some type of metric for how much more water is needed.

Figure 21.2 is this same piping system with Section E's diameter increased based on demand requirements. A couple of distinct changes have taken place as a result of actions aimed at increasing the flow of water through this piping system. First, clearly more water is flowing through this system and collecting in the receptacle. But the most important change of all is the location of the new system constraint (i.e., the bottleneck). As you can see in the figure, the new constraint in this system is now Section B. I hope it's clear to you that if you needed even more water to satisfy demand, your focus must now be on Section B. So how does all of this apply to the real world?

# Focus

The basic principles of understanding constraints are all around us. For example, instead of using the piping system to demonstrate the constraint, we could have substituted an electric circuit with different-sized resistors

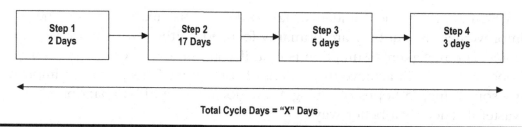

**Figure 21.3**

and measured the flow of electricity through the circuit. The resistor location with the highest resistance to electrical flow would be the equivalent of Section E in the piping diagram. You could easily demonstrate that the flow of electricity through that system is completely dependent on how much more electrical current was needed to satisfy the demand. And, in order to increase the electrical output, you need to reduce the resistance of the resistor that was limiting the electrical flow.

Figure 21.3 is another simple visual example of the same concept. Here, we have a four-step process used to produce some kind of product or deliver some kind of service. If we apply the same *systems thinking* and ask the same series of questions about this system, then we can effectively conclude that Step 2, at seventeen days, is the process that is limiting the output from this system. By understanding this concept, you now know where to *focus* your improvement efforts. Improving any other process in this system, except for Step 2, yields no system improvements *at all*. Globally, the system will improve only when Step 2 requires less time.

## Rolling it ALL Up

With the foundational concepts of the three improvement initiatives laid out and defined, where does this take us? If you apply the methods of TOC first and use TOC to analyze the system and spend the necessary time to do it correctly, then you can employ the other methods of Lean and Six Sigma to help exploit the constraints. If the constraint quickly moves to a new location, then go back to Step 1 and start over. It is possible that the "fix and move" cycle can repeat several times before the system is stabilized and requires the implementation of Step 3 – subordination.

If your current Lean or Six Sigma initiatives are suffering from a lack of real bottom-line improvement, then what has been presented here should be of interest to you. Why? Because the biggest reason many Lean and

Six Sigma improvement initiatives fail to deliver sustainable bottom-line improvement is that they are primarily focused on the *wrong* improvement point. The mistaken assumption is that, if you improve everything, then hopefully you will achieve the benefit of something. This notion of improving something, in hopes of saving a few dollars, should be abandoned as wasteful. There is a better way.

The necessary condition is that you take the time to understand what the problem really is. If you don't understand and *focus* on the real problem, it will be impossible to come up with the correct *leverage* to implement a solid solution. Take the time to slow down your thinking and understand precisely where to focus your improvements. If you think in terms of TLS (that is, the combination of TOC, Lean, and Six Sigma), your results will be much more gratifying.

Just for a moment, imagine what would happen using the focusing power of the Theory of Constraints, coupled with the improvement potential of both Lean and Six Sigma. The crucial component to real bottom-line improvement is to increase throughput through the system. Remember, throughput is not the same as output. Throughput only materializes when the sale occurs, and fresh money is received from the customer and put back into your system. So, by identifying and focusing the full improvement potential of Theory of Constraints, Lean, and Six Sigma on the global system, it is possible to increase the throughput – perhaps exponentially.

## The Importance of Three

The Ultimate Improvement Cycle (UIC) effectively combines all three methodologies into a single improvement consortium, and it allows you to use the best practices of each to solve most of the problems involved with implementing improvements. But exactly how does this integration of methodologies work? Figure 21.4 below provides the comprehensive answer to just how my UIC works in the form of a Goal Tree/IO Map, which was discussed at length in a previous chapter.

Using the Goal Tree/IO Map, I have defined each of these three methodologies as being Critical Success Factors toward achieving your goal. The instructions to the left in Figure 20.4 state, "In order to achieve My Goal, I must achieve all of my Critical Success Factors. And in order to achieve My CSF's, I must achieve my Necessary Conditions, at all levels. Each entity supports the other in being able to move to the next level, until ultimately is the

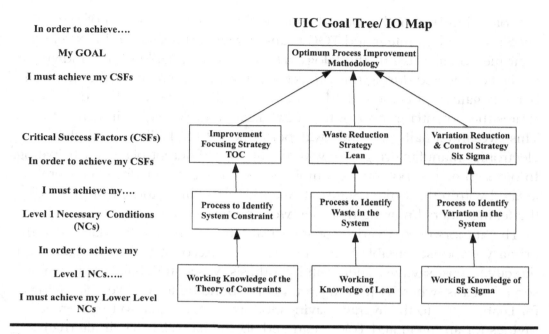

**UIC Goal Tree/ IO Map**

In order to achieve....

My GOAL

I must achieve my CSFs

Critical Success Factors (CSFs)

In order to achieve my CSFs

I must achieve my....

Level 1 Necessary Conditions (NCs)

In order to achieve my

Level 1 NCs.....

I must achieve my Lower Level NCs

**Figure 21.4**

creation of the Optimum Process Improvement Methodology (OPIM). Each method, if used only in isolation, will fall short of the optimum method. But, when these methods are combined, the optimum method and corresponding results will be achieved. Having just one method, or even two of these improvement methods, is not sufficient to complete the journey to the OPIM. All three working in tandem is the optimal approach.

To review, the Goal Tree/IO Map succinctly defines all of the Critical Success Factors (CSFs) that must be in place if we are to achieve the Optimum Process Improvement Methodology. The CSFs are supported by the Necessary Conditions of the need for an improvement-focusing strategy, a waste-reduction strategy, and a variation-reduction strategy. The first layer of Necessary Conditions translates into the need to have a working knowledge of the Theory of Constraints, Lean, and Six Sigma. TOC provides the methods used to focus your improvement efforts on the constraint, whereas Lean and Six Sigma, with their many tools and techniques, can be used to reduce the waste and variation at the constraint and eventually within the system until the constraint moves to another location within the system.

Russ Pirasteh and Bob Fox have published a wonderful book on the integration of TOC, Lean, and Six Sigma, entitled [2] *Profitability with No Boundaries*. Pirasteh and Fox outline the results of a significant study (the first of its kind), aimed at providing a head-to-head comparison of Lean, Six Sigma, and an integrated TOC-Lean-Six Sigma (Pirasteh and Fox refer to their method as iTLS) methodology. The response variable for the individual studies conducted during this project was the measurement of the financial benefits gained. It is the only documented study I have seen that demonstrates the potential power of this TOC, Lean, and Six Sigma integration. This two-and-a-half-year study was performed at the facilities of a global electronics manufacturing firm with twenty-one different plants participating. In order to negate potential cultural effects, all twenty-one facilities were located within the United States. It was a double-blind study, with none of the team leaders knowing that they were participants.

The authors used a variety of statistical tools to analyze the data, with the primary response variable being a coded, Cost-Accounting-based metric tied directly to cost savings. Their null hypothesis was a straightforward comparison of means, whereby $\mu_1 = \mu_2 = \mu_3$ corresponding to the average savings for Lean, equal to the average savings for Six Sigma, equal to the average savings for an integrated TOC, Lean and Six Sigma (iTLS). Their alternative hypothesis was that the three averages were not equal ($\mu_1 \neq \mu_2 \neq \mu_3$).

The authors first used One-Way Analysis of Variance (ANOVA) to demonstrate that there was no statistical difference between Lean and Six Sigma ($\mu_1 = \mu_2$) results. Since, statistically, the Lean and Six Sigma results appeared to come from the same population, the authors combined both sets of results and then compared the combined results to the iTLS results (Integrated TOC-Lean-Six Sigma). The results of this comparison clearly indicated that there was a statistically significant difference between Lean-Six Sigma and iTLS. In fact, the savings contribution from iTLS accounted for 89% of the total savings. The inescapable conclusion from this study was that the interactive effects of iTLS were far superior to the individual results obtained from using either Lean or Six Sigma.

For the past two decades, I have been using a comparable improvement methodology, first reported in my book, [3] *The Ultimate Improvement Cycle* (UIC), and discussed in Chapter 17 of this book, and have achieved analogous results. Although my step-by-step method, or pathway, is somewhat different than the Pirasteh and Fox method, the basic beliefs are exactly the same. Significant bottom-line improvement can be achieved when using an integrated approach of TOC, Lean, and Six Sigma, as compared to using TOC, Lean, Six Sigma or Lean-Six Sigma methodologies in isolation from each other.

Figure 21.5 is a graphic of the integrated Theory of Constraints, Lean, and Six Sigma methodology that I refer to as the *Ultimate Improvement Cycle* (UIC). Each box within this graphic explains the actions which should be taken as you work to improve your system. The contributions of each of the individual methodologies are made known within the three concentric circles.

Figure 21.6 displays the UIC improvement tools, actions, and focus, which can be used to successfully combine these three distinctly different methodologies (i.e., Lean, Six Sigma, and TOC). There are other tools that can be used, so, as I always say, when you learn a new way, make it your own. In doing so, you may come up with new and better ways of doing something.

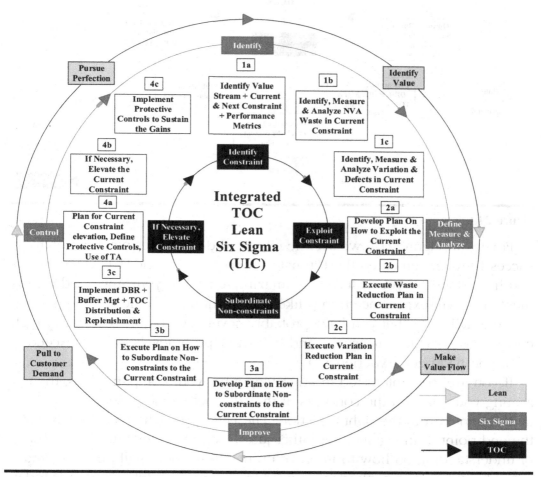

**Figure 21.5**

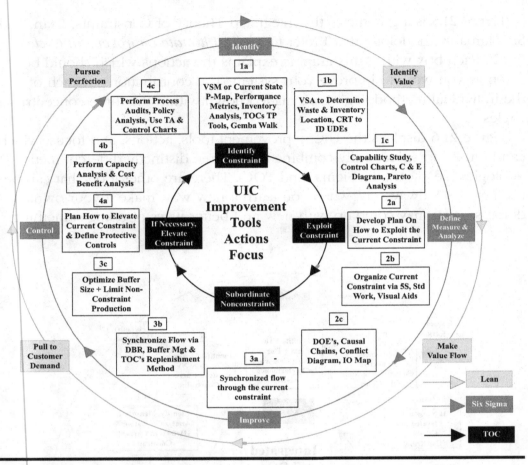

**Figure 21.6**

Finally, in Figure 21.7, we see the expected deliverables when you have successfully implemented the Ultimate Improvement Cycle (UIC). And when you have done so, you will see an amazing return on your improved investment. You will experience things like significant improvements in flow, on-time deliveries that you have probably never seen before, extremely high customer satisfaction measures, and ultimately profit levels that far exceed what you had been experiencing.

If you are truly interested in improving what your company does, then arming yourself with the concepts of the UIC methodology should certainly point you in the right direction. The UIC approach is most likely not the end point in this game, but rather just a step to achieve the next level of understanding on how to improve profitability. There will be more, and possibly even better methods proposed for future use. But as it stands today, understanding and implementing the Ultimate Improvement Cycle carries

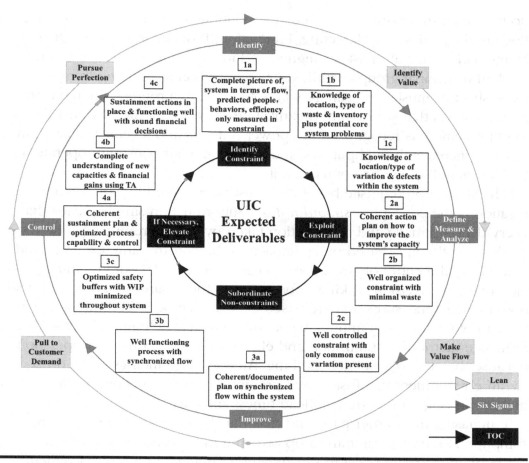

**Figure 21.7**

the potential to lift your organization to heights not even dreamed of in your company's past years. Before we leave this final chapter, I want to discuss something very important, which is how to establish the right environment for change before you begin your improvement journey. In this journey, there will be many changes that must take place, so be prepared.

# Prerequisite Beliefs

If your entire operation is able to accept the prerequisite beliefs of constraint focus and leverage, then you have taken the first step. When I say the entire operation, I am referring to everyone! All of the individual departments, functional groups, and employees in your organization must become focused on the leveraging power of the constraining operation. If you can't do that, then there simply is no need to continue. Accounting, Purchasing, Engineering, Sales and Marketing, Production, Production Control, Quality, Maintenance, etc., all must be aligned and in total agreement. Unless and until all functional groups within your organization are singing from the same sheet of music, you simply will not make any progress. So, the first prerequisite is that your entire organization must accept the idea that the key to improvement is recognizing the power of focus and leverage. That is, in order to increase throughput, you must leverage your constraint operation by focusing all of your resources on it.

The second prerequisite belief that must be accepted by your entire organization is the concept of *subordination*. Subordination simply means that every decision made and every action taken by the entire organization must be done so that it is based on its impact on the constraining resource. And when I say the entire organization, I mean everyone! Accounting must provide real-time decision-making information to the organization and not hold onto financial measures that are based on what happened last month, as is the case with Cost Accounting. Accounting must also eliminate outdated performance metrics like utilization and efficiency in non-constraint operations because they mean absolutely nothing. All these two metrics really do is create an environment that fosters and promotes over-production, resulting in higher carrying costs, extended lead times, and excess inventory.

Purchasing must order parts and materials based upon the rate of consumption at the constraint and stop ordering in large quantities, or only on the basis of the lowest cost to satisfy another outdated performance metric, *purchase price variance*. Sales and Marketing must understand that unless and until the current constraint is broken, they must not make hollow promises on delivery dates, in order to obtain more orders to supplement their sales commissions.

Engineering must respond quickly to the needs of production, in order to ensure timely delivery and updates to specifications. Maintenance must always prioritize their work based on the needs of the constraining operation, including preventive and reactive maintenance activities. If there is an inspection station that impacts the constraint throughput, then inspectors (if they exist) must always provide timely and accurate inspections, so as to never cause delays that negatively impact the flow of materials into and out of the constraint. Finally, Production Control must stop scheduling the plant on forecasts that we know are wrong, using the outdated algorithms contained within the MRP system.

If your entire organization believes in and is ready to subordinate to the constraint, then you have taken the second step. If your organization is like so many others, where individual departments exist as silos, then letting go of the apparent control that they now have will be a difficult pill to swallow, but one that is absolutely necessary. If you're not ready, then do not proceed any further!

The third prerequisite belief that must be accepted by the entire organization is that *improvement is never-ending*. The Ultimate Improvement Cycle is predicated on the fact that, once your constraint is broken, a new one will appear immediately, so all organizational resources must be prepared to shift to it and subordinate actions and decisions toward the cycle of breaking the new constraint. This cyclical process has no end, so be prepared to accept the idea of always getting better.

The fourth prerequisite belief that the organization must accept is one of *involvement of the entire workforce*. If your company is like many other companies, then you've probably been taught that improving profits means reducing expenses. And reducing expenses has typically involved reducing the size of the labor force. This is exactly the opposite of the behavior that is needed to successfully navigate through the Ultimate Improvement Cycle. Why would anyone be willing to participate in improving the operation to the point that they lose their job? So, if in the past, yours is a company that uses layoffs as a way of reducing or controlling expenses, then you are doomed to failure! You must accept the fact that the key to making money now is increasing throughput and, without everyone's involvement, it simply won't happen. So, if you can't accept this belief, then stop here.

As you identify the constraint and subordinate the rest of the organization to the constraint, there will be idle time at the non-constraints. If you are like many organizations that use total system efficiency and utilization as key performance metrics, then you will see both of them predictably decline. You are normally trying to drive efficiencies and utilizations higher and higher at each of the individual operations under the mistaken assumption that the total efficiency of the system is the sum of the individual efficiencies. In a TOC environment, the only efficiencies or utilizations that really matter are those measured in the constraint operation. You may even be using piece-work incentives, in an effort to get your operators to produce more, and I'm sure many of you are using variances as a key performance metric. Efficiencies, utilizations, incentives, and variances are all counterproductive! So, the fifth prerequisite belief in preparing for the implementation of the UIC that must be accepted is *abandoning outdated performance metrics,* incentives, and variances. If you are unwilling to do this, then don't attempt to use the UIC!

The sixth and seventh prerequisite beliefs that must be accepted involve *waste* and *variation.* You must accept the premise that every process contains both excessive amounts of waste and variation that are waiting to be identified, reduced and, hopefully, removed. No matter how perfect you might believe your process is, believe me, it has variation and is full of wasteful activities. Your job will be to locate, reduce, and, hopefully, eliminate the major sources of both. Variation corrupts a process, rendering it inconsistent and unpredictable. Without consistency and control, you will not be able to plan and deliver products to your customers in the time frame you have promised. Waste drives up both operating expense and inventory, so improvements in both of these go directly to the bottom line as you improve the throughput of your process and more specifically your constraining operation. Yes, you will observe waste in your non-constraint operations, but, for now, focus your resources only on the constraint!

The eighth prerequisite belief that your organization must embrace is that *problems must be addressed* instead of being swept under the carpet. You can no longer accept temporary fixes to your problems and, believe me, problems will be uncovered as you progress through the Ultimate Improvement Cycle. If you're like many companies, there are problems that have been hidden with excessive amounts of inventory used to guard against their negative effects. This way of thinking can no longer be accepted. Your organization must be committed to determining the root cause of problems and implementing effective and sustainable solutions or the UIC won't work for you.

The ninth prerequisite belief that your organization must accept if you are to be successful involves the *type and location of the constraint.* Constraints can be either internal or external to your organization and they can be either physical or policy-related. If they are external, then this typically means that you have more capacity than you have orders. If this is the case, then you must use your improved process to leverage this constraint. That is, your improved process will result in less lead time which your sales team can use to leverage more sales. If you have excess capacity, then your sales team can even quote a lower sales cost to leverage additional sales. Think about it; as long as your expenses or truly variable costs are less than the sales price, you are adding more money directly to your bottom line. Yes, the margins will be lower than normal, but it all flows to your company's bottom line. If your constraint is found to be a policy constraint, then you know it involves a conflict that must be resolved. You now have the tools to resolve conflict, so you must be ready to use them. All of what's involved in the Ultimate Improvement Cycle requires out-of-the-box thinking for your organization. As discussed in a previous chapter, if you have excess capacity, try creating a *Mafia Offer* to generate more sales.

The tenth and final prerequisite belief is the understanding that the organization is a chain of dependent functions that requires *systems thinking* rather than individual thinking. There are interdependencies that exist within the organization, with all functions playing a role in the final outcome. Unless and until individual functions desist from protecting their own turf and begin collaborating as a team, real and sustainable progress will not be achieved.

Let's review the ten prerequisite beliefs that your organization must be prepared to accept if you are to successfully implement and navigate through the Ultimate Improvement Cycle:

1. Believing that leveraging the constraint and focusing your resources on the constraint is the key to improved profitability.
2. Believing that it is imperative to subordinate all non-constraints to the constraint.
3. Believing that improving your process is a never-ending cycle.
4. Believing that involving your total workforce is critical to success.
5. Believing that abandoning outdated performance metrics, like efficiency and utilization, reward or incentive programs, and variances, is essential for moving forward.
6. Believing that excessive waste is in your process and that it must be removed.
7. Believing that excessive variation is in your process and that it must be reduced.
8. Believing that problems and conflicts must be addressed and solved.
9. Believing that constraints can be internal, external, physical or policy-related, or any combination of the four.
10. Believing that the organization is a chain of dependent functions and that systems thinking must replace individual thinking.

If your organization has truly accepted these ten prerequisite beliefs, and all that goes with them, then you are ready to begin this exiting journey that has no destination. But simply saying you believe something can be hollow and empty. It is your day-to-day actions that matter most. Review these ten prerequisite beliefs as a group on a regular basis and hold people and yourself accountable to them. Post them for everyone to see. Utilizing the Ultimate Improvement Cycle and true acceptance and employment of these ten prerequisite beliefs will set the stage for levels of success you never believed were possible!

Other key points I have made in this book include the Theory of Constraints Replenishment Solution, which, when implemented, will result in a reduction of raw material part levels in the neighborhood of 50% while virtually eliminating stock-outs. Another methodology is again based upon the Theory of Constraints, which is a different way to schedule your manufacturing facility. This method is referred to as Drum-Buffer-Rope and, as you will see, it is far superior to your current scheduling methodology. My advice, as you read each of the chapters in this book, is to take notes and imagine how all of these methods will work in your facility.

Good luck to you on your adventure into the future of improvement and maximum profitability. But, as I always say in all of my books, luck is Laboring Under Correct Knowledge ... you make your own luck!

# References

1. Eliyahu M. Goldratt and Jeff Cox, *The Goal*, The North River Press, 1999.
2. M. Reza, (Russ) Pirasteh and Robert E. Fox. *Profitability with No Boundaries*, ASQ Quality Press, 2010.
3. Robert A. Sproull, *The Ultimate Improvement Cycle*, CRC Press, 2009.

# Index

Note: Page numbers followed by 'f,' and 't' refer to figures and tables respectively.

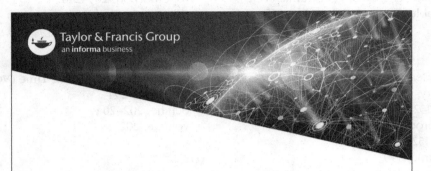